LIFE ON PLANET EARTH
BEFORE THE FALL OF SATAN
(God's Plan From Eternity to Eternity)
(In Past Eternity People and Dinosaurs
Lived Together on the Earth)

By
Albert W. Olema, B.A., B.S., M. Th., D.D.

Companion Press
P.O. Box 351
Shippensburg, PA 17257

ISBN 0-914903-27-6

For Worldwide Distribution
Printed in the U.S.A.

Life On Planet Earth Before The Fall Of Satan
may be obtained for an~~ amount~~ donation from:

Albert W. Olema
Trinity Church
P.O. Box 6062
Beaumont, TX 77705

Please add 10% for postage and handling.
If five (5) or more copies are ordered, author will pay postage.
Please allow 2-4 weeks for delivery.

INTRODUCTION

(Must be read)

In 1967 I had a very interesting conversation with a young Pastor in Waxahachie, Texas, U.S.A., about the age of the planet Earth. He maintained the position that according to the geneology in Genesis 5:3-32 the Earth can be no more than 6,000 years old. All my arguments were rejected as untenable and contrary to the biblical teaching. Finally, I asked him: "When God created Adam and Eve and placed them in the Garden of Eden 6,000 years ago, Satan was already there to tempt them. Where did he come from?" The young man was a little puzzled and exclaimed: "I don't know."

This is the problem with those that maintain the relatively young age of planet Earth. They never make any reference to the fall of Lucifer in past eternity, much less any reference to the destruction of the Earth billions of years ago. The purpose of this study is to find out the age of our planet Earth — which is more than 15,500,000,000 years old, and has undergone some terrific convulsions in the past, destroying the first perfect Earth, and leaving it in a chaotic condition. Genesis 1:2 says: *"...the earth was waste and void, and darkness was upon the face of the deep...."* The Hebrew word "hayah" from which "was" has been translated, is not the verb "to be," but "to become." Thus, the correct translation should be "And the Earth became a waste." From this terrible catastrophy, the age of the universe and of the Earth can be proven by three irrefutable facts.

1. The biblical evidence
2. The geological evidence
3. The astronomical evidence

I would like the reader to participate with me in this study which includes the creation of the universe and of our planet Earth, the creation of Satan and of angels, and the fall of Satan and of angels. We will also explore the judgment upon the original Earth over 15,500,000,000 years ago, the recreation of our planet Earth about six thousand years ago, the creation of Adam and Eve, and the fall of man into sin.

We will look at the redemption of man through faith in Christ, the Millennium and the renovation of the universe and of planet Earth by fire, and the creation of a new universe and of a new Earth. This study also includes the question of God's purpose in creating the universe. Why did God create the billions of galaxies in the universe, the Earth and the angels? There was a definite purpose.

We will also study the ambition of Satan to be worshipped as God. We will see that during the Tribulation when Antichrist, Satan's minister, sits in the rebuilt Temple in Jerusalem, Satan will be worshipped as God.

We will also include a brief study of the New Jerusalem and life on the new Earth. This is a unique study which I believe will be a blessing to the reader.

To avoid confusion, the reader should keep two things in mind when studying this book.

1. The pre-Adamic race, people that lived on Earth before the fall of Satan in past eternity.

2. The Adamic race, people living on planet Earth now, of which we are members.

I will use the American Standard Version which is a revision of the King James Version of 1611, completed in 1885. I consider it to be the best Bible for studying God's Word.

The author is very grateful to all the publishers that have allowed me to use material from their publications.

Albert W. Olema
February, 1989

LIFE ON PLANET EARTH BEFORE THE FALL OF SATAN

Scripture Text:

Genesis 1:1
"In the beginning God created the heavens and the earth."

Isaiah 45:18
"For thus saith Jehovah that created the heavens, the God that formed the earth and made, that established it and created it not a waste, that formed it to be inhabited...."

Psalms 104:5
"Who laid the foundations of the earth, that it should not be moved for ever."

Ecclesiastes 1:4
"...the earth abideth for ever."

Genesis 1:2
"And the earth was waste and void, and darkness was upon the face of the deep: and the Spirit of God moved upon the face of the waters."

Jeremiah 4:23-26
"I beheld the earth, and, lo, it was waste and void; and the heavens, and they had no light.

"I beheld the mountains, and, lo, they trembled, and all the hills moved to and fro.

"I beheld, and, lo, there was no man, and all the birds of the heavens were fled.

"I beheld, and, lo, the fruitful field was a wilderness, and all the cities thereof were broken down at the presence of Jehovah, and before His fierce anger."

Job 28:9
"...He overturneth the mountains by the roots."

CONTENTS

CHAPTER I

THE ETERNAL
SELF-EXISTENT GOD

The Person of God

The study of Deity in the Holy Scriptures is the most wonderful and unique of all studies. The eternal self-existent, omnipresent and omniscient triune God existed in three persons from all eternity. The Father, the Son, and the Holy Spirit constitute the council of God. The existing Godhead is a mystery which no human mind can adequately comprehend, but which should be accepted by faith.

The self-existing God is not created because no creator beyond God can be conceived; therefore He is not created. If God was created, then He would not be God, but a creature created by something greater than God and on the level of creatures which have been created by the First Cause. God, therefore, is an eternally existing Almighty Being. He is infinite, eternal, and unchangeable in His Being. He is wisdom, power, holiness, justice, goodness, and truth, and perfection. There never was a time when God did not exist. Psalms 90:2 says: *"Before the mountains were brought forth, or ever Thou hadst formed the earth and the world, even from everlasting to everlasting Thou art God."*

God is the First Cause of all the existing phenomenon and, without Him nothing can exist. John 4:24 says: *"God is a Spirit...."* Therefore, God is a Spirit Being Who has no physical body — bones or flesh — like humans. God is a Person and not just a power which travels through the universe to a certain destination and manifests itself through some phenomenon. God's Person is revealed in the Holy Scriptures. They represent God as possessing the psychological characteristics of personality.

1. His intellect. The Bible reveals that God is omniscient and possesses wisdom and understanding. He is intelligent. Psalms 136:5 says: *"To Him that by understanding made the heavens...."* Years later King Solomon wrote in Proverbs 3:19-20: *"Jehovah by wisdom founded the earth; by understanding He established the heavens.*

"By His knowledge the depths were broken up, and the skies drop down the dew."

This shows that God is wise, all-knowing, possessing all wisdom which no other in the universe can possess. Romans 11:33 says: *"O the depth of the riches both of the wisdom and the knowledge of God! How unsearchable are His judgments, and His ways past tracing out."*

That God possesses wisdom is revealed through creation. The universe God created is a masterpiece and reveals an infinitely wise Being. The universe is a master plan revealing the wisdom of the First Cause that brought the universe into existence out of nothing. The universe reveals a design, and a design implies a Designer, and that Designer is God. Hebrews 3:4 says: *"For every house is builded by some one; but He that built all things is God."*

2. His volition — God's willpower. The Bible reveals that God has a will. The prophet writes in Daniel 4:35: *"...and He doeth according to His will in the army of heaven, and among the inhabitants of the earth, and none can stay His hand...."* King David knew that God had a will and wrote in Psalms 143:10: *"Teach me to do Thy will, for Thou art my God...."* In Matthew 6:10 Jesus says: *"...Thy will be done, as in heaven, so on earth."* The First Cause, Who has revealed His existence in nature, also had willpower, to bring a universe into existence out of nothing.

3. His sensibility — God's feeling. Does God have any feeling? He certainly has feeling. John 3:16 says that *"God so loved the world...."* Love implies feeling. God hates everything that is contrary to His holiness. Hate implies feeling.

4. His creative power. God's creative power is seen in the creation of the universe and all intelligences. When the Godhead decided to create a universe, He had the power to bring such a beautiful universe into existence out of nothing. No wonder that the Apostle Paul writes in Romans 1:20, *"For the invisible things of Him since the creation of the world are clearly seen, being perceived through the things that are made, even His everlasting power and divinity...."*

Thus, the creation has revealed three great attributes of God: His wisdom, His willpower, and His creative power.

Personal names are given to Him. Genesis 1:1 says: *"In the beginning God...."* Personal pronouns are used for all three persons of the Divine Trinity, both singular and plural. In Genesis 1:26 the Lord says: *"...let Us make man in Our image, after Our likeness...."* This should suffice to show that God is a Person.

The Scriptures ascribe qualities and relations of personality to God. He is represented as speaking. Genesis 1:3 says: *"And God said, Let there be light, and there was light."* He is represented as seeing. Genesis 11:5 states: *"And Jehovah came down to see the city and the tower, which the children of men builded."* Psalms 12:2 reads: *"Jehovah looked down from heaven upon the children of men, to see if there were any that did understand, that did seek God."* Psalms 94:9 says: *"...He that formed the eye, shall He not see?"* The Lord is represented as hearing. Psalms 94:9 states: *"He that planted the ear, shall He not hear...?"* God is represented as angry. Deuteronomy 1:37 states: *"And Jehovah was angry with me for your sakes...."* God is represented as jealous and compassionate (Exodus 20:5, Psalms 111:4). God is a Preserver. Nehemiah 9:6 shows that the Lord is the one that upholds all things. God is a Ruler Who rules over all things (Psalms 75:6-7, Daniel 4:32). Psalms 104:27-28 shows that the Lord is the Sustainer Who supplies the needs of His creatures.

The Eternal Plan of God

In past eternity, when nothing existed except the Father, the Son and the Holy Spirit, the Godhead had a conference during which a unique and most marvelous plan was decreed. This unique plan included the creation of a beautiful universe and the planet Earth, on which God's marvelous grace in man's redemption was to be displayed through Christ Jesus.

The Almighty, omniscient God has revealed this plan to us in the Holy Bible. In the mind of the eternal God existed the plan of having a people for His name — the Church.

In the execution of this Divine plan the Lord created a universe and the planet Earth, where a great drama was to develop. God created Lucifer, Son of the Morning, who later became Satan. He also created the myriads of angels, and life on the perfect Earth. Already in past eternity, before the creation, God knew that Lucifer was going to rebel against His authority and become apostate.

Christ Jesus says in Matthew 25:41: *"...the eternal fire which is prepared for the devil and his angels."* This shows that when God brought our planet Earth into existence, hell fire was included right from the beginning of the creation. This shows the fore-knowledge of God because the Lord saw the rebellion of Satan in advance. In Ephesians 1:4 the Apostle Paul writes: *"Even as He chose us in Him before the foundation of the world...."* This also shows God's eternal plan in regard to the Church.

In Revelation 13:8, the Apostle John shows that God had the death of Christ in His Divine plan. The Apostle writes about the worshippers of Antichrist during the tribulation period. *"And all that dwell on the earth shall worship him, every one whose name hath not been written from the foundation of the world in the book of life of the Lamb that hath been slain."* It shows clearly God's plan of a Lamb, the Son of the living God, the Lord Jesus Christ Who would come to die on the cross for the present human race. God had already chosen a Church for Himself, in Christ, of the present Adamic race on the recreated planet Earth.

The Decrees of God

The decrees of God are His eternal purpose, based on His most wise and holy counsel, whereby He freely and unchangeably, for His own glory, ordained — either efficaciously or permissively — all that comes to pass. In regard to the decrees of God I would like to bring forth five points. The late Dr. Henry C. Thiessen teaches that:

1. The decrees are God's eternal purpose. He does not make His plans or alter them as human history develops. He made them in eternity and they remain unaltered.

2. The decrees of God are based on His most wise and holy counsel. He is absolutely holy and so cannot purpose anything that is wrong.

3. The decrees originate in God's freedom. He is not obligated to purpose anything.

4. The decrees have as their end the glory of God. They do not primarily aim at the happiness of the creature nor at the perfecting of the saints, although both these things are included in His aims, but at the glory of Him Who is absolute perfection.

5. There are two kinds of decrees: efficacious and permissive. There are things which God purposes that He also determines efficaciously to bring about; there are other things which He merely determines to permit. The decrees embrace all that comes to pass. They include all the past, the present, and the future. They embrace

the things which He brings about according to His power and the things which He merely permits. [1] We now understand why the Lord allowed the fall of Satan and the destruction of the first Earth.

Efficaciously means God having the power to produce intended effect. God, Who in His eternal plan purposed to bring into existence a universe and the planet Earth, had the power to do so. God alone, and only He could bring things into existence out of nothing. In God's eternal plan there was to be a universe a planet Earth, a great host of angels, and life on the first perfect Earth.

Permissively means that God allows some things to come to pass. The Lord permitted Satan to decide in his mind to stage a rebellion against the Mighty Creator, which resulted in the destruction of the planet Earth, and all life on it. On the recreated planet Earth, the Lord permitted Satan to tempt Eve and Adam, who subsequently fell into sin. Thus, the Lord in His purpose and work manifests a two-fold will.

1. His perfect will. This means that things which God has decided in His eternal plan must come to pass. They cannot be altered.

2. His permissive will. This refers to things which He permits to pass. God did not tell Satan to tempt Eve, but He permitted it to happen.

The occurrence of God's permissive will depends on the existing conditions. This is beautifully illustrated in Jonah 3:4-10. Because of Nineveh's sin, the city had to be punished. The prophet Jonah proclaimed that in forty more days the city would be overthrown. The people repented in all sincerity, including the King, and turned from their wicked works. Jonah 3:10 says: *"And God repented of the evil which He would do unto them and He did it not."*

If the Ninevites had not repented but continued to live in sin and wickedness, the judgment would have come. The Lord would have permitted a disaster to strike the city. Because the people repented in all sincerity, God postponed judgment, and the city remained 106 years more, and did not perish until 612 B.C.

The Creation of the Universe

The view of the universe that dominated the minds of men in the ancient and medieval world has, as its main features, the notion of a tiny immovable, spherical Earth situated at the center of a vast rotating sphere carrying the fixed stars — the latter in effect

---

1. Henry C. Thiessen, *Introductory Lectures in Systematic Theology,* (Grand Rapids, Wm. B. Eerdmans Publishing Company, 1952), pp. 147-148.

constituting the finite boundary of the universe. However, the current conceptions of the beginning of the universe differ greatly.

Encyclopedia Americana says that "many theorists who favor an evolutionary view of the universe refer to the present epoch of expansion as having begun somewhere between 10,000,000,000 and 20,000,000,000 years ago. Such a beginning of the universe took the form of a highly condensed state, called the primeval atom. From this original point, the universe has undergone an explosive disintegration. The presently observed expansion of nebulae and the distribution of the relative abundances of the elements throughout the universe are taken as evidence of this process of development." [2]

The New Encyclopedia Britannica says, "In the 1920's, the big-bang model, widely-held theory of the evolution of the universe, was promulgated. Its essential feature is the emergence of the universe from a state of extremely high temperature and density, the so called big-bang that occurred at least 10,000,000,000 years ago. The big-bang model is based on two assumptions.

"1. That Einstein's general theory of relativity correctly describes the gravitational interaction of all matter.

"2. The cosmological principle. Light travels in a year 5,880,000,000,000 miles or 9,460,800,000,000 kilometers.

"This principle states that an observer's view of the universe depends neither on the direction in which he looks nor on his location. This principle applies only to the large scale properties of the universe, but it does imply that the universe has no edge, so that the big-bang origin occurred not at a particular point in space but rather throughout space at the same time.

"These two assumptions make it possible to calculate the history of the cosmos after a certain epoch called the Plank time. Scientists have yet to determine what prevailed before Plank time. According to the big-bang model, the universe expanded rapidly from a highly compressed primordial state, resulting in a significant decrease in density and temperature soon afterwards. The dominance of matter over antimatter may have been established by processes that also predict proton decay. During this stage many types of elementary particles may have been present. After a few seconds the universe cooled enough to allow the formation of certain nuclei, and definite amounts of hydrogen, helium, and lithium were produced." [3]

2. "Study of Cosmology" *Encyclopedia Americana,* XXVII (1982) p. 182.
3. "The Universe" *The New Encyclopedia Britannica,* II (1987) p. 205.

According to this theory, the universe is the result of an explosion. Immediately after the explosion, the universe consisted chiefly of strong radiation. This radiation formed a rapidly expanding sphere called the primordial fireball.

According to those scientists who hold this theory, the primeval atom must have belonged to some previous age, and from this original point the universe has undergone an explosive disintegration. They seem to be unable to recognize the fact that the primeval atom must have had a beginning. It implies matter, and matter cannot produce or create itself, acting before it ever existed. These smart men fail to explain who brought the primeval atom into existence? The minds of these educated men are so blinded by the evolutionary theory that they fail to see God's handiwork in the heavens.

The big-bang theory is most unrealistic. Explosion implies a violent bursting with a noise, throwing particles of different shapes in every direction. If a big bomb explodes, sharpnel of all sizes and shapes fly in every direction. The universe, however, does not appear to be the result of such an explosion. If there was an explosion, where did the matter come from to explode? Instead we see an orderly universe, which reveals a design. If there is a design, there must be a designer, and God is the Designer of the universe.

Let's examine for a moment the Earth and its place in the solar system. The sun is the center of our solar system. It, along with billions of stars, is part of our great galaxy called the "Milky Way." This galaxy is about 100,000 light years long and about 20,000 light years across at the center. It is interesting to notice the precision with which the solar system functions.

Our Earth requires 365 days, 5 hours, 48 minutes, and 46 seconds to complete one revolution around the sun. It takes 23 hours, 56 minutes and 4.09 seconds to complete one rotation on its axis. The Earth's revolution around the sun establishes our year; its rotation on its axis establishes our day. The 23½ degree inclination on the Earth's axis and its journey around the sun cause the change of seasons, and varying lengths of night and day. It is important to understand the delicate balance of our planet. The Earth is exactly the right distance from the sun for human life. If it were about 16,000,000 kilometers (10,000,000 miles) closer to the sun, the temperature would be too hot to sustain life. If it were 16,000,000 kilometers farther away, it would be too cold to sustain life.

The size of the Earth is exactly right to maintain the atmosphere, with exactly the proper density to filter through just enough actinic rays of the sun to kill harmful bacteria, but not enough to kill man.

Our planet Earth is hung upon nothing, yet it travels in space with unerring precision, revolving around the sun at the speed of 107,280 kilometers (66,600 miles) an hour in its orbit. And the Earth is rotating on its axis at just the right speed for the right length of day and night. With any change, life could not be maintained on our planet. To think that this intricate design could be the result of an explosion is quite illogical, in my opinion. The universe did not just happen by chance, it was carefully designed and created by Almighty God.

Psalms 19:1-2 says: *"The heavens declare the glory of God; and the firmament showeth His handywork.*

"Day unto day uttereth speech, and night unto night showeth knowledge."

Romans 1:20 states: *"For the invisible things of Him since the creation of the world are clearly seen, being perceived through the things that are made, even His everlasting power and divinity; that they may be without excuse."*

These Scripture passages reveal that the invisible God has manifested His Person through His works, the creation of the great universe. The worlds which He has created manifest His wisdom and might because He brought matter into existence out of nothing. Anyone who has even a little understanding will agree with me that the material universe could not create itself, acting before it ever existed. Therefore, there must have been a First Cause that made these things come into existence. The material universe is an effect and argues back to a cause, adequate to bring the great universe into existence.

The Expanding Universe

The astounding fact is that the universe is expanding. The galaxies are moving away from one another at terrific velocities. According to Merit Students Encyclopedia, Mr. Hubble made one of the greatest astronomical discoveries of the 20th century. He discovered that nearly all the galaxies appear to be receding from the Milky Way system at very high speeds, some in fact, at velocities close to the speed of light. This fact is known from a phenomenon called the red shift, or Doppler shift, of spectral lines. Characteristic lines in the spectrum of a galaxy speeding away from the Milky Way are displaced toward the red end.

By measurements made in the laboratory and from the light of nearby galaxies, astronomers are able to identify and assign definite wavelengths to certain characteristic lines that appear in the spectra of galaxies. When a known line in a distant galaxy is shifted toward the red, it is concluded that the galaxy being observed is speeding away from the Milky Way, with the extent of the shift giving the precise velocity of recession.

From observations made on a very large number of galaxies, Hubble and another American astronomer, Milton Humason, discovered a simple relation between a galaxy's distance and its speed of recession. This relation may be simply stated: The farther away a galaxy is, the faster it moves. [4]

Einstein found the idea of an expanding universe sinister because it implies that it must have a beginning, and that there must have been a point in time when expansion began. Only in 1930, after seeing Hubble's spectrograms, did Einstein become convinced that we live in a dynamic, not a static universe. In this expanding universe, every point moves away from every other point. The center of this universe is nowhere and everywhere. No star system is privileged over another. The galaxies travel at incredible velocities. A spiral nebula in Ursa Major has a radial velocity of 15,000 kilometers per second, or 900,000 kilometers per minute, or 54,000,000 kilometers an hour. A galaxy with its spectrum lying at a distance of 230,000,000 light years from the Earth has a velocity of recession of 39,000 kilometers per second, or 140,000,000 kilometers an hour.

This continuing expansion of the universe implies that billions of years ago the galaxies must have been much closer together. The theory of the expanding universe suggests that there was a zero point when the entire matter of the universe was concentrated at one point in space. It can then be concluded that in time past all galaxies originated at a single point. According to my calculations this must have been over 15,500,000,000 years ago. A newly discovered quasar (quasistellar radio source) lies at a distance of about 15,500,000,000 light years away, at the edge of the known universe.

The number of galaxies that are in space cannot be numbered. Some scientists believe that there are over 10,000,000,000. However, only the Almighty Creator knows how many galaxies there are in the universe.

4. "The Red Shift of Galaxies" *Merit Students Encyclopedia,* 18 (1982) p. 616.

According to the newly discovered quasar, the universe is more than 15,500,000,000 years old. However, the scientists cannot see beyond that. So the Earth and the universe could be much older than 15,500,000,000 years. The exact date, of course only God knows. Isaiah 45:18 says: *"For thus saith Jehovah that created the heavens, the God that formed the earth and made it, that established it and created it not a waste, that formed it to be inhabited...."*

Thus, the Lord has revealed to us that the Earth the Lord formed or created was not created a waste, but was created in beauty for an habitation for people. Yet we read in Genesis 1:2 that *"...the earth was waste and void...."* This implies that some terrific catastrophy destroyed the original Earth sometime in the past. Thus in Genesis 1:2-28 the student of the Word of God finds the story of the restoration of our planet Earth, not its original creation.

Dividing of the Land

Several topographical changes have taken place in the history of the Earth. Genesis 1:9 says: *"...Let the waters under the heavens be gathered together unto one place, and let the dry land appear: and it was so."* This reveals that on the third day a great topographical change took place. There was a lifting up of the land, and all the water gathered together to one place.

This was the second topographical change in the history of planet Earth. The first took place at the time of the fall of Satan billions of years ago, when all the land area sank and the entire planet was covered with water. The main point I wish to bring to the readers attention is the fact that at the recreation of our planet, the inhabitable Earth was just one big piece of land, and was not divided into several continents as it is now.

So, before the Flood the present day U.S.A. and Canada were under water. After the Flood, the inhabitable Earth was one piece of land and remained so for 148 years before the land was divided into several continents. Genesis 10:25 says: *"And unto Eber were born two sons: the name one was Peleg; for in his days was the earth divided...."* The Hebrew "Pelegh" means "division."

The Flood took place about 2348 B.C. and the land was divided in 2200 B.C. just 148 years afterward. The land between South America and Africa sank and the North American continent was lifted up. There are several islands in the central Indian Ocean, about 650 kilometers to 1,500 kilometers east of Madagascar. More than

300 years ago, when the Europeans landed on the three main Islands (The Mascarene Islands), Reunion, Mauritus, and Rodrigues, they found an abundance of Dodos, heavybodied flightless birds that inhabited the Mascarene Islands. This shows that at one time these islands and Madagascar were united to Africa. Before the division of land these birds walked that far east, and when the land sank, only small islands remained. In the Indonesian Islands, there are many animals that migrated that far before the dividing of the land. Many of the animals that inhabit Indonesia are also found in India and many other parts of the world.

CHAPTER II

THE AGES OF PLANET EARTH

The Antechaotic Age

The Scriptures reveal six different ages of Earth's history which I want to examine in this chapter. First, the reader must recognize the difference between an age and a dispensation. An age, in Scripture, means a long period of time in the history of Earth, from one violent change to another in the Earth's crust, involving all the Earth's inhabitants. An age of the Earth might be billions of years, or less than 2,000 years. For instance, the Antediluvian Age, which began with the restoration of planet Earth and ended with the Flood, lasted 1,656 years.

The dispensational study of the Bible consists of the identification of certain well-defined time periods which are divinely indicated, together with the revealed purpose of the Lord relative to each. The history of present mankind from the creation of Adam to the end of the Millennial reign of Christ has been divided into seven dispensations.

The Antechaotic Age of the Earth began from the creation of the universe and ended at the fall of Lucifer, an undetermined period of time. I want to make five points regarding the Antechaotic Age:

1. The creation of the spirit world. There has been confusion regarding God's first act in His creative work. Some believe that the universe was created first; others hold that the spirit world was created first, then the universe. A third group says that the universe was created first, then the spirit world and then the planet Earth.

However, it will not be difficult to prove that the spirit world was God's first creation. Job 38:4-7 says: *"Where wast thou when I laid the foundations of the earth? Declare if thou hast understanding.*

"Who determined the measures thereof, if thou knowest? Or who stretched the line upon it?

"Whereupon were the foundations thereof fastened? Or who laid the cornerstone thereof.

"When the morning stars sang together, and all the sons of God shouted for joy?"

Here the Lord revealed to the old Patriarch that when the Earth was created, the morning stars, or the angels were already there to sing. They were created before the Earth.

Because this passage mentions "the earth," some Bible scholars say that the universe must have already been created. When, however, the Scriptures speak of the heavens, it always means the universe, and when the Earth is spoken of alone, as in Job 38:4, it means the entire universe. In Proverbs 8:22-31, Christ speaks of Himself and several times makes reference solely to the Earth. This would then lead to the conclusion that the Earth was the first act of God's creative work, because it is not until in Proverbs 8:27 that the Lord speaks of the creation of the heavens. It is true that many times, in the Scriptures, the Earth alone has been spoken of separately as a single planet, and sometimes the heavens is spoken of as the universe — apart from the planet Earth.

The Apostle Paul speaks of the creation of the universe and all moral agents in Colossians 1:16. *"For in Him were all things created, in the heavens and upon the earth, things visible and things invisible, whether thrones or dominions or principalities or powers; all things have been created through Him, and unto Him."*

2. The creation of the material universe. Genesis 1:1 says: *"In the beginning God created the heavens and the earth."* This reveals a complete act of God. The entire universe was brought into existence by one creative act, including the planet Earth. Nowhere is it revealed in the Bible that the Lord created some part of the universe at a later date, all was brought into existence at the same time. Psalms 102:25 says: *"Of old didst Thou lay the foundation of the earth; and the heavens are the work of Thy hands."* Here David writes as if the Earth were first created, and then the heavens or universe. The conclusion is simple. These phrases have been used interchangeably to denote the entire universe. The prophet writes in Isaiah 40:26: *"Lift up your eyes on high, and see Who hath created these, that bringeth out their host by number: He calleth them all by name; by the greatness of His might, and for that He is strong in power, not one is lacking."* Again the

prophet writes in Isaiah 45:12: *"I have made the earth, and created man upon it: I, even My hands have stretched out the heavens; and all their host have I commanded."* And the Apostle Paul writes in Hebrews 11:3: *"By faith we understand that the worlds have been framed by the Word of God, so that what is seen hath not been made out of things which appear."*

This great creation occurred billions of years ago, and included all the stars, or billions of galaxies, the sun, the moon, and planet Earth.

3. The creation of the social order on Earth in past eternity. The Bible reveals that when the creation of the universe was completed, the Lord also created the social order — or human beings — on the perfect Earth, billions of years ago. The Apostle Peter saw this when he wrote: *"For this they wilfully forget, that there were heavens from of old, and an earth compacted out of water and amidst water, by the Word of God;*

"By which means the world that then was, being overflowed with water perished" (2 Peter 3:5-6).

Here the Apostle Peter used the Greek word "kosmos" which means "orderly arrangement," by implication the world including the inhabitants. The Greek word "kosmos" occurs 196 times in the New Testament, 91 times in the gospel of John alone. John 1:9-10 says: *"There was the true light, even the light which lighteth every man, coming into the world.*

"He was in the world, and the world was made through Him, and the world knew Him not." The word "kosmos" occurs 4 times in this passage translated "world." This is referring to social order, inhabitants of the world. *"The world knew Him not,"* does not speak of the planet Earth, but the inhabitants living on Earth. John 3:16 states: *"For God so loved the world...."* or "kosmos." God certainly did not love the material Earth and Christ did not die for the planet Earth. Jesus spoke of the people who live on Earth. In 1 Peter 1:4 the Apostle writes about the salvation of the Christians saying: *"...having escaped from the corruption that is in the world by lust."* Again the Apostle used the word "kosmos." 1 John 2:2 says: *"And He is the propitiation for our sins, and not for ours only, but also for the whole world."* Again John uses "kosmos," social order or people. These few Scripture passages will suffice to prove the fact that when the Apostle Peter spoke of the ancient world, he was not referring to the Noachian Flood which occurred in 2348 B.C. but to a social order or Earth's inhabitants then living. His statement *"the world that then*

was" has no reference to the social order before the Flood, because nothing was destroyed — as far as the social order was concerned. After the Flood, everything continued in the same way it was before the Flood. Only about 1,000,000,000 people perished, along with all the animals outside of the ark — including the birds.

Therefore, the world or "kosmos" (social order) in 2 Peter 3:5-6 has to do with the pre-Adamic race, people on the perfect Earth before the fall of Satan. Isaiah 45:18 confirms this very clearly. *"For thus says Jehovah that created the heavens, the God that formed the earth and made it, that established it and created it not a waste, that formed it to be inhabited...."* God did not create the Earth billions of years ago to let it remain empty and without use. He created it for people to live on.

Jeremiah 4:23-26 is the best Scripture passage to prove the existence of the pre-Adamic race. *"I beheld the earth, and, lo, it was waste and void; and the heavens, and they had no light.*

"I beheld the mountains, and, lo, they trembled, and all the hills moved to and fro.

"I beheld, and, lo, there was no man, and all the birds of the heavens were fled.

"I beheld, and, lo, the fruitful field was a wilderness, and all the cities thereof were broken down at the presence of Jehovah and before His anger." Here, the prophet was privileged to see the destruction of the original planet Earth and of the inhabitants in past eternity at the fall of Satan.

4. The rule of Lucifer on the perfect Earth. Isaiah 14:12-14 reveals that Satan, before his fall, was a ruler. He had a throne to sit on. Ezekiel 28:12-17 shows that he was the anointed cherub; he was a priest and a king before his fall. He was the most powerful and beautiful of all the created beings in God's universe. However, I will explain his position in past eternity in Chapter V.

5. The length of the Antechaotic Age. How many years the rule of Lucifer lasted can in no way be determined. I can only say that his rule began at the time when the planet Earth was made ready for human habitation, and the first parents of the pre-Adamic race were placed on Earth. His rule lasted until his fall. All I can say is only conjecture, but it will give the reader some idea about the possible length of time between the creation of the universe and the fall of Satan.

If we were to study the human multiplication on Earth from the time of the Flood to our present time, we would have some idea about the rate of increase of the human race. It is accepted that the population before the Flood was about 1,000,000,000. That might be true because people lived more than 900 years then. If one accepts the theory that the population was about one billion, then only 1,656 years were needed to reach that number, beginning with two people. The one billion figure is not an absolute fact but a possibility which I do accept.

The Flood occurred about 2348 B.C. Only eight people escaped death by drowning. From the Flood until 1986 is about 4,334 years, and the population then was nearing five billion. Now, let us study the growth of the world population.

In the year 1 A.D. the population was about 250,000,000. It required about 2,348 years to increase from eight people to that number.

In 476 the population was about 290,000,000, an increase of only 40,000,000 in 476 years.

In 1215, the population was about 350,000,000, an increase of about 60,000,000 in 739 years.

In 1776, the population was about 850,000,000, an increase of about 500,000,000 in 561 years.

In 1830, the population was about 1,000,000,000, an increase of about 150,000,000 in 54 years. The population needed 4,178 years to reach 1,000,000,000.

In 1930, the population was 2,000,000,000, an increase of about 1,000,000,000 in 100 years.

In 1960, the population was about 3,000,000,000. The third billion needed only 30 years.

In 1975, the population was about 4,000,000,000. The fourth billion needed only 15 years. The present population is estimated to be about 5,000,000,000, and in 2,000 there will be more than 6,000,000,000 on planet Earth.

It is estimated that during the past 300 years about 23,000,000,000 people were born. The rate of growth of the world's population is about 2% a year. This is sufficient to double the world's population every 35 years. By the end of this year there will be about 100,000,000 more people on Earth, not including the murdered, unborn babies some 50,000,000 world-wide.

This tremendous population growth can be attributed to the increase of medical science. Today, doctors treat a human being like a worn out car motor. A motor stops because a certain part is worn-out; replace it and it will run again. Likewise, human beings have had worn-out parts of their bodies replaced. Doctors transplant hearts, livers and kidneys, so that people may live longer.

The rule of Lucifer on the original Earth over the population or the social system must have lasted several thousand years. How long a time he ruled on Earth cannot be established. However, if we assume that the pre-Adamic race multiplied like the present Adamic race, it must have taken considerable time to reach billions of people. I assume that God created only one couple on the perfect Earth as He did on the present Earth (Adam and Eve). If the period of pregnancy required the same time as it does now, the multiplication was very fast indeed.

Before the fall of Satan, there was no sin and no death; so the people lived until the Earth was destroyed. The Earth's surface must have been larger than it is today because there was so much water vapor in the atmosphere. Before the destruction of the Earth, there was no winter, only perpetual summer, a temperate climate. Fossils of tropical trees and plants have been found in Greenland and Alaska. The harvests in those days may have been great and plentious, probably three harvests a year. The vegetation on the perfect Earth must have been the same as it is now. Many fossils have been found of plants and grass of the prehistoric era. Elephant grass, found in the disinterred mammoths in Siberia, is the same as elephant grass found today.

If the world's population and wealth were distributed equally, the Earth could easily sustain about 10,000,000,000 people. However, on the first perfect Earth, there were no deserts, no winter. They had a temperate climate with three harvests a year, and much greater land area. The probability is that before the fall of Satan, the population may have reached 30,000,000,000 or more. This is only a conjecture. However, the population must have been vast.

Antarctica, a vast continent, was habitable in those days because of a world-wide tropical climate. Coal has been found under the ice, confirming the fact that life once existed there.

On these assumptions, I conclude that the Antechaotic age may have lasted 15,000 years, although an exact age cannot be established. Lucifer enjoyed quite a long period of rule on the perfect Earth, the first Eden in God's universe.

However, I would like to present another viewpoint to the reader based on the Antediluvian age of marriage. Genesis 5:15 and 21 show that the marriage age before the Flood was 65 years. People did not mature as fast as they do now. Moses writes: *"And Mahalalel lived sixty and five years, and begot Jared...."*

"And Enoch lived sixty and five years and begot Methusela." It is estimated that the population before the Flood was about 1,000,000,000 — maybe even more. So, it took 1,656 years to reach that number. On this basis, it can be computed again that Satan may have ruled on Earth 15,000 years or more, because in past eternity, the marriage age may have been the same as before the Noachian Flood.

The Ice Age

The length of the Ice Age extended from the fall of Satan to the restoration of planet Earth in Genesis 1:2-28. This period runs into billions of years and ended about 6,000 years ago. The study of this age reveals three points.

1. The cause of the Ice Age. The cause of the Ice Age was the rebellion of Satan against the Almighty God many billions of years ago. His rebellion resulted in a world-wide judgment in past eternity which destroyed the entire planet Earth. Job 9:5-7 describes such destruction. *"Him that removeth the mountains, and they know it not when He overturneth them in His anger.*

"That shaketh the earth out of its place, and the pillars thereof tremble.

"That commendeth the sun, and it riseth not, and sealeth up the stars."

That the waters froze in all the oceans is confirmed by Job 38:30. *"The waters hid themselves and become like stone, and the face of the deep is frozen."*

I have explained this passage in Chapter VIII and will not dwell on it here, except to say that verse seven shows that the rotation of the Earth stopped, and God extinguished the sun. There was no more heat and the waters froze to solid ice. Genesis 1:2 says: *"...and darkness was upon the face of the deep...."* When the Lord began His restoration work about 6,000 years ago, He reactivated the sun. Genesis 1:4 says: *"...let there be lights in the firmament of heaven...."*

The prophet Jeremiah confirms the extinguishing of the sun in Jeremiah 4:23. *"I beheld the earth, and, lo, it was waste and void; and the heavens, and they had no light."* Because the sun was extinguished, there was no more heat to warm the atmosphere, and the Ice Age was ushered in. Only our solar system was darkened, other galaxies were not effected.

2. The length of the Ice Age. No one can say for sure how many billions of years the Ice Age lasted, but I would say that it may have been 15,500,000,000 years or more. Scientists say that the most distant galaxy man has detected lies 15,000,000,000 light years away, but they cannot see the end of the universe. It may run several billion light years more. Only God knows the length of the Ice Age. I suggest that the Ice Age began over 15,500,000,000 years ago, and extended over the entire planet Earth.

Now, let us see what present day scientists say about the Ice Age. The World Book Encyclopedia has included some of the theories promoted by scientists. "The earliest known Ice Age occurred during the Precambrian time, which began more than 600,000,000 years ago. Another Ice Age occurred during the Carboniferous and Permian periods between about 350,000,000 and 230,000,000 years ago.

"The most recent Ice Age occurred at approximately the same time as the Pleistocene Epoch which began about 1,750,000 years ago and ended about 10,000 years ago. The term Ice Age usually refers to the Pleistocene Ice Age. Fossils and other evidence from that period have been less disturbed by changes in the Earth than have signs of the earlier Ice Age." [1]

As to the development of the Pleistocene Ice Age, scientists say: "In the late Tertiary Period, about 3,000,000 to 3,500,000 years ago, the Earth became colder. Glaciers began forming in the mountain and polar areas. This was not sudden change. The world had been cooling down since about 65,000,000 years ago. But this last cooling was marked by a series of ice sheets over parts of the northern continents, beginning about 1,500,000 years ago." [2]

Scientists say further: "A typical glaciation lasted about 40,000 to 60,000 years, and a typical interglacial lasted about 40,000 years. The last ice retreat began less than 20,000 years ago.... In North America the main center was near Hudson Bay (Canada). Ice piled up to 2,400 to 3,000 meters (8,000 to 10,000 feet) thick, and covered

1. "Ice Age" World Book Encyclopedia, X(1982) p. 6.
2. Ibid., p.6.

most of North America down to about the present valleys of the Missouri and Ohio rivers.

"In Europe the Scandinavian Peninsula was the center of glaciation. Ice piled up 3,000 meters (10,000 feet) thick, and flowed southeast about 1,300 kilometers (800 miles), about to Moscow. It also covered northern England, Denmark, and Germany." [3]

3. The results of the Ice Age. The result was a total annihilation of all life. If anything escaped the watery death, especially plants, grass and trees all froze and died. At the fall of Satan, when the Lord overturned the Earth, all the animal kingdom perished. Not one animal or human being was saved at that time. The Apostle Peter stated that *"the world that then was, being overflowed with water perished."*

This implies some instant topographical changes. The continents sank at once and all animals and humans drowned. The mammoths disinterred in Siberia had congested blood in their blood vessels, which implies that they must have died by drowning. The fish in the world's oceans died because of the tremendous cold. How much the continents sank under water at the fall of Satan cannot be determined, but the water must have covered all the continents of the world. This can be called Lucifer's Flood. Thus the Bible shows two Floods in the history of planet Earth — the other being the Noachian Flood in 2348 B.C. Genesis 1:9 says: *"And God said, Let the waters under the heavens be gathered together unto one place, and let the dry land appear: and it was so."* Here is clear evidence of Lucifer's Flood. When God began His restoration work 6,000 years ago, there was no dry land. It was at His command that dry land appeared.

Genesis 1:10 reveals that *"...God called the dry land earth...."* The planet Earth was covered with ice for many billions of years.

Now, let us see what the scientists say about the results of the Ice Age. Again, I will borrow information from the World Book Encyclopedia, which refers to the effect of the ice sheets. "At their height the ice sheets turned so much water to ice that the level of the oceans dropped at least by 91 meters (300 feet). When the ice melted, water flowed back into the oceans and filled them to their present level. As the glaciers slowly spread out, they pushed soil and loose rocks ahead of them like giant bulldozers. They left scratches on the rocks over which they moved. Soil and rocks, left behind when the ice

3. Ibid., p.7.

melted, formed mounds and ridges, called moraines. As the glaciers retreated, the low places they had scoured out filled up with water, forming lakes such as the Great Lakes (in the U.S.A. and Canada).

"The glaciers ground countless rocks into powder. The wind picked up this fine dust and blew it far and wide. Thick deposits of this fine silt, called loess* are found in Kansas (U.S.A.). The Ukraine and northern China have large areas covered with loess." [4]

As to the animals, scientists say: "The modern horse, camel, and elephant first appeared in the Ice Age. The horse and camel originated in North America. Then they crossed the Bering Strait to Asia. Elephants, bison, deer, and bears that evolved in Europe and Asia came to North America. Horses, Llamas, giant ground sloths, and armadillos went to South America.

"When the ice caps pushed down from the north, they drove the animals southward. But, during the interglacial periods, the animals could follow the melting ice northward. At times, arctic musk oxen and wooly mammoths ranged as far south as Michigan and New York (States in the U.S.A.). Some scientists think that the change of climate caused the big Pleistocene mammals to die out. Others believe that human beings killed them off, at least in North America. According to most experts, human beings entered North America about 20,000 to 15,000 years ago. Bison, ground sloths, mammoths and other large mammals lived on until that time, but then these animals soon disappeared.

"In Europe, however, such animals lived side by side with human beings throughout most of the Pleistocene Epoch." [5]

It all sounds most interesting, but the scientists offer no proof whatsoever. It is all an undocumented human philosophy which could be called, more correctly, a lie. The scientists give no evidence or proof of their statement "the first Ice Age began about 600,000,000 years ago." This is totally contrary to the biblical revelation. They also say that 65,000,000 years ago the Earth began cooling down and was marked by a series of ice sheets over parts of the northern continents, beginning about 1,500,000 years ago. They call it "the

* Loess is an unstratified deposit of yellowish-brown loam covering areas in North America, Europe, and Asia, now generally thought to be chiefly an aeolian deposit (Webster).
4. "Ice Age" *World Book Encyclopedia*, X (1982) p. 7.
5. Ibid., p. 7.

last cooling." They say that a typical glaciation lasted about 40,000 to 60,000 years.

According to scientific theories there must have been three or four different ice ages. This would imply that the sun was still hot and the ice melted, then a cold period came again, and there was another Ice Age. It would be impossible to have different ice ages without an active sun. The Bible, however, reveals that God extinguished the sun and a universal cold, absolute Zero (-273°C or 459°F) set in. Therefore, the Ice Age was a continuous period of over 15,500,000,000 years, because God never reactivated the sun until His restoration work began, about which we read in Genesis 1:2-28.

As to the loess, I must reject it at once because it cannot be proven that the glaciers ground some of the rocks to powder, nor that the wind carried this fine dust far and wide, depositing it in various parts of the Earth. Every intelligent person knows that winds are caused by air movements of cold and warm air. When cold and warm air collide, strong air currents, which we call wind, result. Were there winds on a planet that did not rotate and had no warm air?

My answer to this is that there were no winds on a dead planet, with a temperature of -273° Centigrade; therefore, there could be no moving of dust by air. However, the Bible has revealed to the student of the Word of God that the entire Earth was covered with ice down to the bottom of the seas. How, then, could the wind pick up the dust, even if there were any wind?

I accept the fact that there had been some movement of ice during that age. The entire Earth was covered with ice. How, then, could the ice move? Where would it go? Yet, the evidence shows clearly that rocks have been scooped up and carried to certain areas and deposited by the moving ice. This evidence is seen in my native country, Estonia, which has no rock such as is found in Scandinavia. All those huge boulders were transported by ice to Estonia.

When God began to recreate our planet Earth and the sun was reactivated, the ice began to melt. In the Middle East area, the ice could not have been very thick and melted quickly, or else God just said a word and all ice became water in the Middle East and in the southern areas. At the time of the recreation of planet Earth, the Lord acted quickly and instantaneously. Genesis 1:9 says: *"...and let the dry land appear...."* This shows that rapid topographical changes took place. The Middle East was warmed by the sun, and the Lord restored that area to its original state; while farther away, in Europe and in America, the ice melted more slowly. When the ice began to thaw in the southern area and the melting ice moved northward, then the continental ice sheet retracted southward, pushing rocks before it and scouring out deep depressions which filled with water, forming lakes. Falling water from the top of the ice sheet scoured out the sand and left deep lakes in many parts of Europe. In my native country, Estonia, I saw lakes that were several meters deep. The bank of some lakes was in a vertical position, as if it had been dug out by an excavator.

As to the animals, scientists are quite fanciful. They name a number of animals that evolved in Europe and came to America. However, I have no intention of wasting time refuting this unrealistic view, except concerning horses. They say that horses evolved in North America, and then some of them went to South America. They don't seem to know that before the Spaniards came to America in 1519, there were no horses in North America nor in South America. The Spaniards brought the first horses to America. Some of them broke loose and became wild horses in North America. Even today there are some wild horses in the U.S.A.

One of the Conquerors of Mexico, Bernal Diaz del Castillo (1494-1584) says in his excellent work, entitled "The Discovery and Conquest of Mexico," that the Indians had never seen a horse before and "...thought that the horse and its rider was all one animal, for they had never seen horses up to this time." [6]

The Antediluvian Age

The Antediluvian Age began with the restoration of planet Earth and ended at the Flood of Noah, about 1,656 years later. This age began in glory and ended in a world-wide judgment. Studying the Antediluvian Age, three things must be taken into consideration.

1. The dispensation of Innocence. The first human couple were placed by God in the Garden of Eden. They were innocent, sinless, without consciousness of evil, harmless, and free from guilt or sin. An innocent person is one who is free from guilt or violation of any law. Adam and Eve were upright and pure. How long this state of innocence lasted cannot be determined. It may have been a very short time, possibly only a few days, because Satan wanted to regain his dominion as soon as possible. When he fell in past eternity, he lost his

6. Bernal Diaz del Castillo, *The Discovery and Conquest of Mexico*, (Mexico City: Genaro Garcis, 1956), p.59.

position as king and priest. But now, a new creature had been planted on Earth, a human being who was ruler of all the Earth. Satan certainly would try to lead the first couple into sin as quickly as possible.

Satan succeeded in leading the first couple into sin, and they forfeited eternal life. Satan regained his position as king. He became the king and god of this world. 2 Corinthians 4:4 says: *"In whom the god of this world hath blinded the minds of the unbelieving, that the light of the gospel of the glory of Christ, Who is the image of God, should not dawn upon them."* The fall of Adam brought a curse on Earth and death.

2. The promise of a Redeemer. The Lord said to Satan: *"And I will put enmity between thee and the woman, and between thy seed and her seed: he shall bruise thy head, and thou shalt bruise his heel."* This was the first prophecy of the coming of the Lord Jesus to die on the cross for sinners. However, I will not concentrate on this subject here because I will take up this subject in another chapter.

3. The Noachian Flood. Because of all the evil of the Antediluvians the Lord had to destroy them. Genesis 6:5 says: *"And Jehovah saw that the wickedness of man was great in the earth, and that every imagination of the thoughts of his heart was only evil continually."* The main reason for destroying the Antediluvians was the union of the fallen angels with the daughters of men which produced a kind of half celestial and half terrestrial race. I will discuss this subject again in Chapter XII.

The Present Age

The Present Age runs from the Flood (1656 B.C.) to the second coming of Christ in glory to set up His kingdom, the Millennium, roughly about 4,344 years. In studying this age, I will include only three points.

1. The call of Abraham. About 1921 B.C. Abraham received his call to go to Canaan. Abraham was to be the primogenitor of the Hebrew race, from which Christ was to come. The nation of Israel was to be the channel through which God would give His revelations to the world, and bestow His blessings upon mankind. In due time the prophets wrote His marvelous revelations, and the nation Israel learned of the coming of the Messiah.

2. The descent of Christ. Galatians 4:5 says: *"But when the fulness of the time came, God sent forth His Son, born of a woman, born under the law,*

"That He might redeem them that were under the law, that we might receive the adoption of sons."

Christ Jesus, the second Person of the holy Trinity, came down from His eternal glory to assume a human physical body in order to die on the cross for lost humanity.

On the cross, the Lord Jesus, the Son of the living God, paid the penalty for our sins, so that now, by faith, men and women all over the world may receive forgiveness of sins and eternal life.

3. The calling out of the Church. Jesus said: *"...I will build My Church."* [7]

On the Day of Pentecost, the Holy Spirit was poured out, and the risen Christ took His abode in the hearts of the believers. We now have the dispensation of grace, which will end at the time of the first resurrection, and the translation of the Church of Jesus Christ. This dispensation will be followed by the tribulation period of seven years — when the Antichrist will rule in Rome over the revived Roman Empire.

At the conclusion of the tribulation, the battle of Armageddon will be fought. Then the Lord Jesus will appear in the clouds in great glory to defeat the armies at Palestine. Christ then will regather Israel to the holy land. The judgment of Israel and of the nations will take place, the unconverted will be separated and the righteous will enter His glorious reign, the Millennium.

The Millennium

The Millennium will last for about 1,000 years from the return of Christ, when He will set up His own kingdom, spoken of in Daniel and in many other Old and New Testament books. The prophet Daniel writes: *"Then was the iron, the clay, the brass, the silver, and the gold, broken in pieces together, and became like the chaff of the summer threshing-floors and the wind carried them away, so that no place was found for them: and the stone that smote the image became a great mountain and filled the whole world."* [8] Concerning the Millennium I will include only three points.

1. The kingdom concept in the Old Testament. Many passages in the Scriptures reveal God's position as absolute sovereign King. Psalms 10:16 says: *"The Lord is king forever and ever...."* David writes in Psalms 74:12: *"Yet God is my king of old...."* Jeremiah 10:10

---

7. *Matthew* 16:18.
8. *Daniel* 2:35.

says: *"But Jehovah is the true God; He is the living God, and an everlasting king...."* Thus, we see that God has an eternal kingdom. He rules with absolute sovereignty over all intelligences in heaven and on Earth who are willingly subject to Him. God's universal kingdom was challenged by Lucifer in past eternity.

This program of God to demonstrate His sovereignty and manifest the universality of His kingdom is called the theocratic kingdom program. The theocratic kingdom was demonstrated in the Garden of Eden, when God had sovereign rule. Sovereignty that belonged to God was delegated to man, who was to rule over the Earth in an exercise of mediate authority. When Adam sinned, man rid himself of the sovereign rule of God, his King.

2. The New Testament also speaks in many places of the kingdom of God, or the Millennium. The Lord Jesus spoke of it as did the Apostles. However, I will continue with this subject in another chapter.

3. The Millennium will end with the last test of man, when man will, under Satanic influence, rebel against God. Then judgment will come, the final Great White Throne Judgment, and the renovation of the universe by fire.

The Eternal Age

The Eternal Age is a period of time without end. God's eternal kingdom will never end. The Eternal Age is God's rule, and the saints with Him shall rule forever, under the Lord Jesus Christ. The Eternal Age begins with another change in the universe. I want to bring three points to the readers attention.

1. Renovation of the universe and of the Earth by fire. 2 Peter 3:10 says: *"...the heavens shall pass away with a great noise and the elements shall be dissolved with fervent heat, and the earth and the works that are therein shall be burned up."*

2. Christ, King of all eternity. I have already showed from the Scriptures that the Lord is an everlasting King. He has ruled over His universe as absolute Sovereign, and He will rule over all the universe as a absolute Sovereign. This is all revealed in the Scriptures, but I will discuss this subject in Chapter XX. It is enough here to say that after the Millennium when the Earth has been renovated, the New Jerusalem will descend from heaven to Earth. This golden city will be God's capital city of His universe and of His Church, the bride of Christ.

3. The position of the Church in the Eternal Age. The Church will

be His queen or co-ruler throughout the Eternal Age. There will be several different groups on the newly recreated Earth. The Church will be co-ruler with Christ; the nation Israel will be transferred to the new Earth. Old Testament saints that died by faith in the Lord will also rule with Christ, but are not considered part of the Church. The tribulation martyrs will also be placed on the new Earth and the saved Gentiles that remain loyal to Christ at the conclusion of the Millennium, when Satan will make his last attack against humanity — after he has been loosed from prison.

We will study this interesting subject further in Chapter XX.

CHAPTER III

THE AGE OF PLANET EARTH

The Biblical Evidence of the Age of Planet Earth

The exact age of our planet Earth cannot be established. The theory that the Earth is 6,000 years old is misleading. The advocates of this theory base their belief and teaching on the creation of Adam and Eve, who were created nearly 6,000 years ago. But the creation of Adam and the creation of the universe are two different things. The universe, including our Earth, was created billions of years ago, and then the Earth was destroyed by a judgment in past eternity.

Our federal head Adam was created and placed on a restored Earth nearly 6,000 years ago. The genealogy of Adam and his descendents given in Genesis 5:3-32 confirms this fact. Genesis 5:4-8 says: *"And Adam lived a hundred and thirty years, and begat a son in his own likeness, after his image; and called his name Seth:*

"And the days of Adam after he begat Seth were eight hundred years: and he begat sons and daughters.

"And all the days Adam lived were nine hundred and thirty years and he died.

"And Seth lived a hundred and five years, and begat Enoch:

"And Seth lived after he begat Enoch eight hundred and seven years, and begat sons and daughters.

"And all the days of Seth were nine hundred and twelve years: and he died."

This genealogy runs through Genesis 5:32, tracing the genealogy from Noah to Adam. The Flood occurred about 1,656 years after the creation of Adam, or 2348 B.C. From the Flood to Christ was 2,348 + 1,656 or 4,004 years. From Christ to 1986 was 1,986 + 4,004 or 5,990 years. According to this genealogy, the age of mankind seems to be almost 6,000 years.

There is, however, no Scripture passage that states the age of the universe. Isaiah 45:18 says: *"For thus saith Jehovah that created the heavens, the God that formed the earth and made it, that established it and created it not a waste, that formed it to be inhabited...."* In this verse, 3 important factors are revealed to the reader.

1. That God is the creator of the universe and of the Earth
2. The Lord did not create the Earth a waste or desolation
3. God created the Earth to be inhabited

The biblical evidence gives the student of the Word of God only the fact that the Earth and the universe were created in the timeless past. The evidence is found in the statement of Genesis 1:2: *"And the earth was waste and void...."* Isaiah 45:18 says that God created it not "a waste." This confirms the fact that sometime in the past, billions of years ago, terrific convulsions shook the Earth, destroying the original beauty and usefulness of the planet and all life on it. The Earth was left in a chaotic condition.

In Genesis 1:1 Moses used the Hebrew word "bara," which means in a strict sense, "production out of nothing," or "to bring into existence out of non-existing matter." It would be inconceivable to think that the Lord would create or bring into existence the Earth in a chaotic condition, and let it continue billions of years before making it inhabitable and useful.

The statement in Genesis 1:2, *"and the earth was waste and void...,"* "was" has been translated from the Hebrew "hayah" which is the verb "to become," and not the verb "to be." So, the correct translation should be: "And the earth became waste," or a desolation. The Earth was covered with water and darkness. When Satan fell, the Lord extinguished the sun and there was no more light. This, however, does not confirm any age of the Earth, except to prove the fact that the Earth originally was not created a desolation or waste.

The Geological and Astronomical Evidence of the Age of Planet Earth

Can geology reveal the approximate age of Earth? Every year about 4,850,000,000 metric tons of dissolved salts are removed from the continents and deposited in the seas, and every year approximately 32,500,000,000 metric tons of detrital material are stripped from the continents and deposited in the seas. This represents 13.5 cubic kilometers (3.3 cubic miles) a year of sea water that is displaced by continental sediment. The Collier's Encyclopedia says: "The material of continents are redistributed by a combination of weathering which destroyed the structure of the rock; erosion which mechanically wears away the rock, and transported by rivers, wind, sea, carries the material loosened by weathering and erosion and sedimentation, the process by which the loose material is deposited to form new rocks. All these processes operate with reference to a base level, usually sea level, below which erosion ceases.

"Sedimentation is one of the most important of the constructional processes at work on the Earth. It is the process whereby new rocks are formed from old rocks. Waves and currents sort and modify the materials; and it is eventually deposited in layers (strata) of particles of sand, silt, and clay. In general, the silts and clays are carried out to the sea where they settle on the sea floor. When the deposits are later uplifted, they form shale rocks. Sands are deposited mainly as the beach sands, and they eventually form sandstones. When they are not sorted, the eroded material accumulates and becomes bedded into what will later be a conglomerate." [1]

Geology colum gives many different ages and epochs. It is totally unreliable. The Antechaotic Age lasted presumably 15,000 years. It was during this age that silt and leaves of trees were carried by the ancient rivers to the seas, and the rocks were formed. During the Ice Age, the planet Earth was dead, water froze to the bottom of the seas. No rocks were formed during that time. The rocks which God created were the first rocks from which detrital material was stripped and transported to the seas.

Modern knowledge of radio carbon dating gives some idea of the age of Earth. The oldest rocks studied so far are more than 3,500,000,000 years old. According to scientists, the disintegration of a radioactive element occurs at a rate which is dependent on the chemical or physical environment. For example, uranium -238 decays to lead 206 at a rate which results in the reduction of one half of the uranium to lead in 7,600,000,000 years. Thus, by careful comparison of the amounts of these isotopes of uranium and lead present in a rock, one can determine the age of the rock.

The maximum time required for the formation of all the elements in the crust of the Earth has been determined to be about 5,500,000,000 years. According to this theory, the Earth is about 5,500,000,000 years old. However, I am not a scientist, but a

1. "Geology" *Collier's Encyclopedia* X (1987) pp. 658-661.

preacher, and as such I reject all these supposed dates in the light of the Word of God.

Astronomical studies reveal that the Earth is even older. The scientists say that the most distant galaxy detected lies at a distance of 15,000,000,000 light years. This means that the galaxy must have been there 15,000,000,000 years ago. A light year is the distance which light travels in one year at the rate of 300,000 kilometers or 186,000 miles per second, or 9,460,800,000,000 kilometers (5,880,000,000,000 miles) a year.

Scientists have detected a distant quasar which lies at a distance of 15,500,000,000 years from the Earth. But, even this cannot establish the age of our Earth, because the end of the universe cannot be seen. Our planet is no doubt much older than 15,500,000,000 years. Only the Lord knows the exact age of the universe and of planet Earth.

At this point I would like to draw the reader's attention to the discrepancies and contradictions of the sciences. It is believed and accepted by scientists that our sun is about 5,000,000,000 years old and that it will last another 5,000,000,000 years more before it burns out. The most distant galaxy is 15,000,000,000 years from us, according to astronomers. This makes a difference of 10,000,000,000 years.

Scientists say that the maximum time required for the formation of all the elements in the crust of the Earth has been determined to be about 5,500,000,000 years. This is totally wrong because Ezekiel 28:13 shows that every precious stone was Satan's covering *"...the sardius, the topaz, and the diamond, the beryl, the onyx and the jasper, the sapphire, the emerald, and the carbuncle, and the gold...."*

This statement refers back to the time before the fall of Satan. Lucifer had a gold palace which was covered with these precious stones. Thus, we learn from the Word of God that precious stones and gold were in existence over 15,500,000,000 years ago. Genesis 1:1 confirms this. *"In the beginning God created the heavens and the earth."*

This reveals a complete action. Everything was brought into existence at that time. Nowhere is it revealed in the Bible that God created some things later. No! The Almighty God, the Great Creator created everything at once.

The Bible never contradicts trustworthy science, but it does contradict mere suppositions of men. So, I conclude that all the minerals and precious stones were created by God and are as old as the Earth.

There are, however, some scientists and Christians that object to the antiquity of planet Earth. They use several scientific methods to disprove the early ages of Earth, including the sun.

The Shrinking Sun

On the basis of scientific studies, many Christian scientists have concluded that the Earth is comparatively young, no more than 10,000 years. Many scientific articles have been written in magazines, books and newspapers about the possible age of our planet. I would like to include a few of the wrong objections which are based on wrong interpretation of the Holy Bible.

It is estimated that the sun is shrinking about 1.5 meters (5 feet) an hour, or 36 meters (120 feet) per day, or 13,140 meters (43,800 feet) a year. Some scientists have concluded that the sun is about 5,000,000,000 years old and will last another 5,000,000,000 years before it burns out. The diameter of the sun is 1,393,000 kilometers (865,000 miles). If the sun shrinks about 13 kilometers a year, then in 100,000 years the sun will have shrunk about 1,300,000 kilometers, leaving a diameter of only 93,000 kilometers. This is not the case.

I have stated many times that the Earth and the universe are more than 15,500,000,000 years old. According to this, the sun would have shrunk about 185,606,520,000,000 kilometers, which is absolutely impossible. This calculation leads to the conclusion that something is wrong somewhere. The mistake lies with the scientists who don't know the Bible well enough. One cannot draw a conclusion without the biblical revelation, which gives concrete evidence that the sun was extinguished at the fall of Satan.

Job 9:7 says: *"That commandeth the sun, and it riseth not, and sealeth up the stars."* Jeremiah 4:23 states: *"I beheld the earth, and lo, it was waste and void; and the heavens, and they had no light."* These Scripture references confirm the fact that the sun was extinguished. There was no shrinking of the sun during these 15,500,000,000 years. When God restored our Earth to its original usefulness, He reactivated the sun to give light and heat. So, the sun has again been shining almost 6,000 years, with a possible shrinking of nearly 79,000 kilometers. Thus, in the light of the Holy Scripture, the age of the Earth based on shrinking of the sun must be rejected as untenable and unscriptural. At the time of the creation of Adam, the diameter of our sun was about 1,472,000 kilometers.

Cosmic Dust and Comets

With the use of satellite technology, scientists have been able to measure the amount of cosmic dust filtering into the Earth's atmosphere each year. Scientists have calculated that over the estimated billions of years of Earth history, more than 17 meters of cosmic dust may have fallen to the Earth. On our Earth, cosmic dust cannot accumulate because of erosion caused by wind and rain.

Because scientists believe that the Earth and the moon are of the same age, it was expected that lunar landing modules would encounter a problem trying to land in 17 meters of cosmic dust on the moon. When the first landing on the moon took place, scientists were shocked to find that the accumulation of cosmic dust was only 10 centimeters (5 inches), indicating a period of accumulation of about 10,000 years. Scientists assume that the present rate of accumulation is the same as it was in the past. The amount of accumulated cosmic dust indicates that the age of the Earth and of the moon cannot be billions of years.

Job 9:7 states: *"That commandeth the sun, and it riseth not, and sealeth up the stars."* The sun did not rise. This implies that the Earth stopped rotating on its axis, and the stars in our solar system were darkened because the sun was extinguished by God. So, for over 15,500,000,000 years there was no falling cosmic dust. This is the reason the dust layer on the moon was so thin. As to the comets, I must say that because the solar system stopped functioning, there were no comets to circulate in our solar system.

The Earth's Magnetic Field and Erosion

The measurement of the strength of the Earth's magnetic field is another method by which Christian scientists conclude that the Earth is young. Analysis of the data recorded during the past 130 years reveals that the strength of the magnetic field is getting weaker each year. Scientists assume that the rate of magnetic decay has been the same in the past as it is today, so the strength of the Earth's magnetic field would have been equivalent to a magnetic star. No life could exist under such conditions.

It is assumed that another result of the Earth's decreased magnetic field would be the effect which it would have on the Van Allen radiation belts that surround the Earth. These belts determine how much cosmic radiation comes in upon the surface of the Earth. It is estimated that the Earth's magnetic strength decays by one-half every 1,400 years. Scientists say that if this decay has remained constant, 10,000 years ago the Earth's magnetic strength would have been as strong as that of a magnetic star. No life could have survived on Earth with magnetism of that intensity.

This is correct and cannot be rejected. What scientists do not understand is the long Ice Age, lasting many billions of years. During that time, the Earth was a dead planet and there was no decrease of the Earth's magnetic strength. The magnetic strength of our Earth has been decreasing for only 6,000 years.

Erosion has also been used to indicate a relatively young age of the Earth. It is estimated that at the present rate of erosion, the continents could be completely eroded to sea level within 14,000,000 years. However, when our Earth was under the ice for billions of years, there was no erosion whatsoever. Erosion has only existed for some 4,500 years.

I hope that these explanations will help the reader to see how easily scientists can miscalculate without knowing the Bible, the Word and revelation of God.

The Greenhouse Effect

Many 20th century writers have misunderstood Genesis 1:6-7 where Moses writes: *"And God said, Let there be a firmament in the midst of the waters, and let it divide the waters from the waters.*

"And God made the firmament, and divided the waters which were under the firmament from waters which were above the firmament: and it was so."

In Genesis 1:20 God says: *"...let the waters swarm with swarms of living creatures, and let birds fly above the earth in the open firmament of heaven."*

On the basis of these Scripture verses, it is believed by some that there was a layer of water surrounding the Earth before the Flood. Genesis 1:20 shows that there was a firmament or expansion — an atmospheric layer divided a layer of water which was above from a layer of water below. According to the belief of some, there was a ball of water surrounding the Earth and thus the Earth was protected by a canopy of water — which produced a subtropical greenhouse effect from Antarctica to the North Pole — before the Noachian Flood. This is indeed a very interesting thesis and requires close examination to see if it "holds water."

The first question to those that advocate this theory should be:

Was there any evaporation before the Flood? The second question has to be: Was there any winter or cold before the Noachian Flood? These two questions must be understood and answered correctly. Then the "greenhouse" theory will be found untenable and unacceptable. I personally reject this teaching.

Genesis 8:22 is of paramount interest. God says: *"While the earth remaineth, seedtime and harvest, and cold and heat, and summer and winter, and day and night shall not cease."* Notice these statements:

1. Seedtime and harvest
2. Cold and heat
3. Summer and winter
4. Day and night shall not cease

Here the Lord ascribed the same character of permanency to all four things. This implies a continuation of the formerly existing conditions. There was seed time and harvest time before the Flood. There was day and night because of the rotation of planet Earth on its axis, and the Earth's journey in its orbit is always the same. The Lord restored the function of the solar system at the time of the restoration of planet Earth 6,000 years ago, and it has been functioning ever since in the same way. It has not undergone any change.

In light of the biblical revelation, there could not be the so called "greenhouse effect" which would have produced a subtropical climate from pole to pole before the Flood. A wise student of the Word of God realizes that before the restoration of our Earth, the planet was covered with ice several kilometers thick. Both the South and North Poles were covered with ice, as was the present day Europe and North America.

The Lord said that "winter and summer shall not cease." He did not say that from the Flood on the winter and summer shall not cease, as if it started after the Flood. The indication is clear that winter existed before the Flood. It is estimated that the thickness of the ice in Europe was about 3,000 meters or about 120,000 inches. If the ice layer melted about 2.5 centimeters (1 inch) per day, it would have taken about 330 years to free Europe of ice. However, summer in Europe is short, only a few months. The ice could melt only half a year. In that case it would have taken about 660 years before all the ice disappeared. There certainly was no subtropical climate at that time.

The 23½ degree inclination on the Earth's axis and its journey around the sun causes the change of seasons and varying lengths of day and night. As the solar system functioned before the Flood, so also after the Flood.

It is contended by some Christian writers and believers that there was a water ball around the Earth, and long wave radiation would pass through the layer of water in the upper atmosphere and be diffused and scattered in many different directions. Light would reach all latitudes with an equal intensity. Heat from the Earth's surface would be trapped inside the water canopy. This produced a subtropical climate from pole to pole, and subtropical plant and animal life existed over the entire planet.

Radiation is a process for the transportation of energy from one place to another in the form of electromagnetic waves. These waves of radiant energy can pass through solids, liquids, and gases, as well as through a vacuum. A layer of water surrounding the Earth would filter harmful cosmic radiation penetrating the earth's atmosphere. Long wave radiation would be able to pass through the canopy layer, but short wave radiation (heat from the Earth's surface) like ultraviolet light would not.

The question is: Was there a water ball surrounding the Earth before the Flood? Was there any evaporation during the Antediluvian age? Evaporate means to pass off in vapor. This is the result of heat. Since the sun gave off heat before the Flood, it caused evaporation. Water vapor is invisible, but clouds are visible to the human eye. According to this assumption there was a continuous evaporation of water for 1,656 years. Since there was no rain before the Flood, this water vapor must have stayed up in the atmosphere.

It is estimated that the total surface area of the Earth is 510,000,000 square kilometers (197,000,000 sq. miles) of which 153,000,000 square kilometers is land, and 357,000,000 square kilometers is water or oceans. The total volume of the world's water resources, including both fresh water and salt water is about 1,400,000,000 cubic kilometers (330,000,000 cubic miles). The ground water is estimated to be about 10,500,000 cubic kilometers, a total of 1,410,500,000 cubic kilometers. Each year about 445,000 cubic kilometers of water enters the atmosphere by evaporation from the world's oceans and seas, and by transpiration, and returns to Earth in the form of rain.

If the rate of the evaporation before the Flood was the same as it is now, then during the Antediluvian Age of 1,656 years about 736,970,000 cubic kilometers of water entered the atmosphere. This would be more than half of all the water on Earth. This cannot be possible. Therefore, there must have been a different system in operation which did not draw so much water into the atmosphere. There is no evidence whatsoever, that the water vapor constituted a water ball around the Earth. If all the water vapor transformed into a water ball, the ball would have been several hundred meters thick and would have reduced the penetration of the sun's rays to such a point that it would have resulted in an ice age, which is unthinkable.

Rain began with the Flood. Rain is condensed water vapor that falls from clouds and reaches the ground in the form of liquid water drops. According to meterological measurements, heavy rain measures about 8 millimeters (0.3 inch) and more per hour. Let us say that heavy rain measures about 1.25 centimeters (0.5) inch) per hour. This would make about 30 centimeters (12 inches) per day and night. Genesis 7:12 shows that it rained 40 days and 40 nights. According to that, it rained about 12 meters (40 feet) during 40 days.

At the present time, there is enough water vapor in the atmosphere to cover the Earth about 2.5 centimeters (1 inch) with water. This leads to the inevitable conclusion that the evaporation before the Noachian Flood was very small in comparison to the present meteorological system.

Genesis 1:7 reads: *"And God made the firmament and divided the waters which were under the firmament from the waters which were above the firmament...."* The firmament itself means expanse, the atmospheric layer. At the time of the restoration of the planet Earth, the Lord reactivated the sun, and the radiation warmed the cold climate in the Middle East area, and it produced fog. On the second day, the Lord set laws in motion which separated the fog from the waters below, and the fog in the upper atmosphere became the unseen water vapor.

It seems to me that those that advocate the water canopy theory, "greenhouse effect," do not know the Bible properly. Because of the lack of biblical knowledge, the advocates of this theory believe that all the dinosaurs and tropical tree fossils found in Antarctica and animal fossils in other parts of the world perished at the time of the Flood. People who believe and teach so seem to know nothing about Satan's position in past eternity or of life on Earth before the fall of Lucifer, billions of years ago. So, the "greenhouse effect," must be rejected as untenable and unacceptable.

Genesis 1:14 reveals a very important statement of God. *"...Let there be lights in the firmament of heaven to divide the day from the night; and let them be for signs, and for seasons, and for days and years."* "Seasons" is a key word to unlock the truth about the different seasons before the Flood.

Season is one of the divisions of the year, as spring, summer, autumn, and winter. It is also a period in which a special type of agricultural work is normal and a particular type of weather prevails.

Season is translated from the Hebrew "mowadah," and means "an appointment," "a fixed time or season," "an appointed time." For example: Exodus 13:10 says: *"Thou shalt therefore keep this ordinance in its season from year to year."* Here the Lord indicated a certain appointed time for each year when the passover was to be kept. The same Hebrew word "mowadah" has been translated plural (seasons) in Genesis 1:14. This then refers to different seasons in each year, such as summer, autumn, winter, and spring. In Psalms 104:19 David writes: *"He appointed the moon for seasons...."* Here again, the same Hebrew word "mowadah" has been used.

The conclusion is that before the Noachian Flood all four seasons operated according to the laws of God, and have never been changed.

CHAPTER IV

THE CONDITIONS ON THE ORIGINAL PLANET EARTH

The Meteorological Conditions on the Original Planet Earth

The Bible teaches that whatever the Lord God does is good. He does nothing that is not good. When the Lord began to restore our Earth to its original usefulness, it is stated seven times in Genesis 1:4-31 that *"God saw that it was good."* In Genesis 1:1 the statement, *"In the beginning God created the heavens and the earth,"* refers to the timeless past when the entire universe came from the hands of God in perfect beauty. Notice that "the heavens" is in the plural, and not in the singular as in the King James Version.

Isaiah 45:18 reveals that the Lord formed the Earth to be inhabited, not to be empty. The word "formed" has been translated from the Hebrew "yatsar," which in a way means "to mold into a form," "to shape," as a potter does the clay. That there was life on planet Earth is a fact which can be established by biblical evidence, as well as by geological evidence. The prophet Isaiah wrote about Satan's original state. Isaiah 14:14 reads: *"I will ascend above the heights of the clouds; I will make myself like the Most High."* That is what Satan said in his heart before his fall in past eternity. "Clouds" is translated from the Hebrew "ab" which means "darkness" or "density," "a cloud." "Ab" comes from the Hebrew "uwb," a primitive root, "to be dense," "cover with a cloud." "Ab" is used in many places in the Bible to denote clouds. In Judges 5:4 the writer says: *"...yea, the clouds dropped water."* "Clouds" is translated from the Hebrew "ab." Psalms 18:11 says: *"He made thick clouds of the skies."* The same Hebrew word is used for the clouds. In Isaiah 5:6 the

Lord says: *"...I will also command the clouds that they rain no rain upon it."* Clouds is translated from the Hebrew "ab" which means "clouds that give rain."

There are Scripture references that speak about the clouds in past eternity, confirming the fact that there were meteorological conditions on the original Earth. Proverbs 8:28 says: *"When He made firm the skies above, when the foundations of the deep became strong."* This is a reference to the time of creation, when the Lord brought the universe into being. "Skies" is translated from the Hebrew "shachaq" which means "a thin vapor," "sky," "cloud," "firmament." The translation "skies," does not seem to be an accurate translation because "shachaq" is in the singular not in the plural. In Proverbs 3:20, Solomon wrote: *"By His knowledge the depths were broken up, and the skies drop down the dew."* Again "skies," is translated from the Hebrew "shachaq." But here the skies dropped down dew, which means moisture. Job 36:27-28 says: *"For He drawest up the drops of water, which distil in rain from His vapor.*

"Which the skies pour down and drop upon man abundantly." "The skies" is translated again from the word "shachaq." But in the Hebrew "shachaq" is in the singular, sky, cloud and not in the plural. So, the more correct translation should have been "clouds." It is so translated in the King James Version of 1611. Proverbs 8:28 reads: *"When He established the clouds above: when He strengthened the foundations of the deep."* It is so translated in Finnish: "...He established the clouds...." and not skies. The New International version translates it "clouds" and not skies. It is translated "clouds" in the Estonian language, in Swedish and in Danish.

When talking to Job the Lord said: *"When I made the clouds...."* (Job 38:9). Here the Lord referred to the time of the creation of the universe and the Earth. It was at that time that He also put the hydrologic cycle into operation. The clouds point out that there were meteorological conditions on Earth. If there were clouds, there must have been rainfall to sustain life on Earth. The presence of clouds implies the hydrologic cycle, which contains three steps in its operation. The meteorological conditions are the same now as they were on the perfect Earth in past eternity.

1. Evaporation, water converted into vapor
2. Condensation, vapor becoming more compact

3. Precipitation, water vapor falling to the Earth in the form of rain

The three basic human needs on planet Earth are:

1. Food
2. Shelter
3. Clothing

The pre-historic animals ate grass, as do animals on Earth at the present time. The mammoths disinterred in Siberia had grass in their stomachs, showing that there was grass, flowers or vegetation on Earth then. This proves the fact that the digestive system was just the same on Earth then as it is now.

The pre-Adamic race needed shelter, food and cover for their physical bodies. As humans, they had houses like we have today to protect them from rain. There were clouds, which implies precipitation, water vapor falling to the Earth in the form of rain. There were communities on Earth then just like we have today. Jeremiah 4:26 states: *"I beheld, and, lo, the fruitful field was a wilderness, and all the cities thereof were broken down at the presence of Jehovah, and before His fierce anger."*

Before the fall of Satan, there was a warm climate throughout the Earth, and heavy snow and rain storms were unknown, since winds are caused by warm and cold air mixing. All the evidence studied and included in this book confirms that on the perfect Earth, before the fall of Lucifer, there was a temperate climate, tropical trees and flowers grew, and great forests flourished all over the world. Remains of tropical trees have been found on Greenland and in other parts of the world, where it is now impossible for tropical trees to grow.

As the reader continues to read and to study this book it will soon be clear that what is written in this book is established fact, and not fiction.

Fossilized Plants and Animals, Evidence of Life on the Original Earth

Fossils are remains of past life on Earth. Occasionally, whole organisms are preserved in their original state. Carcasses of pleistocene elephants and rhinoceroses have been found preserved in the asphalt deposits of eastern Galicia, Russia. Fossils of plants and trees have been found in many parts of the world. The World Book

Encyclopedia writes that "fossil palms and magnolia found in Greenland indicate a warm moist climate at that time." [1]

The mammoths disinterred in Siberia had grass in their stomachs. Their destruction must have come so suddenly that some of them had grass in their mouths. This must have happened at the time Satan fell. The judgment that fall brought with it was so sudden that animals had no time to swallow their food. This is evidence that there was life on the perfect Earth before the fall of Satan, called the "Day-star, Son of the Morning" in the American Standard Version and "Lucifer" in The King James Version. Isaiah 14:12 says: *"How art thou fallen from heaven, O Day-star, Son of the Morning...?"*

The prophet Jeremiah confirms the fact that there was life on the perfect Earth in past eternity. Jeremiah 4:25 says: *"I beheld, and, lo, there was no man, and all the birds of the heavens were fled."* This implies that at one time they were in existence, but had disappeared. The World Book Encyclopedia writes further about fossil discoveries. "A bird fossil was found in limestone rocks in southern Germany. The bird was about the same size as a crow. Fossil shell fish indicate that the rocks containing them formed under the ocean. Paleontologists find such rocks high in the Alps in Europe, the Andes Mountains in South America, the Himalaya in the Far East, and the Rockies in North America. They know that these areas, once under water, were lifted up to form mountain ranges.

"The long series of fossil animals and plants found in succeeding layers of the Earth's crust builds up the story of past life." [2]

Large fossil beds have been found in the States of Illinois and Iowa, U.S.A. On the 13th of October, 1988, I called the Department of Geology of Beloid College, Beloid, Wisconsin, U.S.A. and talked to the geology professor about the fossils found in the State of Iowa.

In 1884, a blast in the quarry at Le Grand, Iowa, exposed a bed of stone flowers on the dislodged limestone slab. These were marine animals related to starfish, fossils of crinoids. In 1931, another blast uncovered a greater fossil bed. One slab saved from the crusher bore on its face the fossil imprints of over 180 starfish, 12 sea urchins, 2 trilobites, and some other organisms.

In 1933, a third extensive fossil bed was discovered. In the next four years, thousands of specimens were taken from it. They included

1. "Fossils" *The World Book Encyclopedia,* VII (1982) pp. 366-367.
2. Ibid., pp. 366-367.

many species of the closely related blastoids, 40 species of crinoids, as well as bryozoands, brachiopods, and corals. [3]

The Mazon Creek region near Chicago, Illinois, yielded 320 animal species — jellyfish, shrimps, worms, fish, the earliest squid, the only fossil hydra, as well as the fossil lamprey. The same area has also yielded plants — bark, roots, seeds, and ferns. Finding jellyfish on a hillside and marine animals in a coal mine, 1,600 kilometers from the sea, is truly strange. It shows that in past eternity vast areas of the United States were covered by water, and marine animals swam in those areas.

Thus we learn, the Earth's crust is a great depository of evidence of a life of the past which perished at the fall of Lucifer over 15,500,000,000 years ago. These remains of past life confirm the fact that there was life on planet Earth billions of years ago.

Dr. Henry M. Morris writes about "the fossil fish beds which have been found, extending miles in every direction, and contain fish buried in whole shoals by the millions. The fish have every appearance of having been buried alive and with great suddenness." [4]

This is evidence that in past eternity the seas were filled with living creatures, but all perished when Satan fell. Dr. Morris writes about the mammoth beds in Siberia saying, "that literally millions of these mammoths have been entombed in the vast wilderness of Siberia. The remains of the last meal, consisting of elephant grass and other plants, now utterly foreign to the region, have been found in their stomachs. From the evidence of the congested blood in the blood vessels of all these frozen mammoths, scientists say that they must have died by drowning. The hippopotamus beds in Sicily, the horse beds of France and other parts of Europe, to say nothing of the shells of the marine organisms, which probably form the greater part of the stratified deposits of the globe, all point to a great, world-wide catastrophe.

"The Siberian mammoths are an especially vivid illustration of one outstanding fact that paleontology unquestionably reveals, that at one time in the history of the globe there was a world-wide temperate climate. The remains of coral reefs formed by sea

3. Department of Geology, Beloid College, Wisconsin, U.S.A.
4. Dr. Henry M. Morris, *The Bible and Modern Science* (Chicago: Moody Press, 1951), p. 71.

creatures that can live only in warm waters have been found so far north, that it is believed now that they underlie the very poles themselves. Tropical animals have been found in large numbers as fossils in Greenland, Alaska and practically every region in the world. Fossil ferns and other tropical and temperate vegetation have likewise been found in large numbers in the polar region. Even in the very coldest region of the globe, the great continent of Antarctica, extensive coal beds have been found, extending almost to the South Pole itself." [5]

In 1977, the writer of this thesis visited a park in the State of Arizona, the United States of America. In that park there were multitudes of petrified wood. Big, long trees were swept together there and then petrified. This is proof that forests grew on the original Earth billions of years ago.

The Mystery of the Siberian Mammoths Resolved

Siberia is a vast land area in the Soviet Union. Encyclopedia Americana says that the land area is about 13,000,000 square kilometers (5,000,000 sq. miles), extending from the Ural Mountains to the Pacific Ocean. The New Siberian Islands, an archipelago in Russia, consists of three groups of islands lying between the Laptev and East Siberian seas and is included in the Yakut Autonomous Republic of the Soviet Union. The New Siberian Islands have an area of 28,500 square kilometers (11,000 sq. miles).

The northeast group, the De Long Islands, has steep cliffs and small glaciers, but the other islands are low and free of glaciers. The Lyakov Islands constitute the southern group. The center group of the New Siberian Islands proper consists of three large, flat islands and several smaller islands.

The islands of this group are best known for the thick deposits of fossil ground ice that are partly buried beneath silts. The abundant frozen silts contain mammoths, rhinoceros, musk-ox, and other fossil remains. Winters are long, windy, and cold, with little snow and much fog. The damp summer lasts two months, and temperatures rarely rise above freezing. The vegetation consists of an impoverished tundra, entirely lacking trees. [6]

The Lyakov Islands are about 150 kilometers from the Siberian mainland. It was on this island that Lyakhov in 1770 uncovered a

5. Ibid., pp. 72-73.
6. "The New Siberian Islands" *Encyclopedia Americana,* XX (1986) p. 221.

vast amount of fossil ivory, other fossils as well. The New Siberian Islands must have been all one continent where vast hords of mammoths thrived. The East Siberian Sea bottom no doubt conceals millions of buried mammoths. Encyclopedia Americana shows that the mammoths roamed over four continents.

Mammoths formerly existed throughout Europe, Asia, North America, and North Africa. Two species of mammoths are known. The flatbrowed mammoth of Asia was relatively small and had a flat forehead. The southern mammoth of Europe had a domed forehead, and was gigantic in size, standing 4.3 to 4.6 meters (14 to 15 feet) at the shoulder. One woolly mammoth tusk is 5 meters (16 feet, 5 inches) long. Frozen bodies of woolly mammoths have been found in the arctic ice of Asia and North America. [7]

The huge elephant-like animals in Siberia are evidence of life on Earth in past eternity. The existence of these huge animals in Siberia was known at least 2,000 years ago, because the Chinese merchants bought ivory from the Siberian tribes. They did not know exactly what kind of animal the ivory came from. All sorts of speculation circulated.

Great stretches of Siberia are covered by thick forest, through which great rivers meander. In the north is found the tundra, where nothing grows. The tundra and much of Siberia, is a land gripped perpetually by permafrost frozen cold and rock-hard to depths of up to 308 meters (1,000 feet). Of all the merchandise that came from Siberia, the most precious was ivory from the tusks of mammoths.

Since mammoths, elephant-like creatures, were warmth-loving creatures, they could not possibly live in Siberia now because of the unusually cold climate. This leads to the inevitable conclusion that, at one time in the past Siberia had a warm climate. A great catastrophe destroyed the mammoths and buried them under sand and rocks, where they have been preserved in a frozen tundra for billions of years.

In the vicinity of Jeniseik, and further down toward Mangasea the natives, in 1715, found strange bones like ivory, along the banks of the rivers and in the hollows occasioned by the fall of the earth.

The amount of fossil ivory that Lyakhov and others like him uncovered was incredible. It is reported that the town of Yakutsk was the chief marketplace where the ivory was sold. An average of

---

7. "Mammoth" *Encyclopedia Americana,* 18 (1986) pp. 209-210.

22,650 kilograms (50,000 pounds) of ivory a year went on sale in Yakutsk throughout the nineteenth century. The volume of trade in mammoth tusks grew steadily. At least 23,000 tons (46,000,000 pounds) of ivory was sold over a period of 100 years.

The huge mammoth, found in 1799 at the mouth of the Lena River, was disinterred in 1806. This huge mammoth stood 3.2 meters (10 feet, 8 inches) at the shoulder. Full grown African elephants today average 3 to 3.5 meters in height at the shoulder and weigh 5 to 7 tons. The biggest elephant ever known was killed in 1955 and stood 4 meters, 5 centimeters (13 feet, 3 inches) in height, and weighed 12 tons.

In August of 1900, the natives found a large mammoth near the Beresovka River in northeastern Siberia. The huge beast was disinterred by scientists. From the position in which the mammoth lay, it was possible to guess at the way the animal had met its death. It was sitting on its haunches in a stumbled-looking way, with its right hind leg thrust forward and its front limbs fixed, as if grasping at the ground. The mammoth had broken its right foreleg and its pelvis. The immense stomach still contained about thirty pounds of undigested food. From the food still in the mammoth's mouth and in the stomach when death came, botanists were able to determine its diet. The mammoths ate grasses, herbs, wild flowers, mosses, branches of dwarfed larch, fir and pine. The presence of seeds showed that the animal must have died during the harvest season. When the Beresovka mammoth's blood was tested, it showed a close relationship between Siberian mammoths and modern Asian elephants.

A discovery of a mammoth was made in 1948 on the Taimyr Peninsula in western Siberia. The skeleton was buried amid remains of ancient birch and willow trees, which today cannot grow in that area because of the cold.

The mystery of the Siberian mammoths can be only unlocked in light of the biblical revelation of life on planet Earth before the fall of Satan in past eternity. Before the fall of Lucifer, there was a world wide temperate climate because the Earth was erect. Mammoths roamed the vast areas of Europe and Siberia. All the mammoths found were buried deep under sand, and in the ice. This reveals that a sudden catastrophe destroyed the Earth with all life on it. And this happened over 15,500,000,000 years ago.

Job 9:5-7 says: *"Him that removeth the mountains, and they know it not, when He overturneth them in His anger.*

"That shaketh the earth out of its place, and the pillars thereof tremble.

"That commandeth the sun and it riseth not, and sealeth up the stars."

At the fall of Satan, the Lord extinguished the sun. Large areas of the Earth overturned, burying everything on it — including the mammoths. The destruction came so suddenly that some of the mammoths still had grass in their mouths. Thus, the mammoths in Siberia have been buried for over 15,500,000,000 years. Because of erosion, many skeletons of these animals were exposed in Siberia. That is what led people to those areas: the ivory hunt, which had great commercial value.

The Beresovka mammoth, as restored and mounted in the Zoological Museum at Leningrad.

Did Mammoths and People Live Together in Europe in Past Eternity?

Because of the archaeological discoveries in Europe in the past century, scientists have concluded that huge animals and people must have lived together. However, we shall see if this really was so.

Mr. Silverberg, who believes this, writes in his book, "The Morning of Mankind, Prehistoric Man in Europe," about such archaeological discoveries. About 1850, a farmer name Joseph Crometschek found a vast deposit of bones in Predmost, Czechoslovakia. To the farmer these discoveries had but one use. When ground to powder, bones make excellent fertilizer. There was such a great supply that Crometschek started selling wagonloads of bones to other farmers.

In 1878, Czech archaeologists learned about what was going on at Predmost. They persuaded Crometschek to sell his land to a museum, and by 1884 excavators were at work. 2 to 3 meters below the surface they found a layer of ancient deposits nearly a meter thick. It contained the ashes of many fires and the bones of the great beasts, chiefly those of the wooly mammoths.

The archaeologists realized that they were digging up a hunting camp that had been occupied for hundreds of years by people of the Gravettin culture. The bones of more than 1,000 mammoths were found. Jindrich Wankel and Karl Maska, the archaeologists who led the Predmost work, believed that this had been a settlement of nomadic, prehistoric hunters. The hunting range of the Gravettians was a narrow grassy strip, bordered on the south by the Alpine glaciers and on the north by the great Arctic ice sheet. In 1895, one of the archaeologists digging at Predmost found a piece of mammoth tusk out of which a small figure of a mammoth had been carved. By 1900, nearly every prehistorian accepted the view that the Predmost mammoths were the victims of human hunters.

One discovery, made at Predmost in 1894, showed that mammoth bones were an important building material for the prehistoric hunters. At a depth of 3 meters (9 feet), the archaeologist found a mass grave whose walls were formed from the shoulder blades and skulls of mammoths. Within lay the skeletons of nearly fifty people, close together in a squatting position. Great care had been taken to protect the bodies, surrounding them with the massive bones of the beasts that yielded food, and covering the grave with a blanket of stones to ward off foxes and hyenas. Reverence for the dead indicates a belief in the existence of a soul, a spirit that survives the mere body. A whole constellation of religious and philosophical attitudes can be inferred from a single grave. The Predmost excavations also brought to light thousands of flint tools: knives, choppers, chisels, and other implements in the Gravettian style that were needed in those days.

Elsewhere at Predmost were orderly stacks of mammoth bones,

obviously awaiting use by prehistoric craftsmen. 13 tusks were found lying together, and in another place, a pile of 50 molars. This discovery led the scientists to believe that the mammoths and the people lived at the same time at Predmost.

Other evidence used by archaeologists to sustain their belief includes caves in France and Spain in which were found huge paintings of animals on the walls. Mr. Silverberg writes about a cave at Altamira, Spain, discovered in 1878. Here were vivid paintings of animals, in life size, glowing with color so warm it seemed they could have been painted just days before. Here was a herd of massive humped bison, grazing, running, sleeping, standing. Here were wild horses and charging boars, prancing beasts in red and brown and black, a stupendous gallery of portraits of the creatures that once had made Europe their home. In this cave there were no mammoths.

However, at the cave of Font de Gaume, France another gallery of paintings awaited the archaeologists. There were 80 bisons, 40 horses, 23 mammoths, 17 reindeer, 8 wild cattle, 4 antelopes, 2 woolly rhinoceroses, a bear, a wolf, and a lioness. In one place was shown a procession of mammoths walking in single file, great solemn shaggy beasts with immense tusks and lofty bumps on their heads and shoulders. [8]

According to the archaeologists the mammoths of the cave paintings reveal in a unique way extinct creatures seen through the eyes of the men who dwelled among them.

As far as the Predmost finds are concerned, there is great confusion. The remains of mammoths found are prehistoric, but the ashes of innumerable fires are of the present age. They have found the remains of fifty people in a grave, and think that they belong to the ages past. All these suppositions are wrong and need to be corrected. The archaeologists found the grave deep under ground. The bones of mammoths were placed in a separate place by themselves, and the ashes of fires found at Predmost has led them to the conclusion that people must have lived among them, and killed the mammoths. All must be refused.

The theory regarding the remains of mammoths is correct. It establishes the fact that mammoths did live in Europe in past eternity and perished at the fall of Satan. The people that lived at the present day Predmost are of the Adamic race, and are not of the pre-Adamic

8. Robert Silverberg, *The Morning of Mankind, Prehistoric Man in Europe,* (New York: New York Graphic Society Publishers, LTD. 1967), pp. 80-82.

race, because before the fall of Lucifer in past eternity there was no death. When Satan sinned against the Almighty God, the entire planet Earth was destroyed, with all life on it.

Death came into the world by Adam's sin. The human skeletons found at Predmost are the remains of the present Adamic race, and it was after the Flood that they lived there. Those people found those mammoth fossils and gathered some of those huge bones together. During thousands of years, erosion buried the campsite under deep sand.

As to the cave paintings, they are not of past eternity, as is believed and accepted, but were painted after the Flood. This can be understood only in light of the biblical revelation. Horses, lions, bears, and antelopes are also prehistorical animals, as well as of the present creation. In past eternity, there were not only dinosaurs but mastodons and other animals of that nature. If these cave paintings had been painted before the Flood, the paint would have dissolved during the great Deluge. The cave paintings cannot be older than 3,500 years.

A huge mammoth was disinterred in Germany. This monstrous beast was 14 feet and 4 inches high. The mammoth had a dense fur, forming an overcoat hanging almost to the ground. A fine undercoat of 1 inch long hair covered the mammoth's entire body. Above this was a much thicker layer of hair, 4 to 6 inches long on the lower part of the legs, and up to a foot and a half in length on the back and sides of the body.

It must be concluded, at this point, that the pre-Adamic race did not eat meat, because they were vegetarians. Before the fall of Satan, there was no sin in the universe, and blood shedding and meat eating was unknown. Therefore, the people of Predmost cannot be of the pre-Adamic race. The skeletons found in an underground cave belong to the Adamic race. Death entered into the present world by Adam's sin. The Antediluvian people, those living before the Flood, were all vegetarians. Meat eating was introduced by God after the Flood. Moses wrote in Genesis 9:3: *"Every moving thing that liveth shall be food for you: as the green herb have I given you all."* Later God revealed to Israel which of the animals were clean and edible, and which were unclean and to be rejected.

Therefore, the notion that the people of the past ages killed the mammoths before Satan's fall must be rejected as untenable and untrue. However, I do accept the thesis that people in past eternity lived together with mammoths and dinosaurs in Europe, but when Lucifer fell, all life was destroyed by God, including life in the area we now call Europe.

Dinosaur and Human Footprints in Limestone in Texas, U.S.A.

Geology has given us excellent evidence, absolute facts, that at one time people and dinosaurs lived together. There have been dramatic discoveries of footprints in stone in the Paluxy riverbed near Glen Rose, Texas, U.S.A. Discoveries of human footprints among dinosaur footprints in the Paluxy bottom limestone began in 1909.

Layered rocks in the Dinosaur Valley State Park near Glen Rose Texas, belong to the Glen Rose formation, deposited long ago as seas began their oscillating advance across the eroded terrain of more ancient rocks in central and north-central Texas. As the animals moved from place to place, they left deeply impressed tracks in the soft, limy mud. When filled with new sediments washed in from bordering lagoons, and upon hardening into rock, the ancient footprints became the preserved molds that have been found today in many parts of the world.

Dinosaur tracks from Glen Rose limestone outcrops are present at more than fifteen different localities extending from Kinney County, west of Uvalde, to the Paluxy River in Somervell County. The first tracks were found near Glen Rose in 1909, but they were not widely acclaimed until 1938, when Roland T. Bird of the American Museum of Natural History visited the site. Among the many tracks he found were a remarkable double set of tracks left by a giant sauropod dinosaur followed by a large carnivorous dinosaur. This impressive record of an ancient hunt was collected and placed on exhibit at the American Museum of Natural History in New York City. Other tracks collected nearby were put on exhibit at the Texas Memorial Museum in Austin, capital of the State of Texas.

Three kinds of dinosaur tracks occur in the Glen Rose formation. The most common are three-toed, giant bird-like imprints, measuring from 30 centimeters (12 inches) to 60 centimeters (24 inches) in length and from 23 centimeters (9 inches) to 42 centimeters (17 inches) in width, with a stride length ranging from 1 meter and 12 centimeters (45 inches) to 1 meter and 62 centimeters (65 inches). The only dinosaur known from nearby contemporaneous deposits whose foot structure matches these tracks is Acrocanthosaurus — a 6 meter to 9 meter (20 to 30 feet) long two-legged carnosaur, belonging to the same group as the later, and even larger Tyrannosaurus Rex.

The second category of prints consists of saucer-like depressions, ranging to over 90 centimeters (36 inches) in length and 60 centimeters (24 inches) in width, with stride lengths from 2 meters and 10 centimeters to 3 meters (7 to 10 feet). Only one group of dinosaurs contained representatives capable of leaving such enormous tracks. These were the sauropods, plant-eating forms with serpentine necks, massive bodies on pillar-like legs, and long tails. Their biggest member was a 21 meter (70 feet) long Apatosaurus. Glen Rose deposits contain only one kind of sauropod, a dinosaur, 9 meters to 15 meters (30 to 50 feet) long, with a short neck and tail, called Pleurocoelus. When walking, Pleurocoelus made saucer-like depressions with its four-toed, clawed hind feet, it also left odd, crescent shaped tracks as its sheathed front feet sank into the mud.

The third category of footprints is something of a mystery, although these tracks are attributed to an early ornithopod — one of the two-legged plant-eaters whose later descendents included the duck-billed dinosaur. Like the first kind of tracks mentioned, the impressions are large, three-toed and bird-like, but the toes are not as elongated, and the heel tends to be more rounded in outline. The fossil remains of a 4.5 meter to 6 meter (15 to 20 feet) long ornithopod called Tenontosaurus have been found in adjacent areas, but this dinosaur's size and four-toed foot structure do not match the stubby-toed prints very well. In 1985, a Texas discovery of Iguanodon bones, belonging to a 9 meter long ornithopod previously known only from Europe, may account for the originator of the mystery footprints.

The various dinosaur tracks at the Dinosaur Valley Park near Glen Rose, Texas, and surrounding areas have furnished scientists with fascinating evidence about the habits of creatures long extinct.

Dinosaur and human footprints have been found in India, Australia and the Soviet Union, confirming the fact that at one time on planet Earth humans and dinosaurs lived together. However, almost all the preachers and Christian scientists, geologists and other Christian teachers believe that the footprints belong to the Antediluvian Age — before the Noachian Flood. They are mistaken because they have not understood the biblical revelation correctly when it speaks of the fall of Satan and the subsequent destruction of the Earth over 15,500,000,000 years ago.

In June, 1988, I visited the Paluxy River area and saw with my own eyes the footprints of dinosaurs and humans. The discoveries at Paluxy River area has revealed that at least 12 different types of dinosaurs roamed there some time in past eternity.

On September 6, 1988, I again visited the Glen Rose area to get more information about the dinosaur and human footprints. In 1982, the first clearly defined human footprint among the dinosaur tracks was found by the excavation team. This human footprint was only 46 centimeters from the nearest dinosaur track. It was underneath a layer of limestone, 30 centimeters thick. Sometimes they were overlapping. A human footprint was found underneath a dinosaur footprint. The human toes were protruding beyond the dinosaur track that had landed on top of the human print.

In one place a human hand impression was found. There was a left scoop mark and the placement of the right hand print could be seen. I saw a right foot impression, the large toe print, then the second, third, fourth and little toes. The ridge marks of all five toes, from the large toe all the way to the little toe, could be seen.

At the Creation Evidences' Museum at Glen Rose, I also saw human footprints cut out of limestone, and small clams. These impacted clams have been found in many places in the Glen Rose area. One clam, buried alive, was in the process of extruding its young from the relevant section of its body at the time it was deposited alive. Wood has also been found in the Creataceous limestone, still intact, with all the fibers identical to modern wood. Even the coloration has been preserved.

As I walked around in the Paluxy River area and saw the dinosaur and human footprints, I came to the conclusion that men and dinosaurs lived and walked together. The animal and human footprints were on the same level. Many believe that dinosaurs lived before the Flood, just 5,000 years ago. According to the Creation Evidences' Museum, about 186 dinosaur tracks and 54 human prints have been found in the Paluxy River area.

Skeletons of mammoths have been found all over Europe, buried apparently, by an overwhelming flood. Besides mammoths, other fossil creatures have been found in the same strata — including cave bear, rhinoceros, hyena, horse, deer, oxen, bison red-deer, leopard and several kinds of birds. The evidence of these vast fossil graveyards, extending across an entire continent, points to a water catastrophe of immense proportions. It is believed that it was the Flood that destroyed all these animals at the same time.

Fossil tropical palm trees have been found in Alaska and Greenland. At Prudhoe Bay, Alaska, the ground is frozen to a depth of 583 meters (1,900 feet). Everywhere the oil companies drilled around this area they discovered an ancient tropical forest. It was in a frozen state, not a petrified one. It was located between 338 meters (1,100 feet) and 523 meters (1,700 feet) below the present surface. Pine trees, palm trees, and tropical foliage were found in great profusion, lapped over each other, as though they had fallen in that position. The oil at Prudhoe is found at depths of 2,933 meters (8,700 feet). It comes to the surface without artificial pumping.

Fossilized skeletons of 23 gigantic herbivorous dinosaurs (Inguanodons) were found in a Belgian coal mine. This shows to us, dear reader, that the trees and the dinosaurs perished at the same time. They were swept away together by flood waters. Carbon dating has shown that the coal and oil both are 5,000 years old. I have to say that the carbon-14 dating is very unreliable. Scientists say that coal must be millions of years old. Who is right? Who is wrong? It is reported that at one place gold jewelry, and even a bronze bell, was found inside the coal. According to this report the coal had to be formed after the man-made objects had taken shape. In other words, the coal was formed after man was around, and not millions of years before. The jewelry story must be rejected as false. Dinosaur's footprints have been found all over the world. They have been found in Canada, the U.S.A., Europe, Russia, India and Australia. Some of them have been huge creatures. It is reported that one huge dinosaur was 15.5 meters (50 feet) high at the shoulders with another 6.5 meters (20 feet) of neck. This huge animal of 21.5 meters (70 feet) could look over a 7 story house.

The dinosaur skeletons found in 1877-1878 in a coal mine in Belgium, 300 meters (984 feet) below the surface, are further evidence of a terrific overturning of mountains and land areas.

Fossil bones of Lystrosaurus have been found in South Africa, India and Antarctica. A backbone of Ouranosaurus was found in the Sahara, Africa, exposed by the action of wind.

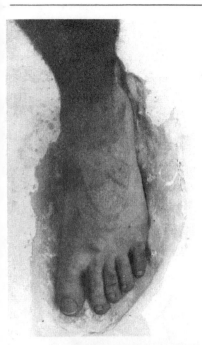

Science teacher Garry Stone puts his foot into the cast of one of the footprints found by the Baugh team between Locus A and B at Glen Rose, Texas. It was virtually a perfect fit.

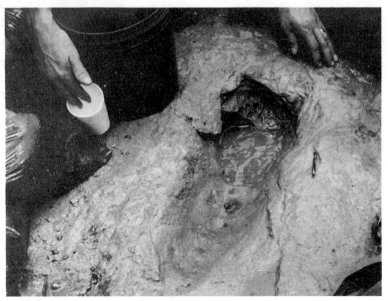

Contrary to some published reports, this photo of the "Ryals" footprint shows all five toes, with mud up-push all around the track, and no stains!

This shows some of the Paluxy River limestone ledges. When the river is very low other levels can be seen. Dinosaur tracks have been found at no less than six such levels.

This is the late Mrs. McFall (right) on whose property much of the Baugh excavation has been undertaken. She is holding a cast of a footprint found on their property some years ago.

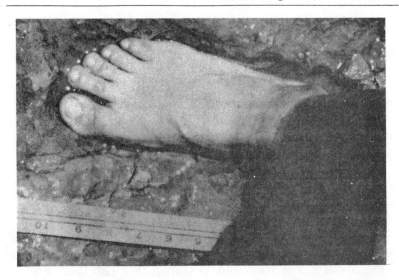

The picture is another footprint at Dinosaur State Park. The modern man whose foot you see put that foot into the footprint from the past. It fitted comfortably.

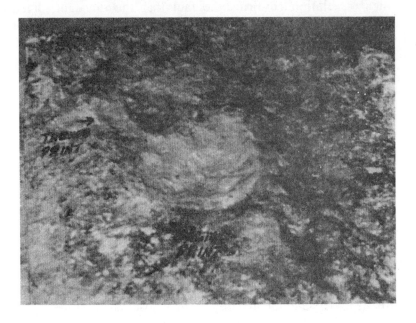

Even a human handprint was identified — as if somebody has fallen when moving into this fast setting layer of limestone. Notice the palm print, the thumb print, and the finger prints.

In the picture you see several **Paluxy River** limestone ledges. Dinosaur footprints have been found on six such ledges.* How can this be possible to have so many limestone ledges with dinosaur tracks on them? To unlock the mystery is not so difficult.

As the pre-historic creatures moved from place to place, they left deeply impressed tracks in the soft limy mud. When filled with new sediments washed in from bordering lagoons, and upon hardening into rock, the ancient footprints became the preserved molds that have been found in the Glen Rose area.

New sediments, washed in by erosion and rainfall, brought a new layer of limy mud, on which dinosaurs again left their footprints. In this process of many thousands of years, several limestone ledges were built by nature.

We shall now study the Scriptures to see if the hypothesis that the dinosaurs were Antediluvian creatures, who lived before the Flood, about 5,000 years ago, is correct. We conclude that this hypotheses must be rejected as untenable and unrealistic. It is the concept of those whose biblical knowledge is very limited. The biblical revelation confirms the fact that the dinosaurs lived billions of years ago on the first perfect Earth before the fall of Lucifer, more than 15,500,000,000 years ago. This can be substantiated by 10 irrefutable facts.

1. The fall of Satan in past eternity
2. The destruction of the first perfect Earth
3. The Siberian mammoths, evidence of a sudden catastrophe
4. Buried forests and oil deep under ground
5. A world wide distribution of fossils
6. No rain before the Noachian Flood
7. A slow increase of the Flood waters
8. Great topographical changes on planet Earth
9. At the Flood, the vegetation kingdom not destroyed
10. The time element involved in forming sandstone

All those who hold to the view that all the fossils derived from the Flood never make reference to Satan's rebellion in past eternity. It is because these sincere men do not know the history of Lucifer and his rebellion against the Almighty God billions of years ago. No one can correctly understand the mystery of the dinosaurs unless he knows

---

* The pictures of Glen Rose area, Texas, have been used by permission of the Creation Evidences' Museum, P.O. Box 309, Glen Rose, TX 76043.

the history of Lucifer (see Chapter V). I will mention briefly the Scriptures where God speaks about His viceroy before his fall.

1. Ezekiel 28:13-17 speaks about Lucifer's past position. Ezekiel 28:14-15 states: *"Thou wast the anointed cherub that covereth: and I set thee, so that thou wast upon the holy mountain of God....*

"Thou wast perfect in thy ways from the day that thou wast created, till unrighteousness was found in thee."

In Isaiah 14:12-14 God speaks about Satan's meditation before his fall in past eternity. I include Isaiah 14:13. *"And thou saidst in thy heart, I will ascend into heaven, I will exalt my throne above the stars of God...."* This shows that he had a throne to sit upon. He was a king on the perfect Earth. He decided to rebel, or dethrone God so that he himself could become the king of the universe, but the Lord cast him down with the angels that joined him in this rebellion. This rebellion resulted in the destruction of planet Earth.

2. The judgment of the perfect Earth in past eternity resulted in total destruction, including all life on Earth. Isaiah 45:18 says: *"...Jehovah that created the heavens, the God that formed the earth and made it, that established it and created it not a waste, that formed it to be inhabited...."* Genesis 1:2 says: *"And the earth was waste and void; and darkness was upon the face of the deep...."* The verb "was" has been translated from the Hebrew word "hayah" which is not the verb "to be," but the verb "to become." So, a more correct translation would have been "and the earth became a waste." We noticed that Moses wrote that darkness was upon the face of the waters. Job 9:6-7 states: *"That shaketh the earth out of its place.... That commandeth the sun and it riseth not, and sealeth up the stars."* Here we see that the rotation of the Earth stopped, and God extinguished the sun. That is how the Ice Age, which lasted for many billions of years, came to be (see Chapter II). I have briefly shown to the reader the destruction of planet Earth at the fall of Satan over 15,500,000,000 years ago. At the time of Satan's fall, tremendous convulsions shook the Earth and buried all who lived here.

3. The Siberian mammoths are vivid evidence of such a sudden destruction. There must have been millions of huge animals that were instantly killed by the most terrible convulsions. Some of those mammoths still had grass in their mouths. They died before they had a chance to swallow the food. During the Noachian Flood, the water rose slowly, and the animals and people went up to higher ground. When the last piece of land disappeared under the water, the animals

and people, in all probability, had to stay a couple of days in the water before it reached over their heads. Then the animals, no doubt, had to swim for quite sometime before they drowned. This certainly does not imply that they had their mouths full of grass when they died.

4. The Earth, in some places, simply overturned and buried all that was on it. In Alaska, the tropical forest, found at depth of over 500 meters, implies tremendous upheaval.

Scientists say that oil is found on the bottom of ancient seas. The Prudhoe Bay, Alaska, oil field is evidence of a terrific confusion of nature in past eternity. The oil is located at a depth of nearly 3,000 meters (8,700 feet). Previously it was a sea bottom, but filled with earth up to 2,413 meters. On top of this huge deposit of sand and rocks great tropical forests were swept together, lapping over each other, just as they had fallen in that position.

On top of this frozen forest, another layer of sand and rocks was heaped up to 338 meters and 523 meters. This catastrophe in no way can be applied to the Noachian Flood. It can be ascribed to the time of the fall of Satan only, when God destroyed the first perfect Earth and overturned mountains and filled the valleys with earth. No wonder Job 28:9 says: *"...He overturneth the mountains by the roots."* Psalms 18:7 states: *"Then the earth shook and trembled; the foundations also of the mountains quaked and were shaken, because He was wroth."*

5. Fossils have been found on every continent. Dinosaur fossils have been found in Canada and the U.S.A. and dinosaur footprints have been found in many parts of the world in Europe, the Soviet Union, India and Australia. This implies a sudden world-wide destruction billion of years ago. During the Flood, there was no such destruction, which would have left animals all over the Earth. We shall see this shortly.

6. It is evident from the Scripture that there was no rain before the Flood. There has been quite an argument between Bible scholars, some saying that there was rain on Earth before the Flood, and others that there was no rain. However, I do accept the thesis that there was no rain before the Flood. Genesis 2:5-6 says: *"And no plant of the field was yet in the earth, and no herb of the field had yet sprung up for Jehovah God had not caused it to rain upon the Earth: and there was no man to till the ground,*

"But there went up a mist from the earth, and watered the whole face of the ground."

Genesis 1:6-7 seems to indicate there was water vapor in the atmosphere. Moses writes that God separated the waters which were under the firmament from the waters which were above the firmament. The waters above the firmament implies water vapor. On the third day, the trees were brought into existence. But, there was no need of rain to bring them into existence. They were created by God. Nowhere is it stated in the first six chapters of Genesis that it rained before the Flood. The first mention of rain is in Genesis 7:12. *"Then it began to rain."* God, Who is Almighty, could order it so that it did not need to rain before the Flood.

Many have referred to Job 38:9 and Proverbs 8:28, where the Lord speaks about making the clouds. This, however, refers to past eternity, when the Lord created the Earth and made the clouds, so that the pre-Adamic race could have rain and the vegetation kingdom could flourish. Some use many other Scripture passages that speak of the clouds, but they are referring to the present age. So, before the Flood there were no significant quantities of mud to form any dinosaur or human footprints.

7. It has been accepted by many Bible scholars that there were great tidal waves which swept animals into areas, where they were fossilized. There were, however, no great hydrodynamic currents and upheavals on the Earth, nor any convulsions. Genesis 7:17-18 shows that there was a slow increase of water. *"...and the waters increased...."*

"And the waters prevailed, and increased greatly upon the earth; and the ark went upon the face of the waters." When the Flood ended, the Bible again shows that there was a slow decrease of the water. Genesis 8:3 says: *"And the waters returned from off the earth continually; and after the end of a hundred and fifty days the waters decreased."* Thus, we see, in the light of the Word of God, that there was no destruction during the Flood, as is believed and taught by many (see Chapter VIII).

8. There have been great topographical changes on the Earth. The study has already revealed to us that there were dinosaurs in Canada, the United States of America, and the tip of South America. Dinosaur footprints and a skeleton have been found in Argentina. Dinosaur skeletons have been found throughout Europe. Dinosaur footprints have been found in Georgia and Uzbekistan in Russia, in Africa, India and Australia. At one place, thousands of footprints of

dinosaurs were embedded on a rock face south-west of Winton, Australia, and dinosaur bones have been found in Queensland and other places in Australia.

This shows us that at one time in past eternity all the continents were united — just one big land mass. Later many big land areas sank and the sea bottom was lifted up. At one time North America was a vast continent. Mammoths and other prehistoric animals roamed the continent. But, at the fall of Lucifer, the continent sank, and at a latter time it was lifted up. This explains why there are fossil fish and clams at Glen Rose in Texas. During the Flood, the fish were not destroyed, but swam freely in the water. So, all the fossil clams and fish are evidence that Texas, in past eternity, was a sea bottom. Before that it was a continent. This is the reason why we have dinosaur and human footprints. (Or we can assume that, at the destruction of the Earth, the waters overran the continent and brought fish and clams with it; and they were buried under sand and petrified).

Before the Flood, there were no significant quantities of mud, and therefore there would be no fossilized dinosaurs — or other fossils, for that matter. For an animal fossil to be formed, death must be followed by a sudden covering with such materials as mud, clay, gravel, or sand. Thus, the body is sealed in a protective cocoon until it is pried open by those living at much later times.

This, no doubt, is true — as far as fossilization is concerned. However, this burying of animals took place at the fall of Satan, not during the Noachian Flood — since, during the Flood, the Earth was not overturned. The water increased slowly, which forced people and animals to go up to higher ground, until the last land area disappeared under the water. All the carcasses of animals and humans were not buried at that moment, but were floating in the open water. In due time, all the bodies dissolved and bones settled on the ground. Therefore, the dinosaur and human footprints belong to the pre-historic times, as do all the fossils.

There is a general opinion that the sediment deposits which formed the limestone strata in Glen Rose, Texas, was deposited during the Flood and buried the footprints and clams under sediments. However, during the Flood no silt or sediments were deposited, because the water was almost stagnant. There was a slow rise of water which hardly stirred up any silt and sand. The only conclusion is that all the sand and silt, which formed the limestone burying the already petrified footprints, must have taken place at the fall of Satan.

There are people that contend that, in the Middle East, sediment deposits have been found which they ascribe to the Flood. However, these same deposits have been made by river inundations (alluvium deposits). Encyclopedia Americana mentions Ur — the city of Abraham — that 4,000 years ago had a seaport and well developed commerce. Ships came into Ur from the Persian Gulf, bringing diorite and alabaster, used in statue making, copper ore, ivory, and hard woods. Ur was situated on the Euphrates River, very close to the Persian Gulf —which reached much farther inland than it does today. The mound, where the ruins of Ur were discovered, is situated about 255 kilometers (160 miles) from the present shore of the Persian Gulf, and 16 kilometers west of the Euphrates River. [9]

9. During the Noachian Flood, nothing was destroyed except living creatures — including humans. The vegetable kingdom was preserved. Grass, trees and all vegetation remained. Moses writes in Genesis 9:20: *"And Noah began to be a husbandman, and planted a vineyard."* There can be no better evidence than this to prove that the vegetable kingdom was not destroyed. When the Lord began to recreate our planet Earth, He had to create everything on the restored planet.

Many contend that, because the grass and all vegetation were under the salt water so long, they perished. I agree with this statement. All vegetation in the lower areas of the Earth perished because of the salt water. On higher ground, however, the water remained only a few days, during which no vegetation perished. When the Flood waters receded, the vegetation spread towards the lower land areas, and eventually covered the Earth again.

When the North American continent was raised, it was only a sea bottom, and salty sand. Now all of the Earth is covered with vegetation, except the arctic areas, too cold for vegetation to exist.

10. The six ledges of sandstone could not be formed during the Antediluvian Age. Before the Flood, there was no rain and forming of sandstone. So, the sandstone ledges must have been formed in past eternity, before the fall of Satan. These sandstone ledges could not be formed in a short period of time. Thousands of years were necessary. The Antediluvian Age was only 1,656 years long. To say that the six

9. "Ur" *"Encyclopedia Americana,* 27, (1982) pp. 793-794.

sandstone ledges at Paluxy River in Glen Rose were formed during the Antediluvian Age would be untenable and unrealistic.

The first fossil fish found in the U.S.A. in 1892, was in a quarry in the Harding sandstone near Canon City, Colorado. There were found bits of petrified bony material, the broken ostracoderm plates. Younger, but wholly intact specimens of similar fish fossils, reaching 30 centimeters (12 inches) in length, have been found in the rocks of Greenland, England, Norway, and elsewhere in the Baltic region, where they have been recovered regularly since the initial history-making find in Colorado in 1891.

Three fossil birds have been discovered in Bavaria, Germany, in the Solnhofen limestone, all from the same locality. A fossil hesperornis was discovered in the Niobrara chalk beds of Kansas, U.S.A. It was a large toothed bird and lived in the waters. The strong hind legs enabled it to swim with ease. The bird had very small wings.

Thus, the study has revealed to us that there are fossils of all kinds of creatures — fish, animals and birds — in many parts of the world. The fossil fish found at Canon City, Colorado, lie at an altitude of about 1,629 meters (5,343 feet). At one time, it must have been a sea where fish swam. This confirms the fact that tremendous topographical changes must have taken place in the past. A fossil fish was found in a coal seam in West Germany. This confirms the fact that forests and living creatures perished at the time of Satan's fall.

In August, 1988, a fossilized skeleton of a 4 meter 27 centimeter-long meat-eating fish was unearthed by the Dallas Museum of Natural History. This fish, known as the xiphactinus, or "bulldog tarpon," was common to the Dallas area billions of years ago. Pieces of xiphactinus fossils are commonly found there.

A museum crew exposed the J shaped, prehistoric fish skeleton from the Austin chalk banks of White Rock Creek in a north Dallas neighborhood. This fish was nicknamed "the bulldog tarpon" because its face resembles a bulldog. The fish was a vicious predator that thrived when this part of Texas was a sea. The xiphactinus's teeth were as long as human fingers. When I visited the Dallas Museum of Natural History in the Fall of 1988, I saw the remains of a fish who lived in that area over 15,500,000,000 years ago.

In 1986, the same museum unearthed a fossil sea serpent in McKinney, 50 kilometers north of Dallas.

Paluxy River limestone in which were found dinosaur and human footprints.

Dinosaur footprint, Paluxy River limestone.

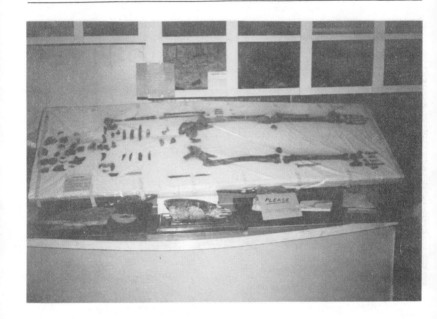

A human skeleton, Creation Evidences Museum Glen Rose, Texas, U.S.A. and half of a fossil fish in front of the skeleton.

A fiberglass replica of Tyrannosaurus Rex. Dinosaur State Park Texas, U.S.A.

Prontosaurus — Dinosaur State Park. A fiberglass replica.

The Unreliability of Carbon-14 Dating

Carbon-14 or radioactive dating is highly unreliable. Carbon-14 — a naturally occurring radioisotope of carbon having a mass number 14, and half life of 5,780 years — is used in radiocarbon dating and in the elusidation of the metabolic path of carbon photosynthesis. Encyclopedia Britannica says that the carbon-14 method was discovered by W.F. Libby in 1947. It is used to measure the age of organic material up to 50,000 years old. Carbon-14, the radioactive isotope of carbon, is created in nature from nitrogen-14 in the upper atmosphere, by the action of cosmic rays. The carbon-14 oxidizes to form carbon dioxide and gradually sinks to the lower levels of the atmosphere. Thus, a certain small percentage of the carbon dioxide in the air is radioactive.

Because of the radioactive carbon dioxide in the air, all living plants contain a certain percentage of carbon-14. Animals, which eat plants, also contain a fixed percentage of carbon-14. When the animal or plant dies, it ceases to obtain more carbon from the air, and the radiocarbon within it decays steadily. By determining what percentage of the carbon in a sample is radioactive, an investigator can calculate the time of death of the organism from which the sample was taken. Nitrogen-14, the decay product of carbon-14, escapes from the sample and cannot be measured. The percentage of radiocarbon in living matter is known.

½ of carbon-14 remains after 5,780 years, ¼ of carbon-14 remains after 11,460 years, and ⅛ of carbon-14 remains after 17,190 years. Typical material dated by the carbon-14 method include mud sediments, wood, charcoal, textiles, leather, paper, and bones. Thus, objects such as fossils, timbers from buildings, ancient campfires, clothing, mummy wrappings, and documents can be accurately dated. [10]

Dr. James Hugg again explains that radiocarbon-14 dating is very unreliable. According to Dr. Hugg the scientist starts with one type of atom which is called radioactive and which presumably changes spontaneously at a fixed rate into another type of atom. If the scientist knows how much of the original radioactive atoms were present in a rock, and if he can also measure how much exists today, how much of the product exists, and the atoms that this radioactive substance changes into, then if he knew the rate at which this radiation took place, he would know how long that rock had been there. There are three assumptions in being able to use this technique for dating. The three assumptions are:

1. One must know how much of the original radioactive substance was present. The scientist does not know exactly how much radioactive element was present in the rocks when they were formed. One cannot assume that there was no radioactive product present in the rock, but this is exactly the assumption of the evolutionists make. The assumption is that there was no product in the rocks, that there was only the original radioactive element present. It is this technique of dating based on this assumption which yields such old dates.

2. According to this system, the rock, in which the radio active element and its products are present, was a closed system. That is, none of the radioactive or the product substances have been taken away or added to the rock since the time it was laid down. That is the assumption. In hourglass analogy, no one has taken the lid off the hourglass and removed any of the sand, either from the top or from the bottom of the hourglass when it was running. This is also not a very good assumption, in many cases, because it is known that ground water will leach these radioactive minerals out of the rocks, giving them the appearance of a great age. In most cases, it leaches

10. "Carbon-14 Dating" *The New Encyclopedia Britannica,* II (1987) p. 850.

the radioactive mineral out of the rocks more than the product. This creates a very serious problem, but one that is generally ignored by the evolutionists.

3. The third assumption is very important to the radioactive dating of rocks. It is the assumption that the decay rate was constant throughout time, that it never changed. The analogy would be the assumption that the sand from the top in the hourglass has always flowed to the bottom in the hourglass at the same constant rate; and nothing has ever changed that process. No force was applied to that sand to make it flow any faster or any slower at any time.

It has been discovered, however, in modern experiments that many things, many processes can change this rate of decay. The most important may be the fact that cosmic radiation, including neutrons and neutrinos, can certainly change the decay rate. One can produce the appearance of fast age just by placing the rock, with its radioactive substance, close to a nuclear reactor —which produces a large number of neutrons, and that rock is aged in a very short period of time billions of years.

Normally, when scientists are dating rocks, they take several samples of a rock and send them to a laboratory and ask for the age to be estimated from this radioactive dating technique. Normally, they get back several different ages, which are vastly different. The different samples may give ages ranging from nearly Z time, which denotes a very recent rock, up to billions of years of time.

Because of the evolutionary assumption, scientists consistently pick the oldest age of the rock or the age that is consistent with how old they think the rock should be. Other conflicting evidence is generally ignored.

One of the most telling facts against radioactive dating is that one can test the technique on some very recent rocks. There are islands in the Pacific Ocean which have been formed by volcanic eruption in recorded history — in the past few hundred years. The radioactive dating techniques, if indeed they work, should give a near Z age for these rocks. Yet, when these rocks were tested, the results showed that the rocks were formed billions of years ago. This technique is totally useless for accurately predicting the age of the Earth. It is totally inaccurate because the assumption involved can never be tested. The assumptions are just too difficult to meet and impossible to prove. [11]

11. Dr. James Hugg, *Science and the Bible,* (McKinney: Lamb and Lion Ministries, 1988). Tape.

The Apollo 16 mission brought back a moon rock, which was dated by three different methods, and gave ages ranging from 7,000,000,000 to 18,000,000,000 years old. In 1970, a carbon-14 test was done on organic material contained in the mortar of an English castle. Although the castle was known to be 787 years old, the carbon-14 date gave an age of 7,370 years old. Mummified seals that had been dead for 30 years dated 4,600 years old.

The Mystery of the Hammer in the Ordovician Sandstone Resolved

In 1938, a man-made hammer was found in the Ordovician sandstone about 2 meters (6 feet) below the surface at London, Texas. The man-made artifacts, both the wooden handle and the metal shaft, were completely encased in the sandstone. This is an irrefutable fact that man was around to make the artifact before the sandstone encased it. Christian scientists ascribe it to the Antediluvian Age because Tubalcain was the first man to make copper and iron artifacts (Genesis 4:22). If this man-made hammer was made before the Flood, the hammer would have never been so many meters under the sand. Geologists say that the Ordovician rock pertains to the period of the Paleozoic era, between the Cambrian and the Silurian, over 440,000,000 years ago.

As a minister, in the light of the Word of God, I have to reject all these suppositions because:

1. After the recreation of the planet Earth, all the land area was one big continent and North America was a sea bottom. The Antediluvians, before the Flood, did not even live in America. It was 148 years after the Noachian Flood (2200 B.C.) that the land between South America and Africa sank, and the land area was split into several continents. Genesis 10:25 says: *"And unto Eber were born two sons: the name of the one was Peleg; for in his days was the earth divided...."*

2. The Bible reveals that there were people and cities on Earth before the fall of Lucifer, more than 15,500,000,000 years ago. Jeremiah 4:23-26 shows the destruction of the first perfect Earth. I include only Jeremiah 4:26. *"I beheld, and, lo, the fruitful field was a wilderness, and all the cities thereof were broken down at the presence of Jehovah, and before His fierce anger."* The pre-Adamic race needed shelter, or houses just as we do today. To build cities or houses implies skill and need of tools. The pre-Adamic race were skillful people and able to invent all the things needed in their daily life. Therefore, this man-made hammer must belong to the pre-Adamic race, and not to the Antediluvian Age.

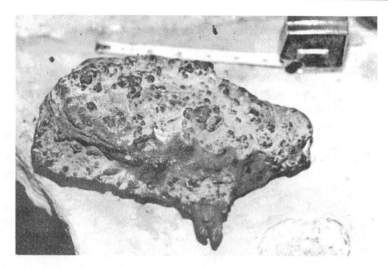

Here is a piece of Ordovician sandstone in which a man-made artefact was found at London, Texas — part of the same Llano Uplift area which the Paluxy River shares. The wooden end of a man-made hammer is projecting out of the stone.

Here is the other side of that man-made hammer. Both the wooden handle and the metal shaft were completely encased in the sandstone — indicating that man was around to make the artefact before the sandstone encased it.

Giants on Earth During the Antediluvian Age

As to the giant footprints of 16 inches under the sandstone at Glen Rose, I have to say that they belong to the pre-Adamic race, and not to the present Adamic race.

1. The footprint was under the sandstone. The giant, human footprint was on the same level as the dinosaur footprints found.

2. Before the fall of Lucifer, there were possibly over 30,000,000,000 people on Earth. Among such a multitude, there must have been some smaller and some larger men. The size of the pre-Adamic race cannot be determined, but it seems that it was the same as that of the present Adamic race. In 1971, a human skeleton was excavated 56 kilometers (35 miles) east of Moab, Utah, by the University of Utah Department of Anthropology. It was found 3.75 meters (12 feet) below the surface in solid stone impacted with azurites (copper carbonate). The skeleton was 2 meters (6 feet) tall, and belongs to the pre-Adamic race.

Just as we have people of different sizes on Earth, so it might have been also during the Antechaotic Age. Peter the Great, Emperor of Russia, was more than 2 meters (6 feet 7 inches) tall. There have been men and women 2.5 meters tall, and even taller. There is no doubt that, before the fall of Satan, there were some people on Earth of great size. Some of them may have been 2.5 meters tall or more.

The size of the footprints of giants before the Flood cannot be determined, although many skeletons of the giants, that died before and during the Flood, have been found. The Bible indeed confirms the fact that there were people, men of immense size, on Earth during the Antediluvian Age. Genesis 6:4 says: *"The Nephilim (giants) were in the earth in those days, and also after that, when the sons of God came in unto the daughters of men, and they bare children to them: the same were the mighty men that were of old, the men of renown."*

Genesis 6:4 revealed that there were giants on Earth before the sons of God married the daughters of men. The sons of God were fallen angels that married women of the human race to produce a kind of half-celestial and half-terrestial race. (The reader can turn to Chapter XII to find an explanation for the giants.) It is difficult, however, to establish a date when the fallen angels began to associate with the women of the present Adamic race. Genesis 6:1-2 says that *"...when men began to multiply on the face of the ground, and daughters were born unto them,*

"That the sons of God saw the daughters of men that they were fair: and they took them wives of all that they chose."

This may have happened before the death of Adam in 3074 B.C. From the death of Adam to the Flood was 1,418 years. People in those days lived over 900 years, so many of the giants died a natural death before the Flood and were buried, like the rest of the Adamic race. This is the reason giant skeletons have been found in many places in Europe.

I have borrowed some information from a book, published over a hundred years ago, entitled "The Mammoth and the Flood" by Mr. Howorth. He writes that according to Eumachus in his Periegesis, the Carthaginians, when surrounding their territory with a ditch, found two skeletons, one 10.75 meters (36 feet) long and the other 10.5 meters in length. During a certain earthquake in the Cimmorian Bosphorus, a hill burst asunder and some immense bones were disclosed, which, when put together as a human skeleton, were 10.75 meters long.

In 1577, the skeleton of a giant was found near the cloister of Reyden, in the canton of Lucerne, under an oak tree which was overturned by a storm. Professor Felix Plator at Basel examined the skeleton and pointed out that the skeleton was the remains of a giant about 6 meters (more than 19.5 feet) tall.

Giant bones turned up in France in 1456. A vast skull, some immense teeth, and other such things were found beside a river near Valence. The skull measured nearly one meter (about 3 feet) wide. A shoulder blade was 2.80 meters (9 feet) across. One expert on giants inspected the relics and concluded that this particular giant must have been seven meters (23 feet) in height.

The greatest giant skeleton find was made in France in 1613, near the castle of Chaumont. It was a nearly complete skeleton of immense size. A local surgeon, Dr. Mazurier, examined the huge skeleton and found it to be nearly 8 meters (25.5 feet) long, 3 meters (10 feet) wide across the shoulders, and 1.5 meters (5 feet) deep from the breast to the back. Each tooth was as big as an ox's foot, and the shinbone alone was nearly 1.25 meters (4 feet) in length. These skeletons were those of the giants that died before the Flood.

In 1705, some huge bones were found in Claverack, New York, and were supposed to belong to a giant. However, it was later discovered that they were bones of a huge mammoth. [12] The 40 centimeter (16 inch) footprint at Glen Rose, Texas, does not belong to the Adamic race, but to the pre-Adamic race.

A miner fell through a hole in a mine in Italy and found this 11' 6" skeleton. He would have had footprints even larger than some of those found at the Paluxy River.

The American Museum of Natural History supplies some information about the animals of the past.

The seas that rolled over the western State of Kansas were the main location of the Mosasaurs, and thousands of specimens have been taken from the chalk bluffs of the region, some of them in such a fine state of preservation that people are well acquainted with their internal structure, and with their outward appearance as well. They were essentially swimming lizards of great size, distant relatives of the Monitors of Africa and Asia, especially adapted to a roving, predatory life by their powerful tails and paddle-shaped feet.

Their cup-and-ball vertebrae indicate great flexibility of the body; their sharp teeth denote ability to capture slippery prey; and the structure of the lower jaw shows that they probably ate in a hurry, swallowing their food whole. The jaws of all reptiles are made up of a number of pieces, but these are usually so spliced together that each half of the jaw is one inflexible mass of bone.

The western sea was full of life in the day of the great Mosasaurs, for with them swam the huge Archelon, king of the turtles. It was

12. Henry H. Howorth, *The Mammoth and the Flood*, (London: Sampson Low, Marston, Searle & Rivington, 1887), pp. 15,21.

about 4 meters (12 feet) in length, with a head one meter long. In the shallow waters, swam great fishes with massive jaws and teeth like spikes. There was also the great toothed diver, Hesperonis, while over the waters flew pterodactyls, with a wing span of 7 meters (20 feet), the largest of all flying creatures in past eternity. [13]

Dinosaur Footprints in Canada

In September, 1987, I visited the Peace Canyon Area of Canada to investigate for myself the dinosaur story.

The dinosaur footprints in the Peace Canyon, British Columbia, have provided a major source of information on dinosaurs and their habits. It is quite different than the information that can be deduced from the study of dinosaur bones alone. Individual footprints help scientists put together a picture of what the living animal was like.

Parallel tracks, found in the Peace Canyon, provide some of the world's best evidence that dinosaurs were herding animals. Trackways also show how individual dinosaurs and herds moved about, how active they were, the ratio of different ages in a herd, and the ratio of different types of dinosaurs in the environment. Peace Canyon is the sole source of evidence in the world of several species in the time of the dinosaurs. Another significant discovery made there was the world's earliest bird footprints, found in 1979. This is the best-documented site of dinosaur footprints in the world.

The first Canadian dinosaur tracks were discovered in the Peace Canyon in 1922 by F.H. McLearn of the Geological Survey of Canada. In 1932, eight species were identified by C.M. Stenberg of the National Museum of Canada. More recently came the 1965 expedition of the Royal Ontario Museum, and four expeditions by the Provincial Museum of Alberta, in the 1970's, to collect rock slabs containing footprints for future study.

There were also strange looking sea creatures in those days. Part of a fossilized skeleton of this marine reptile, the plesiosaur was found in the Peace Canyon in 1976. These long-necked beasts, which were up to 12 meters (39 feet) long, inhabited the inland sea during the time of the dinosaurs. They swam with their large paddles, much the way turtles do.

Hadrosaurs, the horned dinosaurs and the carnivorous ancestors of Tyrannosaurs Rex were some of the species that lived here on the

13. Frederic A. Lucas, *Animals of the Past,* (New York: American Museum of Natural History, handbook series No. 4. 7th edition, 1929) pp. 40-43.

ocean's edge then. The only traces they left behind are their footprints, miraculously preserved as fossils.

In the Museum at Peace Canyon, a life-size model shows what the duck-billed dinosaurs are believed to have looked like. An adult was about 10 meters (32.5 feet) long and 4 meters high at the hip, and weighed 3 to 4 tons. These gentle and slow-moving plant-eaters were good swimmers, but usually preferred to walk, using their hind legs to carry their massive weight and their short front legs for added support. They travelled in small herds, and along with their formidable bulk, this appears to have been their only protection against meat-eating dinosaurs, their natural enemies.

With footprints as the only clue, scientists cannot tell exactly what a dinosaur looked like. Although no dinosaur bones have been found in British Columbia, there have been hundreds of skeletons of dinosaurs found in the Province of Alberta. One particular type of footprint, found in the Peace Canyon, named amblydactylus, is thought to have been made by an early member of the hadrosaur family. Many different kinds of hadrosaurs lived in Alberta at that time.

I want to list 6 different types of dinosaurs of the early career of the planet Earth in past eternity.

1. Ceratosaurus — a large animal nearing 6 meters in length and standing up to 3 meters tall.

2. Apatosaurus — grew to 20 meters in length, was 4.5 meters tall at the shoulder and weighed about 30 tons.

3. Coelurus — a small flesh-eating dinosaur, belonging to the group called coelurosaurus.

4. Stegosaurus — had two rows of large bony plates running along its back and tail. It was 6 meters long, and weighed about 2 tons.

5. Brachiosaurus — stood 12.5 meters high and weighed about 80 tons. The footprints show that the animal walked very slowly — about 2 miles per hour.

6. Camptosaurus — from only 70 centimeters (25 inches) long up to 5 meters long.

About 300 species of dinosaurs have been identified in the world.

Scientists say that the hadrosaurs and the carnivorous ancestors of Tyrannosaurus Rex lived in the time called the Early Cretaceous period, more than 100,000,000 years ago. The dinosaurs in Alberta lived about 50,000,000 years ago. I reject this as false and untenable. In no way can the age of the dinosaurs be established. They are all prehistoric animals that lived on this planet before the fall of Satan, more than 15,500,000,000 years ago.

In the month of January, 1987, I preached for a pastor in Vilna Alberta, Canada. He related the following story to me. Several years ago he was a missionary to the Eskimos on the Arctic Sea Coast, in the Northwest Territories. A family began to build a house on Pelly Island, about 75 kilometers off the Canadian Coast, north of the mouth of the Mackenzie River. As they were digging into the frozen tundra, they found mammoth tusks in the frozen ground. This is evidence that mammoths once lived there, and enjoyed a temperate climate.

Duckbilled dinosaur, Peace River Canyon Museum, British Columbia, Canada.

Plesiosaur found in the Peace River Canyon in 1976. A marine reptile. The skeleton was about 12 meters long.

A dinosaur footprint in the Peace River Canyon, Canada, was made by duck-billed dinosaur, also known as hadrosaurs.

The world's earliest bird footprints were discovered in the Peace River Canyon, Canada.

The birds that made the footprints were only about 10 centimeters tall and looked like modern shore birds such as the killdeer.

An impression in the rock of the skin on the tail of a duck-billed dinosaur.

Human Life on the Original Planet Earth

Whether or not there was human life on the first perfect Earth has been controversial, and is rejected by most because they find no evidence of such life. However, the Bible does show clearly that there was human life on planet Earth before Satan fell. This can be based on three assumptions.

1. Lucifer was a king and a priest upon the Earth. He must have had people to rule over, because he had a throne (Isaiah 14:13).

2. Isaiah 45:18 reveals that the Lord did not create the Earth a waste, but to be inhabited.

3. Proverbs 8:27-31 says: *"When He established the heavens, I was there. When He set a circle upon the face of the deep.*

"When He made firm the skies above. When the foundations of the deep became strong, when He gave to the sea its bound, that the waters should not transgress His commandment. When He marked out the foundations of the earth;

"then I was by Him, as a master workman and I was daily His delight, rejoicing always before Him.

"Rejoicing in His habitable earth; and my delight was with the sons of men."

4. According to the statement of Christ in Matthew 12:44, demons are disembodied spirits, and not fallen angels.

Proverbs 8:28-31 reveals the time of the creation when God brought the universe into existence. The statement, "my delight was with the sons of men," does not refer to the Adamic race on the present Earth, but to past eternity. The statement, "when He made firm the skies above," refers to the very beginning of the creation. This shows the position of Christ in past eternity as He was with the Father and by Him were the heavens created. Proverbs 8:31 shows that there were people on the original planet Earth. "...and my delight was with the sons of men," has reference to the pre-Adamic race. "The sons of men" is a common term in the Old Testament used in general in reference to mankind. King David used this term 6 times. In Psalms 4:2 he writes: *"O sons of men, how long shall my glory be turned into dishonor? How long will ye love vanity, and seek after falsehood?"* In Psalms 57:4 he writes: *"My soul is among lions. I lie among them that are set on fire, even the sons of men, whose teeth are spears and arrows, and their tongue a sharp sword."*

King Solomon used this term 11 times. Ecclesiastes 3:8 says: *"I said in my heart, It is because of the sons of men, that God may prove them, and that they may see that they themselves are but as beasts."* Again, Ecclesiastes 8:11 says: *"Because sentence against an evil work is not executed speedily, therefore the heart of the sons of men is fully set in them to do evil."* Solomon writes again in Ecclesiastes 9:3: *"...the heart of the sons of men is full of evil, and madness is in their heart while they live, and after that they go to the dead."*

From these few Old Testament Scriptures can be seen that the writers had mankind in general in mind, and that mankind is full of evil and falsehood.

The Bible says that God hates sin. Psalms 119:104 says: *"...I hate every false way. "* Proverbs 24:9 states: *"The thought of foolishness is sin.... "* In Isaiah 61:8 the Lord states: *"For I, Jehovah, love justice, I hate robbery with iniquity.... "* The prophet Zechariah writes: *"And let none of you devise evil in your hearts against his neighbor; and love not false oath: for all these are things that I hate, saith Jehovah. "* [14] In Psalms 5:4, David writes *"For Thou art not a God that hath pleasure in wickedness. Evil shall not sojourn with Thee. "*

In these passages, we have seen that a holy God hates everything that is contrary to His holiness. In no way can God have any pleasure in a sinful human race, the "sons of men." Ecclesiastes 5:4 says: *"When thou vowest a vow unto God, defer not to pay it; for He hath no pleasure in fools. "* Through the prophet Malachi, the Lord revealed that He had no pleasure in disobedience. [15] The Apostle Paul also uses the same term in Ephesians 3:5.

The statement in Proverbs 8:31, *"...my delight was with the sons of men, "* is not in reference to the present Adamic race, nor to the Church. It refers to the pre-Adamic race. This must be a reference to a race that was righteous, pure and holy. Therefore, the conclusion is that the "sons of men" spoken of by the Spirit of Christ in Proverbs 8:31 has reference to a clean, holy human race in whom a holy God was delighted.

Before the fall of Satan, there was no sin in existence, no rebellion and wickedness in the hearts of "the sons of men" that lived on planet Earth in past eternity. The worship and service of the pre-Adamic race gave God great pleasure and satisfaction. Therefore, He had delight in mankind on planet Earth, before the fall of Satan.

At this point, I must explain the meaning of parentheses in the Bible. It means an interval between two verses or between two sentences. For instance: In John 5:28-29 the Apostle writes: *"Marvel not at this: for the hour cometh, in which all that are in the tombs shall hear His voice,*

"And shall come forth; they that have done good, unto the resurrection of life; and they that have done evil, unto the resurrection of judgment. "

Between these two sentences "unto the resurrection of life; and they that have done evil, unto the resurrection of judgment," is 1,000 years. This time period is between the words "life" and "and." Many

14. *Zechariah* 8:17.
15. *Malachi* 1:10.

Christians have understood that the Lord taught that all dead — both the righteous and the wicked — will be raised at the same time. The Bible teaches, however, that the wicked dead will be resurrected about 1,000 years after the rapture, or the first resurrection, at the conclusion of the Millennial reign.

There is also interval or parentheses of billions of years between Proverbs 8:31 and Proverbs 8:32. We read: *"...and my delight was with the sons of men,"* and *"Now therefore, my sons, hearken unto Me; for blessed are they that keep My ways."* Reading Proverbs 8:22-32, one does not notice the parentheses at first. A cautious reading, and a careful comparison of Scripture with Scripture reveals the interval, a time period of billions of years. Such a parentheses is found in many places in the Bible.

I want to give two more examples of this problem and cause of much misinterpretation. Daniel 12:2 says: *"And many of them that sleep in the dust of the earth shall awake, some to everlasting life, and some to shame and everlasting contempt."* Here we have the first resurrection and the second resurrection spoken of prophetically. Again with a parentheses of 1,000 years. The Bible teaches no general resurrection, as is taught by some preachers, who interpret John 5:28-29 to mean that the righteous and wicked dead will be raised at the same time.

Hosea 3:4-5 is another Scripture with a great parentheses. The Prophet writes: *"For the children of Israel shall abide many days without king, and without prince, and without sacrifice, and without pillar, and without ephod or teraphim.*

"Afterward shall the children of Israel return, and seek Jehovah their God, and David their king, and shall come with fear unto Jehovah and to His goodness in the latter days." Between verses 4 and 5 is an interval of nearly 2,000 years. At the present they have no king, no temple or place of sacrifice, no ephod or priest. At the second coming of Christ, the Lord will regather His ancient people, and they will seek the Lord. Amos 9:11 speaks also of the regathering of Israel. *"In that day will I raise up the tabernacle of David that is fallen, and close up the branches thereof; and I will raise up its ruins, and I will build it as in the days of old."*

At this point I want to bring a couple of Scripture references to your attention, which will substantiate the fact that there was human life on planet Earth.

Genesis 1:28 states: *"...and God said unto them. Be fruitful, and multiply, and replenish the earth...."* "Replenish"is an important word. It means "to refill again." Thus, the fact stands out that the Earth at one time was filled with people. They perished and the Earth became empty. God's command to Adam was to replenish, or fill the Earth again with people.

The same command was given to Noah. Genesis 9:1 says: *"And God blessed Noah and his sons, and said unto them. Be fruitful and multiply, and replenish the earth."* The connotation is simple. The Earth was emptied of humans by the Flood, and now Noah and his descendents had to fill it again, or repopulate it.

The human footprints, found in Glen Rose, Texas, and in other parts of the world, prove the existence of a pre-Adamic race. In 1938, a human skeleton was found in a rock in the State of Utah. The skeleton was 3.75 meters (12 feet) under rock. It is advocated by many that it was a skeleton of a member of the Adamic race. This must be rejected. There is no evidence whatsoever, that the Flood waters deposited 3.75 meters of sediments which buried that human being, and then petrified to form a cocoon, encasing the human body. There is only one answer. The skeleton belongs to the pre-Adamic race, which perished more than 15,500,000,000 years ago.

As to the jewelry and the bronze bell found in the coal, this must be taken as a hoax. There is no evidence at all in the Bible that the women of the pre-Adamic race wore jewelry. We have no documented evidence of such a find. It is a false story, just like the ones spread by a man in England after World War II who painted a bone brown, buried it, and two years later excavated it —declaring that he had found evidence that people had lived there long before the Brittons came to England. The Radiocarbon dating showed 10,000 years — again proving its unreliability. A two year old bone was suddenly 10,000 years old. Somebody placed the jewelry and bell in the coal seam and then made a fuss over them.

Very little evidence is found of the pre-Adamic race in the form of fossils. One was found in the U.S.A. another in Africa. But, human foot prints have been found in several places in Glen Rose, Texas.

In 1914, a skeleton of a child was found firmly embedded in the limestone of the river bank near the village of Ehringsdorf, Germany.

In 1924, in a quarry in South Africa, a child's skull was found in a rock.

In 1854, fossilized human jawbones were found in Algeria, Africa.

All these skeletons belong to the pre-Adamic race that perished at the fall of Satan. Thus, the Earth has yielded evidence to us that there were humans on Earth in past eternity.

The Giant Sea Turtle Archelon
A contemporary of the Mosasaurs
From the specimen in the Yale University Museum

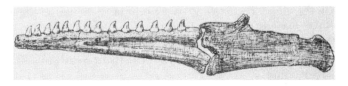

Jaw of Mosasaur showing the joint that increased the swallowing capacity of that reptile.

The Dead in the Sea
Confirms the Existence of a Pre-Adamic Race in the Past

Revelation 20:13 says: *"And the sea gave up the dead that were in it; and death and Hades gave up the dead that were in them: and they were judged every man according to their works."*

This is a unique statement which has never been understood correctly by Bible scholars. Namely: "The sea gave up the dead which were in it." What is meant by the sea and the dead that are in it? My answer to this question is that the sea contains buried in it the pre-Adamic race.

We will now study the Scriptures to prove the fact that the dead in the sea does not refer to those of the Adamic race, who have drowned in the sea during the past several thousand years. The souls of the unsaved, that drown now in the seas and lakes, will land at once in hell or Hades. According to the New Testament, there are four compartments for the dead. First, I want to analyze Revelation 20:13 properly, so that the reader may see the distinctions made by the Apostle John.

1. The sea
2. The dead
3. Death
4. Hades or hell
5. Judgment
6. Every man
7. According to their works

Now, according to a careful conclusion based on what has been said, 5 points stand out.

1. The sea is spoken of in a singular tense, which "gave up the dead that were in it."

2. Death and Hades are spoken of in a plural tense, as two separate compartments containing the dead. "Them" is plural.

3. All the dead that came forth for the judgment from these three places are termed "every man."

4. All the dead resurrected were humans, because the fallen angels were already judged and cast into the lake of fire.

5. The dead in the sea are termed "every man," just as the wicked of the Adamic race that will come forth from death and hell are called "every man."

This establishes the fact that the pre-Adamic race was made up of humans like the men of the present Adamic race. Those that come forth from hell are the souls of the present human race. Thus Revelation 20:13 has shown three separate places of confinement of the dead.

In Luke 16:19-31, Jesus tells a true story of a rich man and of Lazarus, who was poor. Both of them died, and their souls departed to their separate destinations. Both of them landed in hell, which is called "Hades" in the Greek language, but it was divided into two parts. Luke 16:22-23 says: *"And it came to pass, that the beggar died, and that he was carried away by the angels into Abraham's bosom: and the rich man also died, and was buried.*

"And in Hades he lifted up his eyes, being in torment, and seeth Abraham afar off, and Lazarus in his bosom." In hell the rich man was in torment, but Lazarus was comforted. In great suffering he saw Abraham and Lazarus in his bosom. In great agony, the rich man asked Abraham to send Lazarus to bring some water to him to cool his tongue. Abraham replied: *"...between us and you there is a great gulf fixed, that they that would pass from hence to you may not be able, and that none may cross over thence to us."* [16] This proves the fact that Hades was in two parts then. As to the location of Hades, I have no time to concentrate on this point, except to say that before the death of Jesus and His resurrection, Hades was in the heart of planet Earth. When Christ died, He went into Hades and proclaimed to the righteous dead that atonement was accomplished, and transferred paradise from Hades to heaven. The Apostle Paul writes about it in Ephesians 4:8-9. *"...When He ascended on high, He led captivity captive, and gave gifts unto men.*

"Now this, He ascended, what is it but that He also descended into the lower parts of the earth." All the righteous souls of saints that die now, will be carried by the angels into paradise which is now located in heaven. However, the other division of hell where the rich man is suffering, is still in the same place — in the heart of the Earth. The abode of the righteous dead was called "Abraham's bosom," and in Luke 23:43, Jesus calls it "paradise."

Our study has taken into consideration four different places of the dead.

1. Paradise, where the righteous dead are waiting for the resurrection spoken of in 1 Thessalonians 4:14-17 and in 1 Corinthians

16. *Luke* 16:26

15:51-53. Paradise will be emptied at the first resurrection. Only the condemned sinners will be left behind in hell.

2. The sea. This has the pre-Adamic race buried in it. Before the fall of Satan, our planet Earth was erect, and much of the present day sea floor was land surface. At the fall of Lucifer, God destroyed the Earth. The water overflowed the continents and buried the pre-Adamic race. It is this pre-Adamic multitude that will come forth from the sea.

In connection with this, I should bring to the reader's attention a mysterious silence in the Scriptures. Namely, nothing is said about the judgment of the demons. In 1 Corinthians 6:3, the Apostle Paul speaks about the judgment of the fallen angels, but not about the demons. The demons are the spirits of the pre-Adamic race, and at the time of the resurrection of the wicked, the evil spirits will be then united with their bodies, and they will come forth from the sea for the judgment of condemnation.

3. Death. Death means separation, and Satan has the power of this separation — called "the power of death" in Hebrews 2:14. Death, then, holds the bodies of all those who have passed into eternity —both the bodies of the saints and the bodies of the sinners. Therefore, the bodies of the pre-Adamic race will also come forth from the sea, held by death.

4. Hades, or hell. At the resurrection of the wicked sinners, Hades will give up all the souls of the condemned of the Adamic race. They will come forth for judgment, be judged and cast into the lake of fire.

For clarification, I want to say there are 6 steps in the first resurrection. At the rapture, only the dead in Christ will be resurrected. The Old Testament saints will be resurrected seven years later. When Christ descends to Earth at the conclusion of the tribulation period, the Old Testament saints will be resurrected, and will rule with Christ and His Church during the Millennium, and throughout eternity.

The Reason for the Absence of Fossilized Humans

Many people have argued against the existence of the pre-Adamic race because fossils have been found of plants, of fish and of animals, but not of humans. The absence of fossil humans is no proof, whatsoever, that the pre-Adamic race did not exist. One has to understand geography in order to understand the absence of fossil humans. One must know and understand the tremendous changes that have taken place in the Earth's crust. Where there is sea today, at one time there was a continent. The vast Atlantic Ocean once must have been a great continent, but sank and buried everything that lived on it.

Fossil shellfish, found in the Himalayas in the Far East, is evidence that, at one time, the present mountains formed a sea bottom. The Alps in Europe have yielded fossil shellfish, evidence that, at one time, Europe must have been a sea bottom. The Andes Mountains in South America also have yielded fossil shellfish. All this irrefutable evidence shows us the tremendous changes that have taken place in the Earth.

Before the fall of Satan, the planet Earth was erect, and a temperate climate prevailed. It was not only temperate in certain areas, but it was a world-wide temperate climate, confirmed by fossilized tropical trees and plants found in Greenland and in other northern regions — where today there is cold and ice.

In the United States of America, at one place oil wells have been drilled to depths exceeding 20,000 feet. According to scientists, oil is found only in beds of ancient seas. Oil, found at a depth of over 6,000 meters, proves that, at one time, the land was a sea bottom. Great topographical changes have taken place, and that sea bottom was buried under more than 6 kilometers of sand and rock. The Himalayian mountains are nearly 9 kilometers high. At one time, they formed a sea bottom and shellfish lived in their waters. Think for a moment of the tremendous changes that have taken place. If the Far East continent sank, the Atlantic sea bottom would be lifted up and become a continent, as it was before the raising of the Far East continent. The fish beds filled with fossil fish imply a sudden overturning of extraordinary large areas of land, maybe whole continents.

Before the fall of Satan, the North American continent was different. Now, the hemisphere runs from the Arctic Sea close to the South Pole. Before the destruction of the Earth, the Atlantic was a continent and may have run from East to West for thousands of kilometers. Much of present day Alberta, and Western Canada, in general, has been a sea bottom. The oil found confirms this fact.

When Satan fell in past eternity, a part of the angels and the pre-Adamic race fell with him, resulting in the destruction of the original Earth and the pre-Adamic race. The waters that overran the continents swept humans to destruction. The Atlantic continent sank, and all the pre-Adamic race was buried in the deep waters, never to be seen by human eyes, until the day of judgment, when all shall come forth.

That is why we read in Revelation 20:13: *"And the sea gave up the dead that were in it...."*

This theory is substantiated by the statement in Genesis 1:9: *"And God said, Let the waters under the heavens be gathered together unto one place, and let the dry land appear; and it was so."* This reveals the important fact that some vast topographical changes took place at the time of the fall of Lucifer. The Earth's surface must have been smoothed out, so that the entire planet Earth was under water. Because of the terrific cold, the water froze to solid ice down to the very bottom of the seas. The entire planet was covered with ice for billions of years. Every living thing that lived in the seas froze to death. Job 38:30 says: *"The waters hide themselves, and became like stone. And the face of the deep is frozen."*

When God began to recreate our planet Earth, He set the forces into motion, and the dry land appeared, because the basins of the seas were formed by the power of God. The ice melted, and water gathered into the oceans.

CHAPTER V

THE ORIGIN OF SATAN

The Prophet Ezekiel's Description of Satan

The Bible reveals much about the past position of Satan, who once was God's mightiest angel, great in wisdom and perfect in beauty. At one time, Satan was a king and a priest, and perfect in his ways, until pride brought his downfall.

Ezekiel 28:12-17 describes the arch enemy of God, who is called the king of Tyre. The prophet Ezekiel wrote: *"Son of man, take up a lamentation over the king of Tyre and say unto him, Thus saith the Lord Jehovah: Thou sealest up the sum, full of wisdom, and perfect in beauty.*

"Thou wast in Eden, the garden of God; every precious stone was thy covering, the sardius, the topaz, and the diamond, the beryl, the onyx, and the jasper, the sapphire, the emerald, and the carbuncle, and gold: the workmanship of thy tabrets and of thy pipes was in thee; in the day that thou wast created they were prepared.

"Thou wast the anointed cherub that covereth: and I set thee so that thou wast upon the holy mountain of God; thou hast walked up and down in the midst of the stones of fire.

"Thou wast perfect in thy ways from the day that thou wast created, till unrighteousness was found in thee.

"By the abundance of thy traffic they filled the midst of thee with violence, and thou hast sinned: therefore have I cast thee as profane out of the mountain of God: and I have destroyed thee, O covering cherub, from the midst of the stones of fire.

"Thy heart was lifted up because of thy beauty; thou hast corrupted thy wisdom by reason of thy brightness: I have cast thee to the ground; I have laid thee before kings, that they may behold thee."

In this passage of the holy Scripture 10 important factors have been revealed about the former beauty of heaven.

1. The time of the creation of Satan
2. Satan, God's masterpiece of wisdom and of beauty
3. Satan's habitation in the garden of God, in Eden
4. Satan's palace of gold
5. Satan's musical ability
6. Satan's office in past eternity
7. Satan, God's viceroy on the original planet Earth
8. Satan's freedom to travel in the universe
9. Satan's righteous life on the original planet Earth
10. The cause of Satan's sin

The Time of the Creation of Satan

The exact time of his creation cannot be established. Genesis 1:1 says: *"In the beginning God created the heavens and the earth"*. This refers to the creation of the material universe and our planet Earth. Before that, there was nothing except the Triune God — Father, Son, and Holy Spirit.

The phraseology used here reveals that the "heavens," the real heaven where God's throne is located, the starry heaven, the universe and the planet Earth were brought into existence.

But, the Lord says nothing about the creation of the angels in Genesis 1:1. The book of Job reveals that the angels were created before the material universe. The Lord, talking to Job about the creation of the Earth, asked the old patriarch in Job 38:4-7: *"Where wast thou when I laid the foundations of the earth...?*

"Who determined the measures thereof...?

"Whereupon were the foundations thereof fastened? Or who laid the cornerstone thereof?

"When the morning stars sang together, and all the sons of God shouted for joy?"

This shows, to the student of the Word of God, that when the creation of the beautiful universe and of the Earth took place, the angels, called here "the sons of God," shouted for joy.

This confirms the fact that the angelic host, including Satan, was created before the material universe. Scientists say that the most distant quasar detected lies at a distance of 15,500,000,000 light years. The end of the universe cannot be seen, which means that the universe is even older than fifteen billion years. Satan, who was created before the material universe, might be more than 20,000,000,000 years old.

In Ezekiel 28:12-18 the Lord reveals the position of Satan before his fall. He was the anointed cherub. He was a king and a priest on the first perfect Earth, and he led the pre-Adamic race in the worship of the Almighty God.

In Isaiah 14:13 the Morning Star says: *"...I will ascend into heaven, I will exalt my throne above the stars of God...."* This statement shows that Lucifer had a throne. Only royalty sits upon a throne, not ordinary subjects. So Satan, before his fall, had a throne to sit upon. Therefore, he must have had subjects to rule over; and they were the pre-Adamic race. He was the anointed cherub, therefore, he must have been a priest also. Angels need no priest, but the prehistoric human race did need a priest to lead them in the worship of God.

Satan, God's Masterpiece of Wisdom and Beauty

Ezekiel 28:12 says that Satan sealed up the sum, full of wisdom, and perfect in beauty. The statement "full of wisdom," implies the sum total of wisdom. No other being in God's creation has been addressed with such a magnificent phrase. No angel, prophet or apostle has ever been spoken of by God in that way.

The angels are very wise, having more wisdom than human beings, but they are not omniscient. Only the Almighty God is omniscient. 2 Samuel 14:20 says: *"...and my lord is wise, according to the wisdom of an angel of God, to know all things that are in the earth."* This verse confirms the fact that angels are greater than man in knowledge, but not all-knowing.

Satan was the wisest angel God ever created. No creature in God's creation was so wise as was Lucifer, before his fall. However, he is not called "wisdom" as Christ is called "wisdom" in prophecy. Proverbs 8:12 says: *"I Wisdom have made prudence my dwelling...."* The Spirit of Christ calls the Lord Jesus "wisdom" here. The Lord Jesus referred to Himself as "wisdom." Luke 11:45 reads: *"Therefore also said the Wisdom of God. I will send unto them prophets and apostles; and some of them they shall kill and persecute."* In Colossians 2:3, the Apostle Paul wrote about Christ. *"In Whom are all the treasures of wisdom and knowledge hidden."* Christ Jesus, the Son of the living God alone is called "wisdom," and no other.

Satan was great in wisdom and superseded all the rest of the created things, but was never called "wisdom" anywhere in the Bible. He was spoken of as perfect in beauty. No angel, no human being has been called perfect in beauty, but Satan, before his fall, was the most powerful, the most beautiful and the greatest in wisdom. It is a wonder that Ezekiel 28:17 says about Satan: *"Thy heart was lifted up because of thy beauty...."* This unspeakable beauty engendered pride in him, and that pride caused his downfall.

Through the sin of pride, he corrupted himself and became an evil angel, who now opposes God and His work. So, Satan was the most beautiful and wisest of all the angels that the Lord created. His might cannot be totally understood, because it was so great.

The Lord has only one archangel, called Michael. Michael means "who is like to God." This archangel is so great and mighty, that his name is, "like to God." Satan, however was more powerful than Michael. In Jude 9, one reads about Michael: *"But Michael the archangel, when contending with the devil he disputed about the body of Moses, durst not bring against him a railing judgment, but said, the Lord rebuke thee."* In this case, the archangel Michael recognized his former superior and did not remonstrate.

Satan's Habitation in the Garden of God, in Eden

The study of Eden and the garden of God is a very complicated one. The noun "Eden" occurs 20 times in the Old Testament alone. Four instances in the book of Genesis are in reference to the primitive Eden, where there was a garden, the home of Adam and Eve. Eden is not used in reference to paradise only, but also as a name. 2 Kings 19:12 speaks of the children of Eden. King Sennacherib of Assyria wrote to king Hezekiah of Judah saying: *"Have the gods of the nations delivered them, which my fathers have destroyed, Gozan, and Haran, and Rezeph, and the children of Eden that were in Telassar."*

Telassar was a place wrested from the children of Eden by Assyria. It was located somewhere in western Mesopotamia; associated with Gozan, Haran, and Rezeph, in the hill country above the upper Mesopotamian plain, from which rises the river Khabour. Nothing more is said about the children of Eden, whether they were the descendents of Eden spoken of in 2 Chronicles 29:12 or not. Ezra writes about the Levite families: *"...and of the Gershonites, Joah the son of Zimma, and Eden the son of Joah."* Gershon was the eldest of Levi's three sons (Genesis 46:11). 2 Chronicles 31:14-15 reveals that Kore was in charge of the freewill offerings to God, and Eden was under him.

King Sennacherib of Assyria ascended the throne in 704 B.C. and the 10 tribes of the northern kingdom of Israel were deported to

Assyria in 722 B.C. and placed in Hala and in Habor by the river of Gozan, and in the cities of the Medes. [1] According to the historical facts, King Hezekiah of Judah ascended the throne in 715 B.C. and died in 687 B.C. He ruled 29 years on the throne of Judah. It was in 701 B.C. that Sennacherib invaded the kingdom of Judah, he also determined to capture the Judean capital and sent letters to Hezekiah, in which he spoke of the children of Eden at Telassar. From the deportation of the ten tribes in 722 B.C. to Assyria and to the cities of Media would be only 21 years. Since many of the Levites lived in the northern kingdom, it may be possible that many of them were carried to Telassar, including the descendents of Eden; but this cannot be proven.

Eden is used in Isaiah 51:3 in connection with the nation of Israel in the Millennium. *"For Jehovah hath comforted Zion; He hath comforted all her waste places, and hath made her wilderness like Eden, and her desert like the garden of Jehovah; joy and gladness shall be found therein, thanksgiving, and the voice of melody."* Ezekiel 36:29-35 shows that there will be renewed fertility and productivity in the land of Israel. Ezekiel 36:35 says: *"And they shall say. This land that was desolate is become like the garden of Eden; and the waste and desolate and ruined cities are fortified and inhabited."*

The garden of Eden was established before the fall of Adam and Eve. Before their fall, there was no curse and all nature was fertile and proliferated in the newly restored Earth. When Jesus returns to Earth in glory, He will remove the curse from the Earth. During the Millennium all the Earth, including Palestine, will flourish like the garden of Eden.

"The garden of God" has been used only a few times in the Old Testament. In Genesis 13:10 Moses writes: *"And Lot lifted up his eyes, and beheld all the plain of the Jordan, that it was well watered every where, before Jehovah destroyed Sodom and Gomorrah, like the garden of Jehovah...."* Here the garden of Jehovah denotes a very fertile land full of vegetation. It implies fertility and prosperity.

In Isaiah 51:3, the prophet wrote about the land of Palestine *"...like the garden of Jehovah...."* This will be so in the Millennium under the rule of Christ.

Even Egypt is called "the garden of God." In Genesis 13:10 Lot exclaimed about the fertility of the Jordan plain. *"...like the garden*

1. *2 Kings* 17:6

of Jehovah, like the land of Egypt, as thou goest unto Zoar." Lot referred to the fertility of Egypt, which was indeed a country of plenty.

Ezekiel 28:13 states: *"Thou wast in Eden, the garden of God...."* The Lord speaks here about Lucifer or Satan before his fall in past eternity. This Eden must not be confused with the Eden spoken of in Genesis 2:8. *"And Jehovah God planted a garden eastward, in Eden; and there He put the man whom He had formed".* The former refers to an Eden on the perfect Earth in past eternity which was the garden of God; the latter refers to an area called Eden in the Middle East in which there was a garden, and God placed our first parents there to dress and keep it. In connection with the first Eden on the perfect Earth in past eternity, no mention is made of any trees, as in the garden of Eden. Genesis 2:9 says: *"And out of the ground made Jehovah God grow every tree that is pleasant to the sight, and good for food: the tree of life also in the midst of the garden, and the tree of the knowledge of good and evil."*

The location of Eden on the Earth before the fall of Satan cannot be established, because Eden is called "the garden of God," and not "the garden of Eden" like the one spoken of in Genesis 2:8. The connotation is obvious. In past eternity, before the fall of Lucifer, there was no evil, no sin, no curse, so that all the Earth was a perfect garden of God in which Lucifer, with the pre-Adamic race, worshipped the Great Creator, God. Eden is a transliteration of the Hebrew "Eden" and means "pleasure" or "delight." The Eden in which Adam and Eve dwelt, with the tree of life and the tree of the knowledge of good and evil, was located in Mesopotamia. No mention is made about such trees in "Eden, the garden of God." Hopefully, these few Scripture passages will show the reader the connotation of "Eden" and "the garden of God." It was in the first Eden that God's angel, perfect in beauty and full of wisdom, the Morning Star, had his palace of gold.

Satan's Palace of Gold

Ezekiel 28:13 says: *"...every precious stone was thy covering...and gold...."* There is a striking resemblance between Satan's palace and that of the New Jerusalem. Lucifer's palace was of gold, and the New Jerusalem is of gold. In Satan's palace, there were nine precious stones. The New Jerusalem will have twelve foundations, each foundation embellished with a different precious stone, according to Revelation 21:18-20.

The gold and the precious stones were Satan's covering. "Covering" is translated from the Hebrew word "mecukkah" and means "covering" or "garniture." "Mecukkah" is from the Hebrew word "micgereth" and means "something enclosing." Thus, the Scripture reveals clearly the fact that Lucifer had a dwelling made of gold and embellished with nine different precious stones. What a beautiful palace that must have been for Lucifer to dwell in. He was perfect in beauty, and his dwelling place was also perfect in beauty, made by God Himself. Everything that existed, whether material or immaterial was made by God.

This golden dwelling place was not in heaven, where God's throne is, but on Earth, in Eden "the garden of God." There is no Eden in heaven. In heaven there is only paradise, where the righteous souls are waiting for the resurrection morning.

Satan's Musical Ability

Lucifer, the Morning Star, also had musical ability. This is revealed by the statement in Ezekiel 28:13. *"...the workmanship of thy tabrets and of thy pipes was in thee; in the day that thou wast created they were prepared."* By this statement musical ability must be understood. Tabrets and pipes were used in ancient times to produce music. In 1 Samuel 18:6, tabrets is translated "timbrel." The Hebrew word used in Ezekiel 28:13 is "toph," and is translated "tabrets," and actually means "tambourine" or "timbrel." The word "toph" comes from "taphaph," a primary root, "to drum," "play," as on the tambourine. 1 Samuel 18:6-7 shows that when kings Saul and David returned from the battlefield, the women came to meet them with music and singing, playing music on timbrels and other instruments.

"Pipes" is translated from the Hebrew "chaliel," which means "a flute" as perforated. 1 Kings 1:40 shows that at the coronation of Solomon, the people piped with pipes because of the great joy they were experiencing. Tabrets and pipes, then, were musical instruments.

Lucifer had the ability to produce music and lead the pre-Adamic race in the worship of God.

Satan's Office in Past Eternity

The text I have chosen for this interesting study reveals that Lucifer was a king and a priest. Ezekiel 28:14 says: *"Thou wast the anointed cherub that covereth...."* The key word is "anointing." He was the anointed cherub, one who had a very high office. None of the angels have been spoken of as anointed for service, not even the mighty archangel, Michael. In Isaiah 14:13, he speaks about his throne which he wanted to elevate above the throne of God. The throne symbolizes royal authority.

Satan had a twofold office before his fall. He was a king, and he was a priest. In the Old Testament, there were two offices occupied by anointed men. Kings of Israel, and priests that were in service of the Tabernacle, were anointed.

2 Samuel 5:3 says that David was anointed into the royal office, to be king over Israel. Samuel used the Hebrew word "mashach," which means "to consecrate," "to anoint." Consecrate means "to set apart to the service or worship of God." 1 Kings 1:39 speaks about Solomon who was anointed to be king over Israel. 1 Kings 19:15 shows that the Lord told Elijah to go anoint Hazael to be king over Syria.

The Lord even called Cyrus His anointed. Isaiah 45:1 says: *"Thus saith Jehovah to His anointed, to Cyrus, whose right hand I have holden, to subdue nations before him, and I will loose the loins of kings; to open the doors before him, and the gates shall not be shut."* This was a prophecy. Cyrus became king of Persia in 558 B.C. It was at least 160 years before Cyrus ascended the throne of Persia, that the Lord called him into a work that he had to do during his reign. Cyrus was a heathen man who believed in the two opposing powers of good and evil. Yet the Lord called him His anointed. By this statement, it is obvious that it means "consecration to the service of the Lord."

Regardless of the fact that Cyrus was a pagan man, God had called him to do a work for the Lord. He did not even realize it. According to the will of the Lord, Cyrus, king of Persia, liberated the Jews and allowed them to return to Jerusalem to rebuild the Temple. Ezra 1:1-4 reveals that the Lord stirred up the spirit of Cyrus. As a result he made a proclamation saying that the God of heaven had charged him to build God a house in Jerusalem. He liberated the Jews and encouraged them to return to their native country to build the Temple for the Lord God. In this way the Lord used Cyrus. The king did what the Lord laid upon his heart in 536 B.C.

Cyrus was called by the Lord to do this work, and he did it. For this reason, he was anointed or consecrated for the work of the Lord.

Ezekiel 28:14 says that the Day-star, or Satan also was anointed, or consecrated to the service and worship of God.

Satan must have been a priest also before his fall. He, no doubt, led the worship of God, and directed the pre-Adamic race in the service of the Lord. In the Old Testament, the priests were anointed for service. Exodus 28:41 says: *"And thou shalt put them upon Aaron thy brother, and upon his sons with him, and shalt anoint them, and consecrate them, and sanctify them, that they may minister unto Me in the priests office."* Here the priests were dressed properly and anointed to minister unto the Lord. So, Lucifer was also a priest before his fall.

But, can there be a king or priest without people to rule over, or to lead in worship? A king always had people to rule over, and a priest always had a place to minister unto God, to be in the service at the altars, at the Brazen-altar and at the Incense-altar.

Lucifer was called "the anointed cherub that covers." Cherubim are the highest rank of heavenly beings, sitting nearest to the throne of God and leading the worship of the universe. Revelation 4:9 says: *"And when the living creatures shall give glory and honor and thanks to Him that sitteth on the throne, to Him that liveth for ever and ever."* The living creatures here are cherubim.

Lucifer, before his fall, led his subjects in the worship of the Almighty God.

Ezekiel 28:13 says about Satan: *"Thou wast in Eden, the garden of God...."* This was the first Eden on the perfect Earth under the leadership of Lucifer. In this Eden, there was no tree of the knowledge of good and evil, as in the second Eden in which Adam and Eve were placed. It was in the second Eden, on the recreated Earth, that Satan came to tempt Eve to sin against God; while in the first Eden there was no Satan. Lucifer or the Morning-star had not yet fallen.

Satan, God's Viceroy on the Original Planet Earth

Our study has shown that Lucifer was a king and a priest. He was not an absolute monarch on the original Earth, but a kind of viceroy. Ezekiel 28:14 says: *"Thou wast the anointed cherub that covereth: and I set thee so that thou wast upon the holy mountain of God...."*

In this statement "upon the holy mountain of God," God's government must be understood. Mountain in the Bible sometimes symbolizes a kingdom, or government. Mountain is symbolically used in Psalms 30:7. *"Thou, Jehovah, of thy favor hast made my mountain to stand strong...."* David spoke about his government and kingdom, which the Lord had established in his hands. Also, Daniel 2:35 uses mountain symbolically: *"...and the stone that smote the image became a great mountain, and filled the whole earth."* The stone is Christ. At His second coming, He will destroy all the kingdoms of this world and set up His own kingdom, the Millennium, and rule over the entire Earth. The mountain symbolizes the government of Christ and His kingdom, the Millenium. In Jeremiah 51:25, Babylon is called a "destroying mountain." That Satan was on the mountain of God refers to the government of God on the original Earth, before his fall. The original Earth was a real paradise where perfect purity and righteousness ruled under the leadership of Lucifer. He was under the rule of God. Jeremiah 10:10 says that God is *"...an everlasting king...."*

The great Creator was, and is, and will be the everlasting King Who rules over His creation, but Satan was under God as His viceroy. Lucifer ruled over the planet Earth, and the entire domain of Earth was under him.

The Lord called him a "covering cherub." "Covering" is translated from the Hebrew word "sakak" which is a primary root and means "to intwine as a screen," "to fence in," "to cover over." So this Son of the Morning, the Day-star, the viceroy of the Earth in past eternity was over God's government as a guardian. Satan also had a number of angels under his direct command, which later rebelled against God along with him. Isaiah 14:13 shows that he had his own throne.

That he had his own throne to sit upon confirms the fact that he was a king. In the Bible throne always refers to royalty. It is so seen in Genesis 41:40. Pharaoh, speaking to Joseph, says: *"...only in the throne will I be greater than thou."* In 2 Samuel 7:16, the Lord spoke about David's throne which he was going to establish forever.

The Bible speaks also about the throne of God. The Great Creator God also has His own throne, from which He rules the universe. 1 Kings 22:19 says: *"...I saw Jehovah sitting on His throne, and all the host of heaven standing by Him on His right hand and on His left."* David says in Psalms 11:4: *"...Jehovah, His throne is in heaven...."* In Matthew 5:34 Jesus says: *"...the heaven, for it is the throne of God."* In Psalms 103:19 David writes: *"Jehovah has established His throne in the heavens, and His kingdom ruleth over all."* Revelation 5:1 speaks about God Who *"...sat on the throne...."*

Satan also had a throne. The prophet writes in Isaiah 14:13 about Satan's meditation in his heart before his fall in past eternity. *"...I will ascend into heaven, I will exalt my throne above the stars of God...."* This is immutable proof that he was a king, because throne symbolizes royal authority. So, these two things prove that he was a king and a priest:

1. He had a throne to rule from
2. He was anointed into the service of God as a priest, to direct the worship of the pre-Adamic race on the original planet Earth in past eternity

Satan's Freedom to Travel in the Universe

The Bible reveals very little of Satan's past activities on the perfect Earth before his fall. The information is indeed very scarce, but there are some hints to indicate that he had perfect liberty to travel in the universe.

Ezekiel 28:14 says: *"...thou hast walked up and down in the midst of the stones of fire."* The "stones of fire," have a mysterious symbolical implication. What does "stones of fire" mean? A reasonable interpretation would be that it refers to the stars, which seem during the night to be shining fiery stones. The Lord said that Satan "walked up and down in the midst of the stones of fire." This, no doubt, means that God's viceroy, Satan in past eternity, could move freely anywhere in the universe.

He had free access to the throne of God in heaven. Luke 1:19 quotes the angel Gabriel as saying: *"...I am Gabriel, that stand in the presence of God...."* Satan, as the supreme ruler over the angelic host, had access to the immediate presence of God. He ruled from this throne on Earth over the pre-Adamic race, and over the angels that were under his immediate authority.

The same phrase is again used by God in Ezekiel 28:16: *"...and I have destroyed thee, O covering cherub, from the midst of the stones of fire."* This is a reference to Satan's fall, when God destroyed his supreme authority on Earth and the life on it, and turned the Earth upside down. Satan now has no more authority to command the rule in the universe under God's sovereignty. He is now king of this world.

Satan could ascend from his earthly throne to the throne of God at anytime in past eternity. What transpired between Lucifer and the Almighty Creator at those times in past eternity is not revealed.

Satan's Righteous Life on the Original Planet Earth

In the beginning, Satan was holy and righteous. Before his fall, there was no sin in God's universe. All creation was spotless and good. The pre-Adamic race under the rulership of Satan, all the angels and Satan himself were holy and righteous.

Ezekiel 28:15 says: *"Thou wast perfect in thy ways from the day that thou wast created, till unrighteousness was found in thee."* "Perfect" is translated from the Hebrew "tamiym" which means "without blemish," "complete." "Tamiym" is used in reference to Noah. Genesis 6:9 says *"...Noah was a righteous man, and perfect in his generation: Noah walked with God."* In Genesis 17:1, the Lord said to father Abraham: *"...walk before Me, and be thou perfect."* Noah lived a flawless, spotless life before God, and so also did Abraham.

Satan lived, on the original Earth, a life which was without blemish, spotless and righteous.

How long this state of holiness lasted cannot be determined. To say that the original state of righteousness under Lucifer lasted 15,000 years would be only a conjecture. In the beginning, all the created intelligences were holy and righteous, until Satan decided to revolt and overthrow God's government. Satan and all the angels, as well as the pre-Adamic race, had the ability to sin and the ability not to sin. All their interest and affection was directed toward the Almighty God, Who had created them. Satan was placed in the position where he could do either. He was not constrained to do the one or the other. Satan's will was yielded totally to God's interest, until he deliberately decided to elevate his throne above God's. Through his rebellion he lost all righteousness and became corrupt and wicked in his ways.

CHAPTER VI

THE FALL OF SATAN

The Cause of Satan's Fall

How a holy, righteous being could fall into sin is a question that needs to be answered. Ezekiel 28:17 gives an appropriate answer to this question. *"Thy heart was lifted up because of thy beauty, thou hast corrupted thy wisdom by reason of thy brightness...."* The sin of pride and selfishness seems to be the cause of Satan's fall.

The purpose of his revolt against God is revealed in Isaiah 14:12-17. *"How art thou fallen from heaven, O Day-star, Son of the Morning! How art thou cut down to the ground, that didst lay low the nations!*

"And thou saidst in thy heart. I will ascend into heaven, I will exalt my throne above the stars of God; and I will sit upon the mount of congregation, in the uttermost parts of the north.

"I will ascend above the heights of the clouds; I will make myself like the Most High.

"Yet thou shalt be brought down to Sheol, to the uttermost of the pit.

"They that see thee shall gaze at thee, they shall consider thee, saying. Is this the man that made the earth to tremble, that did shake kingdoms;

"that made the world as a wilderness, and overthrew the cities thereof; that let not loose his prisoners to their home?"

It is revealed in this passage of the holy Scripture that Satan's sin consisted of five terrible "I will's" against the will of God, the Almighty Creator.

1. "I will ascend into heaven." This reveals his determination to take up his abode in the heaven of heavens, where God's throne is located. It must be kept in mind that this reasoning took place on Earth, where he had his throne. Therefore, the first sin was

committed on Earth and not in heaven, as is taught by the Bible scholars. Satan determined on Earth to overthrow his Sovereign, the Creator God. Sin was already committed in his heart on Earth, which was manifested by his attack against God's divine government.

"I will exalt my throne above the stars of God." Satan was anointed to the guardianship of the throne of God, but he aspired to the possession of a throne of his own, to rule over the universe, and be the sovereign to receive all the worship which was due to the Almighty God.

"Above the stars of God" means the angels, for the stars also have several different symbolically meanings. Judges 5:20 says: *"From heaven fought the stars, from their courses they fought against Sisera."* The figurative language is so simple that every one can understand that the stars that fought against a Canaanite army under Sisera were the angels of God. God Himself calls them "stars." Job 38:7 states: *"When the morning stars sang together, and all the sons of God shouted for joy."*

3. "I will sit upon the mount of congregation, in the uttermost parts of the north." "Congregation" is translated from the Hebrew "mow'adah" and means "a fixed time or season," conventionally, "a year," by implication, "an assembly as convened for a definite purpose," by extension, "the place of meetings," and technically, "the congregation." This noun is strictly used in reference to Israel. Joshua 18:1 says: *"And the whole congregation of the children of Israel assembled themselves together at Shiloh...."* In Joshua 22:16 Israel is called *"...the whole congregation of Jehovah...."* Many Bible scholars believe that in Isaiah 14:13 "congregation" refers to Israel and means Satan's attempt to get a share of the Messianic rule in the Millennium.

This I reject because there is no implication in the Bible that Satan will have such a privilege. Revelation 20:2-3 shows that he will be imprisoned for 1,000 years, and will have no liberty whatsoever. Furthermore, Isaiah 14:13 says that the congregation is in the uttermost parts of the north. This implies a vast gathering over a large area, because "parts" is plural, meaning many places. Israel had only one place where they congregated to worship God. At first, it was the Tabernacle, later, the Temple in Jerusalem. And Jerusalem is in the center of the world, not in the uttermost parts of the north. The "mount" refers to the divine government in the Earth.

4. "I will ascend above the heights of the clouds." In the Pentateuch, "cloud" is associated with divine glory. Exodus 16:10 says: *"...behold, the glory of Jehovah appeared in the cloud."* Matthew 24:30 states: *"...and they shall see the Son of man coming in the clouds of heaven with power and great glory."* That Satan referred to the heights of the clouds, exposes his desire to secure for himself the glory which belongs to God alone.

5. "I will make myself like the Most High." To be like God cannot mean to be Jehovah, the self-existent One, which no created being can be. But his statement "like the Most High," reveals Satan's ambition to be possessor of heaven and Earth. Genesis 14:22 says: *"...Jehovah, God Most High, possessor of heaven and earth."* Satan's purpose, then, was to gain authority over heaven and Earth.

It was this selfish desire or purpose which put his own personal interests before the interests of God and led Satan to revolt against God. He also induced the angels under his direct command to go along with him, as well as the pre-Adamic race. This revolt failed and ended in terrible judgment, in which planet Earth was totally destroyed. All life on our planet was wiped out in this most awful judgment. In Luke 10:18 Jesus says: *"...I beheld Satan fallen as refers to an act taken place in the past, and does not refer to a future fulfillment. ven."* In the past tense, this It does not refer to Revelation 12:7-8, which speaks of the expulsion of Satan and his angels from the heavens — the atmospheric heavens.

In Ezekiel 28:12, Satan is called "king of Tyre," but in Obadiah 3-4, Satan is spoken of as "Edom." *"The pride of thy heart hath deceived thee. O thou that dwellest in the clefts of the rock, whose habitation is high; that saith in his heart, who shall bring me down to the ground.*

"Though thou mount on high as the eagle, and though thy nest be set among the stars, I will bring thee down from thence, saith Jehovah."

Satan's Former Authority Destroyed

When Lucifer was cast out of heaven, the Lord destroyed Satan's authority to have rulership over God's angels. Ezekiel 28:16 says: *"...thou has sinned: therefore have I cast thee as profane out of the mountain of God; and I have destroyed thee, O covering cherub, from the midst of the stones of fire."* Satan was the guardian of God's throne and leader of the pre-Adamic race on the perfect Earth in past eternity. He had access to God's throne at any time he wanted to commune with his Creator God.

His revolt and rebellion against the Almighty God resulted in the destruction of his authority as guardian over God's government. He was thrown down from heaven by the power of God, with all the angels that followed him. The Lord said: "I cast thee as profane out of the mountain of God, and I have destroyed thee." The Lord did not destroy Satan in the sense of annihilating his person, for he is still loose in the world today working against God and His purpose. But his authority as the anointed cherub was destroyed.

The Scriptures do not reveal the abode of Satan, his angels and demons during the past billions of years when the Earth was covered with ice and thick darkness (the Ice Age). Was he imprisoned in the cold and ice with his imps? Or was he loose in the universe to roam around at will? We cannot say.

At the present he has access to heaven, where he accuses God's people. He has no access to the immediate presence of God, where God's throne is located, but he is seen in the Scriptures to be sometimes in the Lord's presence. Job 1:6 says: *"Now it came to pass on the day when the sons of God came to present themselves before Jehovah, that Satan also came among them."* Both the fallen angels and the good angels are called the sons of God in the holy Scripture. I will discuss the Devils' work and that of the fallen angels and demons in another section. In the New Testament, Satan is seen as the tempter and accuser, leader of the forces of evil. Satan has many names, and each name expresses a quality of character, a method of operation, or both.

Satan's Destiny — the Lake of Fire

Satan's case is a hopeless one. On the perfect Earth in past eternity, there was no one to tempt him to sin. He originated his own sin within himself and became Satan. People of the present Adamic race have an opportunity to be redeemed, because Eve and Adam were tempted to sin against God. Therefore, through faith in Christ there is a way to escape the Lake of Fire. If man had originated his own sin without a tempter like Satan, then man himself would have become a satan, and would be without hope of salvation.

Satan knows that he has no hope of escaping the lake of fire. In his great hatred of God and man, he does all he can to drag as many souls of the Adamic race to hell as possible. Satan, the introducer of sin into the universe, knows that the day of the execution of his sentence is near. The condemnation of Satan is an established biblical fact. In

Matthew 25:41 Jesus says to the condemned: *"...Depart from me, ye cursed, into the eternal fire which is prepared for the Devil and his angels."* This is the first indication of Satan's judgment and destiny. There are five distinct stages in the condemnation of Satan.

1. Cast out of heaven, the very heaven itself in past eternity. It is of great interest to notice that the New Testament speaks nothing about a certain day of Satan's judgment, except to be cast in the lake of fire. When he rebelled against God in past eternity with his angels, he and his angels were cast out of heaven. What kind of sentence God pronounced on him is not revealed in the Holy Bible. But he is condemned to eternal doom. In 1 Timothy 3:6, the Apostle Paul warns church leader not to place a novice, or young convert into a position of responsibility, lest *"...he fall into the condemnation of the Devil."* "Condemnation" is translated from Greek "krima," which means "a decision," "the function against crime." "To condemn" means "to sentence to punishment." God, then, in past eternity at the fall of Satan, sentenced him to punishment. This is the first stage in the process of the execution of Satan's sentence. Pride was Satan's sin.

2. In John 16:11 Jesus says: *"...the prince of this world hath been judged."* The death and resurrection of Christ confirmed the condemnation of Satan.

3. Cast out of the atmospheric heaven. In the middle of the tribulation period, the mighty archangel, Michael, will expel the Devil from his headquarters — the atmospheric heaven, or the lower air. Revelation 12:7-9 says: *"And there was war in heaven: Michael and his angels going forth to war with the dragon; and the dragon warred and his angels.*

"And they prevailed not, neither was there place found any more in heaven.

"And the great dragon was cast down, the old serpent, he that is called the Devil and Satan, the deceiver of the whole world; he was cast down to the earth, and his angels were cast down with him." Satan and his angels will be on Earth during the last half of the tribulation period — 3½ years.

4. Satan will be cast into the abyss. Revelation 20:1-3 says: *"And I saw an angel coming down out of heaven, having the key of the abyss and a great chain in his hand.*

"And he laid hold on the dragon, the old serpent, which is the Devil and Satan and bound him for a thousand years,

"And cast him into the abyss, and shut it, and sealed over him, that he should deceive the nations no more, until the thousand years should be finished...."

It is amazing to see how Satan has lost his power. An ordinary angel shall bind him and cast him into the abyss. The Greek "abyss" means "deep." This place to which Satan will be consigned during the Millennium is in the heart of the Earth. The angel will carry him through the Earth's crust and throw him down into it for a thousand years. The names of the dragon are mentioned in the order in which they occur in Revelation 12:9. As "the dragon" he is the embodiment of cruelty. As "the serpent" he is the personification of guile. As "the Devil" he is the arch-tempter of men. As "Satan" he is the arch-opponent of Christ and His people.

5. Satan will be cast into the lake of fire. Revelation 20:7-9 shows that, at the end of the Millennium, Satan will be loosed for a short time. He will again go forth and deceive the people that were not born-again during the Millennium, and the last revolt will take place. They will come against the City of Jerusalem, and then fire will come down out of heaven and devour them. All the multitude that comes against Jerusalem will be burned up by fire. They will not be cast, however, into the lake of fire, but will appear at the Great White Throne for judgment.

Satan, the old serpent, will be consigned immediately to the lake of fire. Two persons will preceed him to the lake of fire. The Antichrist and the false prophet will be consigned to the lake of fire at the second coming of Christ in glory at the end of the tribulation. Clearly, these two men will be cast into the lake of fire without a trial. Revelation 20:10 says: *"And the Devil that deceived them was cast into the lake of fire and brimstone, where are also the beast and the false prophet; and they shall be tormented day and night for ever and ever."* Satan will be cast into this place of torment without a trial. His angels, however, will not be cast into the lake of fire at that time, they will be judged a little later.

CHAPTER VII

THE FALL OF ANGELS

The Fact of Their Fall

The angels were holy and righteous and all their affection was directed to God. In loving obedience and willingness, they served and worshipped their Creator. Nehemiah 9:6 says: *"Thou hast made heaven, the heaven of heavens, with all their host, the earth and all things that are therein the seas and all that is in them, and Thou preservest them all; and the host of heaven worshippeth Thee."* The Lord created them holy, pure and righteous. How then could a righteous being fall when there was no sin in God's universe? This is indeed a deep mystery in theology. Genesis 1:31 says: *"And God saw every thing that He had made, and, behold, it was very good...."* Genesis 1:31 is in reference to the recreation of the planet Earth, nearly 6,000 years ago. The point, however, is this — what God did was perfect and good. The angels, in past eternity when God created them, were good and holy. He did not create bad angels, and yet they are spoken of in the Word of God as being evil.

Psalms 78:49 speaks about *"...a band of angels of evil."* In Matthew 25:41, Jesus spoke about the everlasting fire which is prepared for Satan and his angels. The Apostle Peter writes about the bad angels in 2 Peter 2:4. *"For if God spared not angels when they sinned, but cast them down to hell, and committed them to pits of darkness, to be reserved unto judgment."* Here the Apostle speaks about the angels that sinned against God. Jude 6 speaks about the same matter. *"And angels that kept not their own principality, but left their proper habitation, He hath kept in everlasting bonds under darkness unto the judgment of the great day."*

These three Scripture passages suffice to confirm the fact that a group of the holy angels sinned against God and fell from their original position of righteousness and holiness. In this connection, two points should be taken into consideration.

1. The time of their fall. The Scripture does not specify any time, but it is clear that they must have followed their commander Lucifer, in past eternity, in rebellion against the Almighty God. It happened over 15,000 years after the creation of the universe, when Satan revolted. Then, a group of the angels that were under his direct command followed him. He certainly had his own angels. Revelation 12:7 speaks about the archangel, Michael, and his angels. Michael has an unspecified number of angels under his direct command, and they will do the command of Michael in the service of the Lord. Thus, the fall of the angels took place at the time of the fall of Satan, billions of years ago.

2. The cause of their fall. There could be no other cause for their fall, except that they were under the command of Lucifer, whom they followed in rebellion against the Lord God. Satan, who was the mightiest and most beautiful angel in God's creation, no doubt persuaded the angels that were with him on Earth to go with him, and dethrone God. Then they, together with him, would be rulers of the universe. Isaiah 14:13 reveals Satan's meditation and purpose. *"...and I will ascend into heaven, and I will exalt my throne above the stars of God...."* This was Satan's deliberate decision to dethrone God. So, the angels that decided to follow their leader, Lucifer, did so knowingly, a self-determined revolt against God. It was their deliberate choice of self and self-interests in preference of God's interests. Undue ambition and the desire to surpass God was the main cause of their fall.

The angels, that were in direct service of Lucifer on the original planet Earth, became the fallen angels. The pre-Adamic race also joined Satan in this rebellion and perished; and the Earth became waste and void.

The Result of Their Fall

Concerning their fall, several factors stand out that should be taken into consideration.

1. They were separated from their Creator forever. They will never get the chance to have their broken fellowship with God restored. The lake of fire will be their place forever.

2. The angels that sided with Satan and fell lost their holiness and became corrupt in nature and conduct. The Apostle Paul writes in

Ephesians 6:12: *"For our wrestling is not against flesh and blood, but against the principalities, against the powers, against the world-rulers of this darkness, against the spiritual hosts of wickedness in the heavenly places."* The Apostle spoke here also of the fallen angels, the rulers of the kingdoms of this world, including the demons.

3. According to 2 Peter 2:4, a number of the fallen angels have been imprisoned in Tartarus, to be kept in chains until the great day of judgment at the conclusion of the Millennium.

4. Some of the fallen angels are still loose and are free to engage in definite opposition to the work of God, and against the good angels. Revelation 12:9 reveals that during the tribulation the evil angels will be cast down to the Earth with their leader, Satan, the world's deceiver. Up to that time they will be free to direct the affairs of the nations under the direct command of Satan. Daniel 10:13 reveals this very clearly.

The angel that brought the message to the prophet Daniel said: *"But the prince of the kingdom of Persia withstood me one and twenty days; but, lo, Michael, one of the chief princes, came to help me: and I remained there with the kings of Persia."* These kings of Persia were satanic rulers, or fallen angels who ruled over the kingdom of Persia. In Daniel 10:20, the angel said to Daniel. *"...knowest thou wherefore I am come unto thee? and now will I return to fight with the prince of Persia: and when I go forth, lo, the prince of Greece shall come."* These few passages have shown to us how the evil angels are engaged in battle against the good angels of God.

5. The fall of angels, with their leader Satan, resulted in the destruction of the original Earth.

6. According to Revelation 12:8-9, the fallen angels, in a future time, will be cast to the Earth, and at the conclusion of the Millennium, will be cast into the lake of fire, to be tormented forever and ever.

The Work of the Fallen Angels

The Bible speaks much about the fallen angels, but very little is revealed of their evil work. The Scriptures does reveal the fact that sometimes God uses even the evil angels to work out His purposes. Psalms 78:49 says: *"He cast upon them the fierceness of His anger, wrath, and indignation, and trouble, a band of angels of evil."* This is a strict reference to Israel's rebellion against God that invited the Lord's displeasure. He allowed the evil angels to attack the stubborn people.

The fallen angels are leaders and chiefs over the nations on Earth now, leading the hosts of demons under the direct command of Satan, the commander in chief. The prophet shows, in Daniel 10:12-13, that they oppose the work of the good angels. *"Then said he unto me. Fear not, Daniel; for from the first day that thou didst set thy heart to understand, and to humble thyself before thy God, thy words were heard: and I am come for thy words' sake.*

"But the prince of the kingdom of Persia withstood me one and twenty days; but, lo, Michael, one of the chief princes, came to help me: and I remained there with the kings of Persia."

This passage of the holy Scripture reveals some of the activities of the evil angels. First, it was the prince of Persia, then the kings of Persia, which seems to reveal the chief of the evil forces operating in Persia in the days of Daniel, and kings or a number of lesser rulers over the Persian Empire.

The Apostle Paul shows, in Romans 8:38, that fallen angels endeavor to separate the believer from the Lord Jesus Christ. *"For I am persuaded, that neither death, nor life, nor angels...."* will be able to separate a Christian from the Lord.

Ephesians 6:12 shows that they co-operate with Satan in the evil work in this world. The Apostle writes: *"For our wrestling is not against flesh and blood, but against the powers, against the world-rulers of this darkness, against the spiritual hosts of wickedness in the heavenly places."*

The Eschatological Aspect of the Work of the Fallen Angels

The work of the evil angels is not limited to the present dispensation, but they will also have a part in the tribulation troubles and judgments. Revelation 9:13-15 says: *"...I heard a voice from the horns of the golden altar which is before God,*

"one saying to the sixth angel that had the trumpet. Loose the four angels that are bound at the great river Euphrates.

"And the four angels were loosed, that had been prepared for the hour and day and month and year, that they should kill the third part of men."

These four evil angels have been bound at the great river Euphrates, and will be turned loose during the tribulation to kill one third of men. The number four is strictly mentioned in this connection. Number four in the Bible symbolizes universality. However, the statement to "kill the third part of men," does not refer to the whole world, the entire globe. It refers to the revived Roman Empire under the Antichrist.

There are two expressions in the Bible which have caused much misunderstanding and misinterpretation.

1. The whole world, used sometimes in connection with the entire globe

2. The whole world, used in reference to Europe, and the Middle East, the then-known world

However, I have no intention to go into theology too deeply here except to concentrate on the part played by the four angelic leaders during the tribulation. They will lead the armies that come to attack the Roman Empire. Revelation 9:16 says that *"...the number of the armies of the horsemen was twice ten thousand times ten thousand...."* Notice "the armies" is plural, indicating more than one army that will attack the Empire of the Antichrist. The total number of the armies will be 200,000,000. This vast multitude will kill one third through three plagues. Revelation 9:18 says: *"By these three plagues was the third part of men killed, by the fire and the smoke and the brimstone...."* Europe now has a population of nearly 600,000,000. About 200,000,000 will be killed under the leadership of these four fallen angels.

The Number of the Fallen Angels

How many of the angels sided with Lucifer cannot be established. Most Christians believe that one third went with Satan, basing their teaching and belief on Revelation 12:4 which says: *"And his tail draweth the third part of the stars of heaven, and did cast them to the earth...."* This will happen during the tribulation period, and is future. I think that the faulty translation of The King James Version of 1611 is the cause of the misinterpretation. It translates Revelation 12:4 *"And his tail drew...."* Here it is in the past tense, as something that happened already. In the American Standard Version, it is in the future tense, which is correct. Stars have several symbolical meanings in the Bible. A star symbolizes pastors. In Revelation 1:20, Jesus says to John. *"...The seven stars are the angels of the seven churches...."* or the stars are the pastors of the seven churches. Daniel 8:9-10 speaks about the stars also. *"And out of one of them came forth a little horn, which waxed exceeding great, toward the south, and toward the east, and toward the glorious land.*

"And it waxed great, even to the host of heaven; and some of the host and of the stars it cast down to the ground, and trampled upon them."

The "little horn" is the Antichrist. And the stars are individual rulers which the Antichrist will overthrow, after he has gained power in Europe after the rapture. This is something that will take place during the tribulation period, and has not yet been fulfilled. The prophet speaks about the same matter in Daniel 7:8. *"I considered the horns, and, behold, there came up among them another horn, a little one, before which three of the first horns were plucked up by the roots...."* The "little one" here, again, is the Antichrist, and the three horns symbolize rulers, because in the Scripture "horn" sometimes symbolizes "authority," or "power" in the abstract. "Horns" symbolize kings and rulers in the historical context. Revelation 13:1 reads: *"And I saw a beast coming out of the sea, having ten horns...."* In Revelation 17:12, the angel explains for John that the horns typify rulers. *"And the ten horns that thou sawest are ten kings...."* Thus, the horns in Daniel 7:8 means rulers in Europe which the Antichrist will topple when he comes to power after the rapture. The stars spoken of in Revelation 12:4 symbolize Christian rulers, nominal not born-again rulers, and ecclesiastical dignitaries. Walter Scott has some good thoughts about this passage. In Satan's tail is the emblem of his soul-destroying influence; in other words, his lies. Satan is said to be a liar. He murders the bodies, and ruins the souls of men. His power is in his head; his malignant influence in false and damnable teachings in his tail. Stars of heaven mean individual rulers set in outward relationship with God in positions and places of authority. These rulers and teachers are caught in Satan's snare, and believe the Devil's lies. He cast them to the Earth. Their moral ruin is complete. [1]

Thus, the Scripture reveals that the stars in Revelation does not mean angels which he took with him at his fall, but individual rulers and ecclesiastical rulers and teachers.

The number of the good angels has not been revealed in the Bible. In Hebrews 12:22, they are spoken of as *"...innumerable hosts of angels."* The Scripture seems to reveal that the number of the angels is so great they cannot be numbered, and are spoken of as "innumerable hosts of angels." On this basis, no one knows the number of the fallen angels.

The Judgment of the Fallen Angels

In 1 Corinthians 6:3, the Apostle Paul writes about the judgment of angels saying: *"Know ye not that we shall judge angels...."* This

1. Walter Scott, *Exposition of the Revelation of Jesus Christ,* (London: Pickering & Inglis LTD, 1914), p. 251.

passage of the holy Scripture has been interpreted in several ways. Some Bible expositors say that this includes both classes, the good and the bad. For the fallen angels, the condemnation, but for the good, a pronouncement of blessing, since they will be united with the Church under one head, Christ. The Apostle Paul writes in Ephesians 1:10: *"...to sum up all things in Christ, the things in the heavens, and the things upon the earth; in Him, I say."*

The idea that the good angels are included is supported by Hebrews 1:14. *"Are they not all ministering spirits, sent forth to do service for the sake of them that shall inherit salvation,"* and in the hypothetical expression found in Galatians 1:8, the Apostle Paul writes: *"But though we, or an angel from heaven, should preach unto you any gospel other than that which we preached unto you, let him be anathema."*

These expressions, in the form of an interpretation, sound very interesting, but nowhere is it stated in the Bible that good angels of God will receive any rewards on the day of judgment. They have been created as ministering spirits who work faithfully for the Lord God Almighty.

The conclusion is that the angels spoken of in 1 Corinthians 6:3 cannot be the good angels, but the fallen angels. According to the holy, just God, every creature must be judged according to what they have done. This is substantiated by 2 Peter 2:4. *"For if God spared not angels when they sinned, but cast them down to hell, and committed them to pits of darkness, to be reserved unto judgment."* Jude 6 also speaks of the same judgment: *"And angels that kept not their own principality, but left their proper habitation, He hath kept in everlasting bonds under darkness unto the judgment of the great day."*

The great day of judgment is spoken of in Revelation 20:11-15, the Great White Throne Judgment where all the pre-Adamic race, the fallen angels, and the Adamic race, lost sinners will be judged. So, the angels spoken of by the Apostle Paul must refer to the fallen angels that sinned against God at the fall of Satan. All of them will be cast into the lake of fire.

I must also say a word about the wrong concept of the statement of Christ recorded in Luke 20:35-36: *"But they that are accounted worthy to attain to that world, and the resurrection from the dead, neither marry, not are given in marriage:*

"for neither can they die any more: for they are equal unto the angels; and are sons of God, being sons of the resurrection."

This passage is used by many people to project the belief that the fallen angels cannot marry and produce offspring, because Jesus said that the angels do not marry. Yes, I agree with that. The angels in heaven do not marry, and the resurrected saints will not marry either. But, the angels of heaven and the fallen angels of Satan are two different categories. The good angels in heaven will never marry. The angels of Satan can, however, because Satan himself prepared bodies for them with sex organs to produce offspring. I think this will suffice to clarify the notion that the fallen angels cannot marry. They will marry no more on planet Earth, for many of such have been imprisoned, but before the Flood Satan did try to corrupt the human seed and stop the coming of Christ. Before the Flood, the fallen angels were the ones that married the daughters of men. This was the main reason the Lord destroyed the Antediluvian race, to cleanse the human race of the corruption — a mixture of celestial and earthly beings.

CHAPTER VIII

THE JUDGMENT OF THE ORIGINAL PLANET EARTH

The Geographical Evidence of a Judgment in Past Eternity

How the Lord judged the perfect Earth is not entirely revealed in the Bible. Sometimes the Lord reveals very little about certain things in only a few passages of the Bible, and we have to consider and evaluate the truth revealed to us.

In the light of the geographical evidence, it can be concluded that the Lord knocked our planet Earth out of its original position, which caused the waters of the ocean to run over the continents, resulting in total destruction. The Earth is now tilting 23 ½ degrees. Before, our planet was erect, and lush forests grew all over it. Where there is cold and snow today and very short summers, there was, at one time, lush forests that flourished.

For instance, Spitsbergen in the Arctic Ocean, about 600 kilometers north of Norway, is a good example of such judgment. This area consists of several islands, with a total area of about 57,600 sq. kilometers (24000 sq. miles). 90% of the islands are covered with ice. No forests grow on the islands. However, Norway has coal mines on some of the islands. Since 1890, this Scandinavian country has been mining coal there.

Every school boy knows that coal is a combustible mineral formed by the partial decomposition of vegetable matter, without free access of air, under the influence of moisture, pressure, and temperature.

When our God, the Great Creator, knocked our Earth out of its former position, the masses of water swept the forests and vegetation into valleys, carried silt and sand onto them, and heavy pressure without air turned wood and vegetable into coal. Coal deposits are found in nearly every region of the world. About 9,500,000,000,000 tons of coal reserves are known to exist throughout the world, and another estimated 7,330,000,000,000 tons are thought to exist in unmapped and unexplored areas, making total world coal reserves about 16,800,000,000,000 tons. In some places, coal seams are several thousand feet under ground.

Petroleum, or crude oil, is more evidence that life existed on Earth billions of years ago. Petroleum is found only in beds of ancient seas, many of which are now thousands of feet below dry land. Crude oil was formed from dead plants and animals which settled to the sea bottoms. Some of this matter was carried from the land, along with clay and sand, to the seas by ancient rivers; and some of the matter was marine life, mostly microscopic in size, but occurring in vast quantities. These organic materials were subjected to tremendous pressures at the sea bottom. The pressures generated high temperature, and heat, together with the action of bacteria converting organic matter into crude oil. Pools of oil have been found in many parts of the world. Oil wells have been drilled in the United States of America to depths exceeding 20,000 feet, or 6,154 meters. Some of those wells are productive.

This shows us the tremendous upheavals and convulsions of nature which occurred on Earth billions of years ago. The soil or crust of the continents simply turned over in some places, burying everything on it. Where there was at one time a beautiful continent, today it is a deep ocean or vice versa.

All the animals of the prehistoric era were buried under sand and rocks, and petrified. That's the reason we have skeletons of dinosaurs in many parts of the world. They have also been found in America and in Canada.

As for crude oil, the present world stock is about 500,000,000,000 tons, and much more is to be found in unproved crude oil reserves, and in oil shale.

The Geological Evidence of a Judgment in Past Eternity

Before Satan fell, the North American continent was a beautiful continent. All the mammoths and dinosaurs that lived on the North American continent perished at the time of Satan's fall. The skeletons of those prehistoric animals have been found in America and in Canada. At the destruction of the first perfect Earth, the North

American continent sank and became a sea floor. At a later date, it was raised again to become a continent. The geological evidence proves the fact that at one time this continent was under water.

Great geographical changes also took place after the Flood. The ocean between Africa and South America, at one time, was a continent, but sank. Genesis 10:25 states: *"And unto Eber were born two sons: the name of one was Peleg, for in his days was the earth divided...."* This occurred about 2200 B.C. or only 148 years after the Flood. It was during this period of time that all the land animals and people that are now in South America and in North America came to this hemisphere. The Indian people we have in the Western hemisphere did not come from India, as believed by antropologists, but came from the Middle East through Africa to South America, before the section of land between Africa and South America sank.

Dinosaur's skeletons have been found in many places in the Province of Alberta, Canada. Some of them were huge, others small. A large sauropod dinosaur was discovered in 1972 in Colorado. The evidence reveals that this huge land animal was more than 15 meters (49 feet) tall and up to 30 meters (97 feet) long. It might have weighed 100 tons or more. This huge animal could have looked over the top of a four-story building.

Dinosaur remains and eggs have been found in the Gobi Desert, in Mongolia, confirming the fact that a great destruction took place billions of years ago.

As I read several encyclopedias, I realized that the Gobi has been visited by many scientists. American and British scientists who investigated the Gobi Desert include Henry F. Osborn, Roy Chapman Andrews, and N.C. Nelson. Their finds of fossil dinosaurs, dinosaur eggs and remains of the giant rhinoceros established the fact that life, in past eternity, existed in that part of planet Earth now known as Mongolia.

Perhaps the most noteworthy expedition was undertaken by Roy Chapman Andrews of the American Museum of Natural History in 1922. The American expedition found remains of a few mammals in the Cretaceous rocks in Asia, north of the Himalayas. These were disarticulated duckbill dinosaurs, as well as giant flesh-eaters. A perfect skull was found of a very primitive horned dinosaur, the long-sought ancestor of Triceratops, and was named Protoceratops Andrews, in honor of the expeditions's leader. But the most exciting discovery was of some dinosaur eggs, proving beyond all doubt that the dinosaurs were egg-laying.

Over two years, 1923 and 1925, they excavated a unique collection of Protoceratops remains, consisting of more than 70 skulls and 12 complete skeletons, showing all growth stages from hatchling to 2 meter long adults. More fossil eggs were found in large numbers, belonging to Protoceratops and other reptiles. Some of these eggs were arranged in concentric circles in clutches preserved in the position in which they had been laid.

In 1964 fossils of Tarbosaurus were discovered. A sensational find in 1971 produced 2 complete skeletons — a small herbivorous locked in a death embrace with the carnivorous Velociratops. These specimen are the only direct evidence of dinosaurs fighting. This all confirms the fact that the destruction, in past eternity at the fall of Satan, was so sudden that even the fighting dinosaurs had no chance to separate one from the other, but were buried instantly and petrified.

Nine different types of dinosaur eggs have been identified. They come from Mongolia, France, Brazil, South America, and the United States.

There was an extraordinarily wide range of creatures on Earth, before the fall of Lucifer in past eternity. Some 600 species have been recognized by scientists, so far.

The world's largest mammal also comes from Mongolia, the Far East. In 1922, Walter Granger, an American working in Mongolia, found 3 partial skeletons of Baluchitherium, one of which included the skull. Mr. Carrol L. Fenton writes about this Baluchitherium (a rhinoceros) in his book entitled, "The Fossil Book." He writes that 365 fragments were removed and shipped to New York, where the pieces were put together. This rhinoceros stood 5.5 meters (18 feet) at the shoulders and was the largest mammal known to have lived on land.

Mr. Fenton writes about the fossils of the Agate Bone Beds in Nebraska, which were found by Captain James Cook in 1877. The stratum lies in two flat-topped hills east of the Agate post office. No one knows how many bones the deposit once contained, since all except the two small hills have been worn away. But there are 4,300 skulls and separate bones in one slab of graybuff sandstone, with an area of 44 square feet; at that rate, one of the two hills contains 3,400,000 skulls and bones belonging to 17,000 skeletons. Of those

17,000 skeletons, at least 16,000 represent a rhinoceros named Diceratherium, which weighed no more than a small hog. [1]

I have to conclude that there must have been large herds of these animals that were swept together at the destruction of planet Earth. It is estimated that before the white man arrived in America, there were at least 60,000,000 buffalos in North America. There were herds which had tens of thousands of animals. So, the Agate Bone Beds confirm the fact that a sudden destruction swept thousands of those animals into one locality where they were buried under sand and rocks and petrified.

All kinds of fossils have been found throughout the United States, including birds, animals and fish. A sea turtle, Archelon, was unearthed in the State of Kansas. It was 3 meters and 67 centimeters (12 feet) long, and weighed nearly 3 tons. Bird footprints have been found in sandstone in the States of Connecticut and Massachusetts.

Baluchitherium, an Oligocene rhinocereos, was 18 feet high at the shoulder. At the left, its femur is compared with a 6-foot man.

At one place in Africa, they found a huge underground depository of bones of prehistoric animals swept together. The mammoths in Siberia were so suddenly killed and frozen that grass was found still in their mouths when disinterred. The Siberian mammoth was about

1. Carrol L. Fenton & Mildred A. Fenton, *The Fossil Book*, (Garden City: Doubleday & Company, Inc., 1958), pp. 406-407.

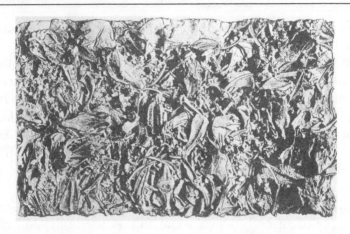

A slab from the Miocene bone bed at Agate Springs, Nebraska. It contains about 4,300 bones and skulls. (Photograph from the American Museum of Natural History)

the size of the modern Indian elephant. A complete specimen of this animal was first disinterred near the mouth of the Lena River in Siberia in 1806. The American mammoth is the largest species as yet identified. It reached a height of about 14 feet. Thus we understand the statement in Genesis 1:2: *"And the earth was waste and void, and darkness was upon the face of the deep...."* This was the result of the judgment on Earth and its inhabitants.

Violent convulsions must have taken place upon the Earth, for it was inundated with ocean waters; its sun was extinguished, the stars were no longer seen above it: its clouds and atmosphere, having no attractive force to keep them in suspension, descended as moisture upon its surface. Not a single living being was to be found in the entire planet. The withdrawal of the sun's heat occasioned the glacial period, or the Ice Age, the vestiges of which are plainly distinguishable.

The geological evidence proves all this.

Scientists say that within three days of the extinction of the sun, there would not have been a vestige of animal or vegetable life on the globe. The first 48 hours would have sufficed to precipitate every atom of moisture from the air in deluges of rain and piles of snow, and from that moment would set in a universal frost — a temperature of between two hundred and three hundred degrees below zero. No animal or vegetable could resist such frost for even an hour.

The water in the oceans froze down to the very bottom. Job 38:30

says: *"The waters hide themselves and become like stone, and the face of the deep is frozen."*

There are eight classifications of strata, from the Tertiary period down to the Silurian. The remains of plants and animals are found in the fossiliferous strata. Geologically, strata means sheetlike mass of sedimentary rock or Earth of one kind, usually in layers between beds of other kinds. According to the geologists, the Silurian period began about 440,000,000 years ago and endured for approximately 40,000,000 years.

The paleontologists say that the first fossiliferous rocks, or rocks containing the earliest evidence of life, were formed during the Peleozoic Era. The first abundant fossils date from approximately 600,000,000 years ago.

The lower and middle Silurian rocks contain a few seaweeds, but no land plants. Yet, the rocks abound in creatures belonging to three of the four sections of the animal kingdom.

1. The molluska: This large phylum contains most of the animals popularly called shellfish, except the crustaceans.

2. The articulata: This is one of the four kingdoms in the classification of cuvier, comprising invertebrates having the body composed of a series of ring-like segments.

3. The radiata: This major category of invertebrates including forms having the parts arranged radially about an axis, such as hydroids, jellyfishes, sea anemones and corals.

When we get to the highest strata of the upper Silurian rocks, land plants begin to appear, and together with them, some specimens of vertebrata, the remaining section of the animal kingdom. In this fossiliferous strata, plant fossils are rare, but remains of every division of the animal kingdom have been found.

Thus, the crust of our planet Earth appears to be a vast mound which God has heaped over the remains of past creation. And geology shows that the creatures on the first perfect Earth were destroyed in an instant by the most terrific convulsions of nature.

As the author of this thesis, I have to reject the dates calculated by the paleontologists and the geologists. They are all highly misleading. According to the paleontologists, the earliest evidence of life dates from approximately 600,000,000 years ago, while science books and some Encyclopedias say that our Earth was hot and began to cool off about 65,000,000 years ago. What a contradiction, a confusion and deception. Sandstone, of course, has been formed from deposits of sediments, and life on the perfect Earth dates from approximately 15,500,000,000 years ago or more.

The Biblical Confirmation of a Judgment in Past Eternity

There is a graphic portrayal of this judgment in Job 9:4-7. *"He is wise in heart, and mighty in strength. Who hath hardened himself against Him, and prospered?*

"Him that removeth the mountains, and they know it not, when He overturneth them in His anger.

"That shaketh the earth out of its place, and the pillars thereof tremble.

"That commandeth the sun, and it riseth not, and sealeth up the stars."

The statement, "that shakes the earth out of its place," has reference to the evidence that our planet Earth is no more in its original position, but is about 23½ degrees out of its original position.

Psalms 18:7 also refers to the same catastrophe. *"Then the earth shook and trembled; the foundations also of the mountains quaked, and were shaken, because He was wroth."*

The prophet Jeremiah also got a glimpse of the desolation of the Earth. He writes in Jeremiah 4:23-26: *"I beheld the earth, and, lo, it was waste and void; and the heavens, and they had no light.*

"I beheld the mountains, and, lo, they trembled, and all the hills moved to and fro.

"I beheld, and, lo, there was no man, and all the birds of the heavens were fled.

"I beheld, and, lo, the fruitful field was a wilderness, and all the cities thereof were broken down at the presence of Jehovah and before His fierce anger."

The prophet Jeremiah saw the planet Earth in its condition, after the destructive judgment billions of years ago. Some say that Jeremiah 4:23-26 refers to the tribulation, when great destruction will devastate our planet Earth. However, my Bible does not reveal such world-wide destruction to hit the Earth during the tribulation. The Bible shows that a great multitude of saved Jews and of saved Gentiles will enter the Millennium, while Jeremiah saw a destruction that had swept all life off the Earth — a total destruction.

Job 9:7 is a great revelation of the change of the natural laws of the universe. *"That commandeth the sun, and it rises not, and seals up the stars."*

At this point two questions must be asked that will help to clarify the statement, "That commendeth the sun, and it rises not...."

1. How could it be possible for the sun not to rise again the next morning?

2. What causes the division of day and night?

The only way the sun could not rise would be when the rotation of the Earth stops on its axis. The Earth's revolution around the sun establishes our year; its rotation on its axis establishes our day. The 23½ degree inclination on the Earth's axis and its journey around the sun causes the change of seasons and varying length of night and day.

In past eternity, when Satan fell, the Lord stopped the rotation of the Earth on its axis, and the sun did not rise again. The Lord extinguished the sun and there was no light. That is how the Ice Age came to be.

In 1450 B.C. the Earth stopped on its axis for the second time in its history. Joshua 10:12-13 says: *"Then spake Joshua to Jehovah in the day when Jehovah delivered up the Amorites before the children of Israel; and he said in the sight of Israel. Sun, stand thou still upon Gibeon; and thou moon, in the valley of Aijalon.*

"And the sun stood still, and the moon stayed, until the nation had avenged themselves of their enemies. Is not this written in the book of Jashar? And the sun stayed in the midst of heaven, and hasted not to go down about a whole day."

This was the only time in the history of the Adamic race that God stopped the rotation of planet Earth on its axis. This shows the mighty power of our God. Everything functions according to His will, the Earth and the entire universe. Praise the Lord, our Great God!

2 Peter 3:5-6 states: *"For this they wilfully forget, that there were heavens from of old, and an earth compacted out of water and amidst water, by the Word of God;*

"by which means the world that then was, being overflowed with water perished." Job 12:15 refers to the same destruction. *"Behold, He withholdeth the waters, and they dry up; again, He sendeth them out, and they overturn the earth."*

The Apostle Peter received a revelation about the judgment of planet Earth which destroyed the first perfect Earth. He was not referring to Noah's Flood, which occurred in 2348 B.C. That Flood did not destroy grass, trees and the rest of the plants. A number of animals and birds and eight human beings were carried through the Flood in the ark. When the water receded and dry land appeared, all vegetation and forests proliferated again on the Earth.

The judgment on planet Earth, in past eternity, destroyed all life here, vegetable, animal and human life. There is no evidence in the Bible whatsoever that on the first perfect Earth there was winter and summer as we have them now. Before the fall of Satan, there was a continuous summer, and all trees and plants were of tropical nature. They perished during the Ice Age. Therefore, the Lord had to create all new plants, and all beings that live and move today on our planet Earth.

Today, we are living on a recreated planet Earth, which is out of its foundations. David wrote in Psalms 82:5: *"All the foundations of the earth are shaken."* Three hundred years later, one of the greatest Hebrew prophets wrote in Isaiah 24:1: *"Behold, Jehovah maketh the earth empty, and maketh it waste, and turneth it upside down, and scattereth abroad the inhabitants thereof."*

Furthermore, the statement in 2 Peter 3:6: *"by which means the world that then was, being overflowed with water perished,"* is of paramount importance. The word "world" is translated from the Greek word "kosmos," which means "orderly arrangement," or "social order," including its inhabitants. The social order that perished in water lived or existed on Earth before the fall of Satan. Notice that the Apostle Peter referred to the social order "that then was" — billions of years ago.

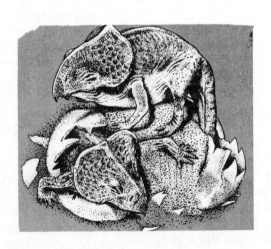

Baby Protoceratops hatching from their eggs, Mongolia.

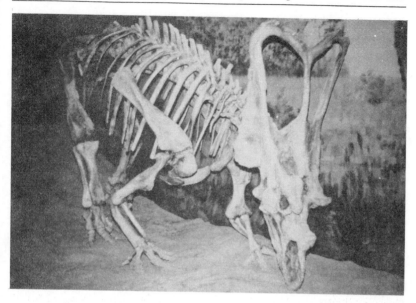

Chasmosaurus, a horned dinosaur, from Alberta, Canada.

A dinosaur from Alberta, Canada.

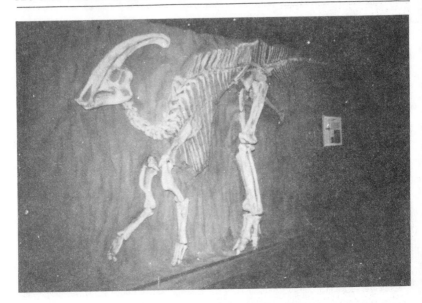

Parasaurolophus, Alberta, Canada.

Scolosaurus, Alberta, Canada.

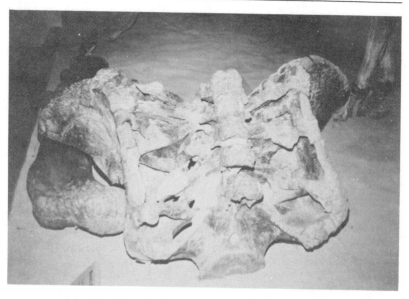

A fossil vertebral colum of a dinosaur, Alberta, Canada.

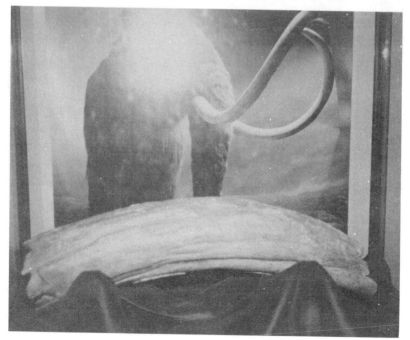

Fossil mastodon tusk. Peace River Canyon, Canada.

A fin-backed pelycosaur, Texas, U.S.A.

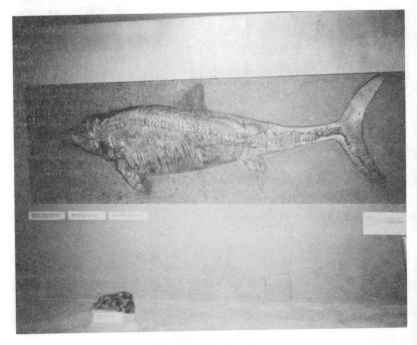

A fossil fish, Canada.

Petrified trees in Arizona, U.S.A.

A piece of a petrified tree, Arizona.

The Contrast Between the Noachian Deluge
and the Judgment of the Original Earth

Almost all distinguished Bible scholars and writers ascribe the catastrophic results of the fall of Satan to the Flood of Noah. They are misled. The great difference between these two catastrophes is clearly revealed in the Bible. The Noachian Deluge is described in Genesis 7:11-24, which reveals seven points of importance.

1. The fountains of the great deep broken up. This implies some great subterranean disturbances that must have taken place. There are vast amounts of water in the Earth's crust. There are great underground lakes and rivers. The greatest subterranean lake is in the United States. It begins in the Texas Panhandle, and runs under the States of Oklahoma, Kansas, Nebraska, South Dakota, and up to North Dakota. It is about 1,300 kilometers (812 miles) long. This vast water reservoir is supposed to be about 413,000 sq. kilometers (172,000 sq. miles). At the time of the Flood, the Lord, by His mighty power, squeezed the Earth and vast amounts of water were ejected.

2. The windows of heaven were opened. This implies a tremendous rain, water poured down on the Earth. Before the Flood, there was no rain. Genesis 2:6 says: *"...there went up a mist from the earth and watered the whole face of the ground."* Rainfall, such as we know it now, did not exist. Rainfall began at the Flood, when a new hydrological system came into operation. Therefore, a great water vapor surrounded the Earth, above its atmosphere. The Lord changed the existing hydrologic law, and it began to rain.

3. It rained for forty days and forty nights. Because of the great water vapor in the atmosphere, it could pour down water for nearly six weeks. At present, there is only enough water vapor in the atmosphere to cover the lands to a depth of a few inches. At that time, a great atmospheric change took place. The scientists say that there is enough water on planet Earth to cover it to a depth of more than 3 kilometers (2 miles) — if the terrestial topography were smoothed to a common elevation.

4. A continuous increase of water for forty days and nights. Genesis 7:17-18 says: *"...and the waters increased, and bare up the ark, and it was lifted up above the earth.*

"And the waters prevailed, and increased greatly upon the earth; and the ark went upon the face of the waters."

5. All the mountains were covered with water. Genesis 7:19 says: *"And the waters prevailed exceedingly upon the earth; and all the high*

mountains that were under the whole heaven were covered." How can it be possible to cover the highest mountain with water? The world's highest mountain is Mount Everest, which is 8,848 meters (29028 feet) high; and the deepest sea is about 11,033 meters deep. This, then, would mean that there had to be over 29,000 feet of water above the present sea level. How could it be possible to have so much extra water on the Earth? If so much water did come down to Earth, where did it go after the Flood ended?

The key to unlock this mystery is found in the statement of a steady increase of water. When it began to rain, the Lord in His mighty power caused the forces to operate. And there were some topographical changes: the mountains sank and the sea bottoms came up, until the mountains were covered up to 15 cubits of water (22.5 feet). [2]

The same structural changes of the Earth's crust are seen in the statement in Genesis 8:3: *"And the waters returned from off the earth continually...."* Here a decrease is seen, which implies a raising of the Earth's crust so the waters began to return to the oceans. Moses again writes about the same in Genesis 8:5: *"And the waters decreased continually until the tenth month: in the tenth month, on the first day of the month, were the tops of the mountains seen."* This shows very clearly the sinking and rising of the mountains. Thus, the Bible proves the fact that the Noachian Deluge was universal, and not a local affair, as is believed and taught by many preachers and teachers.

If the Flood was local only, then all the birds and animals would have fled to the West or to the East, to escape death; but Genesis 7:19 stated that *"...all the high mountains that were under the whole heaven were covered."* Notice the adjective "all." Not just a few mountains, but every mountain on Earth was covered with water. Genesis 7:21 says: *"And all flesh died that moved upon the earth both birds, and cattle, and beasts, and every creeping thing that creepeth upon the earth, and every man."* Notice again the adjective "all," not just a few. It is estimated that before the Flood there were at least 1,000,000,000 people on Earth. Genesis 7:13 shows that only Noah, his wife, his three sons and their three wives were allowed by God to enter the ark, and no more. 2 Peter 2:5 also indicates that only eight people

2. *Genesis* 7:20.

escaped death by drowning. The Apostle writes: *"And spared not the ancient world, but preserved Noah with seven others...."*

6. Did the increasing of the Flood waters cause great tidal waves? It is believed by many that the increasing of the waters caused great tidal waves which swept the animals together into certain areas, where they were fossilized. Dr. Morris writes: "The biblical deluge was both terrestial and atmospheric in nature. Tremendous volumes of water poured from the heavens for forty days and nights. At the same time, "the fountains of the great deep were broken up," most likely implying great subterranean and subaqueous disturbances, which would have created tidal waves and ejected great amounts of juvenile water. The great complex of hydrodynamic currents and forces, thus generated, would then undertake its divinely ordained mission of destruction and purification of the Antediluvian world." [3]

This, however, is not compatible with the biblical revelation. The Bible does not reveal any storms during the Flood, nor any fast currents. The reader has already noticed that there was a slow increase of water, according to the slow raising of the sea bottoms and sinking of the mountains. If there had been fast tidal waves and currents, then the ark of Noah would have drifted to the other side of the world, but Genesis 8:4 says that *"...the ark rested in the seventh month, on the seventeenth day of the month, upon the mountains of Ararat."* From Mesopotamia, where Noah built his ark, to the mountains of Ararat in Armenia is roughly 450 kilometers (300 miles). During five months, the ark drifted only 450 kilometers, or 3 kilometers (2 miles) a day. That is a very short distance. This certainly does not imply fast currents in the water.

7. The animal kingdom preserved. Of every species of animals, birds and creeping things, that existed on Earth before the Flood, Noah took a number into the ark. After the Flood, all the species of the animal kingdom were transferred from the ark back to the Earth. They continued to exist and to multiply as before the Flood. Not one of the species became extinct.

8. All the animals and birds that drowned in the Flood decomposed and did not petrify or fossilize. Some writers say that the Earth turned over in many places and buried the animals and the fish, which then fossilized. This theory has to be rejected as untenable. Because there was a slow increase of water, the animals and birds

3. Morris, op. cit., p. 65.

and men, as well, tried to climb up to higher ground, until all mountains were covered. Then all living creatures and men drowned in the flood waters. All the bodies of all the creatures that died decomposed and disintegrated.

Those who teach that all fossils date back to the Flood are wrong. They do not understand the judgment on the first perfect Earth, at the fall of Satan, and are confused. I have already shown the destruction of the original Earth and all the life that was on it.

9. When the Flood came there were no terrific natural convulsions on Earth. When Satan fell, the destruction that hit the Earth is associated with terrific natural convulsions. Job 9:6 says: *"That shaketh the earth out of its place...."* We know that the planet Earth was erect before, but is now about 23½ decrees out of its original position.

Crude oil is found in beds of ancient seas, and in some places in the United States oil wells have been drilled to depths exceeding 20,000 feet, or 6,154 meters. This means that, at one time, the oil pool was a sea bottom, but vast mounds of land overturned, and buried the sea bottom under sand and rock, exceeding 6 kilometers. I am confident that these 9 points will show the reader the vast difference between the Noachian Deluge, and the destruction of the first perfect Earth. They are two different catastrophes. The original Earth was destroyed over 15,500,000,000 years ago by a flood, but the Noachian Flood occurred about 2348 B.C.

Some writers teach that the Earth tilted during the Flood, and then sudden cold killed the mammoths in Siberia. This is totally unbiblical and must be rejected. The Bible reveals very clearly that all the species that lived on Earth before the Flood were preserved. Not one species became extinct during the Noachian Flood. Genesis 6:18-20 says: *"But I establish My covenant with thee; and thou shalt come into the ark, thou, and thy sons, and thy wife, and thy sons' wives with thee.*

"And of every living thing of all flesh, two of every sort shalt thou bring into the ark, to keep them alive with thee; they shall be male and female.

"Of the birds after their kind, and of the cattle after their kind, of every creeping thing of the ground after its kind, two of every sort shall come unto thee, to keep them alive."

This was God's command to Noah to preserve all species that existed on the Earth before the Flood. In Genesis 7:13-16, the fact, that every species which existed on Earth before the Flood was preserved is reconfirmed. Moses writes: *"In the selfsame day entered Noah, and Shem, and Ham, and Japheth, the sons of Noah and Noah's wife, and the three wives of his sons with them, into the ark;*

"they, and every beast after its kind, and all the cattle after their kind, and every creeping thing that creepeth upon the earth after its kind, and every bird after its kind, every bird of every sort.

"And they went in unto Noah into the ark, two and two of all flesh wherein is the breath of life.

"And they that went in, went in male and female of all flesh, as God commanded him: and Jehovah shut him in."

This is a clear statement made by the Word of God that not one species was exterminated. Every species that existed on Earth before the Flood was preserved. The mammoths and the other fossilized animals disinterred are prehistoric animals, and not part of the present order that exists on Earth now. Therefore, the teaching that the Earth tilted during the Flood is untenable, and must be rejected as irreverent.

Furthermore, during the Noachian Flood the sun was not extinguished, it shined in full force, except during the rain. Therefore, there could not have been ice during the Flood, because of the warm climate. Since there were no convulsions, or turning over of the Earth, during the Flood, the conclusion is that neither the people nor the animals that perished in the Flood were buried, but all of them decomposed.

I think it is advisable to show some contrasts between the prehistoric Flood and the Flood of Noah.

1. At the fall of Satan the Earth was made waste. Genesis 1:2 says: *"And the earth was waste...."* During the Noachian Flood, the Earth was not made waste. Genesis 8:11 says: *"And the dove came in to him at eventide; and, lo, in her mouth an olive-leaf plucked off: so Noah knew that the waters were abated from off the earth."* God says in Genesis 8:22: *"While the earth remaineth seedtime and harvest, and cold and heat, and summer and winter, and day and night shall not cease."*

2. At the fall of Satan the Earth was made empty. Genesis 1:2 says: *"And the earth was...void...."* Jeremiah 4:23 says: *"I beheld the earth, and lo, it was waste and void; and the heavens had no light."* During the Flood, the Earth was not made empty or void. Genesis 8:16-17 reveals God's statement to Noah. *"Go forth from the ark, thou, and thy wife, and thy sons, and thy sons' wives with thee.*

"Bring forth with thee every living thing that is with thee of all flesh, both birds, and cattle, and every creeping thing that creepeth upon the earth; that they may breed abundantly in the earth, and be fruitful, and multiply upon the earth."

This certainly does not imply a destroyed Earth, made empty by a catastrophy. All vegetation was intact.

3. At the fall of Satan, the Earth was made totally dark. Genesis 1:2 says: *"...and darkness was upon the face of the deep...."* The prophet writes in Jeremiah 4:23 that *"...the heavens had no light."* God extinguished the sun at the fall of Satan, and there was no light in the Solar System. During the Flood of Noah, the sun was not extinguished; and the Earth was not made totally dark. Genesis 8:6-12 shows that Noah sent forth a dove that flew around and returned to the ark, through a window which Noah had opened. The second time the dove returned to the ark she had an olive-leaf in her mouth. This does not imply any darkness, because a dove does not fly in darkness.

4. At the fall of Satan, there was no more light in the heavens. The Lord extinguished the sun, and total darkness prevailed. But, Genesis 8:6-22 shows that there was light from heaven at the time of the Noachian Flood, 2348 B.C.

5. After the fall of Satan, there was no day and night. The Earth stopped rotating and the sun stopped shining. Genesis 1:2-5 is the result of the destruction of the perfect Earth — total darkness. During the Flood, the Earth did not stop rotating, and day and night did not cease. Genesis 8:1-22 reveals this very clearly.

6. All vegetation was destroyed at the fall of Satan. Genesis 1:2 and Genesis 2:2-5 show that there was no vegetation left, God had to recreate all vegetation on the Earth. During the Flood, the vegetation was not destroyed. Genesis 9:3 says: *"Every moving thing that liveth shall be food for you; as the green herb have I given you all."* Genesis 9:20 shows that Noah planted a vineyard. This shows clearly that no vegetation was destroyed during the Flood, and God did not need to recreate new vegetation.

7. When God began to recreate the Earth, there was no continued abating of the waters from off the Earth. Genesis 1:6-12 shows that the waters were taken off the Earth in one day. During the Flood, there was a continual abating of the waters from the Earth. Genesis 8:3 says: *"And the waters returned from off the earth continually, and after the end of a hundred and fifty days the waters decreased."*

8. All fish were totally destroyed in the Flood of Genesis 1:2. No fish were destroyed during Noah's Flood, and there was no recreation of fish after the Flood.

9. At the fall of Satan, all the birds and animals were destroyed. Jeremiah 4:23-26 reveals that all was destroyed. During the Flood animals, birds and creeping things were kept alive, in the ark of Noah. Genesis 8:7-17 states that all creatures that were in the ark went forth to live on the Earth.

10. At the destruction of the perfect Earth, no man was left. Jeremiah 4:25 says: *"I beheld, and, lo, there was no man, and all the birds of the heavens were fled."* During the Noachian Flood, eight people were preserved in the ark. The Apostle writes, in 1 Peter 3:20, that eight souls were saved.

11. No social system was left at all, after the fall of Satan. 2 Peter 3:6 says: *"By which means the world that then was, being overflowed with water perished."* A social system was left after Noah's Flood. Genesis 9:1-16 and 1 Peter 3:20 show this very clearly.

12. The cause of all the destruction of the perfect Earth was the rebellion of Satan. The Flood was the result of the wickedness of men. Genesis 6:5-13 confirms that the Flood was a judgment upon wicked men.

CHAPTER IX

THE UNEXPLAINABLE MYSTERIES OF THE CARIBBEAN SEA

Remains of a Prehistoric Forest

During past several decades, discoveries made by the archeologists in the Carribbean Sea, have made national headlines, and have provoked much interest in the hearts of the American people. The underwater caverns in the Bahamas and underwater forests off Panama City, Florida, are mysteries to which scientists cannot find an answer.

As early as 1932, a speleologist dived into a pool of water, deep within the Grotto of Montespan and came up in an underground chamber, containing clay animal statues and other ritual evidence of man's existence there thousands of years ago.

In southern Florida, several springs contain artifacts of an ancient society that once lived there. In a spring called Little Salt — an underwater configuration, resembling a giant hourglass, narrowly constricted in the middle and widening on a ledge 27 meters (90 feet) below the surface — archaeologists found bones of prehistoric bison, mastodon, mammoth, giant ground sloth and giant land tortoise.

Higher up, on the sloping walls of the underwater cavern, they found long, shaped, wooden pins driven into the limestone. The carved tips of the stakes had been sharpened by man. On the 27 meter ledge (90 feet below the surface), a diver found an inverted prehistoric tortoise shell.

In the Warm Mineral Springs, in Florida, a diver put in a small test cut in an undistrubed part of the sedimentary layers, under a ledge 12 meters below the surface. The diver found compact sections of organic wood and leaf material, containing broken stalactites and the skeletal remains of small rodents. A mid-layer produced small pieces of burned wood and fragments of human bones, identified as the vertebra and pelvis fragment of a six-year old child. Carbon-14 dating showed the bones to be between 10,260 and 10,630 years old. In 1960, a diver again explored the Warm Mineral Springs. He found a jawbone of a human, far back, beneath huge boulders on the 12 meter-deep ledge. However, the author cannot agree with the carbon-14 dating.

The only possible solution to this puzzle is that thousands of years ago the water was much lower, and the early inhabitants used the hourglasses as dwelling places. The mastodon and mammoth bones must have been brought into the cavern by the ancient people who lived there.

Since stalagmite remains were found in that cavern, the cavern must have been dry thousands of years ago, when the early inhabitants lived there. The clay animals may have been used for ritual purposes.

In 1961, the crew of a United States navy research ship, sailing in the Gulf of Mexico, 2 kilometers off the coast of Panama City, Florida, saw something strange that no one could explain. Navy scientists aboard the vessel were testing a highly sophisticated type of detecting gear, the then-classified side-scanning sonar. Instead of the flat bottom it had been recording, the instrument suddenly began scribing large waves, which were actually large ridges. What had caused them?

The next day, guided by coordinates from the sonar ship, oceanographers, from the United States Navy Mine Defence Laboratory at Panama City, returned to the site, donned diving gear, and swam down to see what was there — 18.5 meters (60 feet) underwater. They landed in the middle of a strange seascape, a field of sand ripples, larger than any they had ever seen on the ocean floor, about 2 kilometers off the coast. I want to include material from Mr. Burgess's book entitled: "Man 12,000 Years Under the Sea," for comparison, to see if 12,000 years ago man truly lived on Earth and built those mysterious things. Mr. Burgess writes that over a 1,000 ancient trees were found standing on the continental shelf off Panama City, Florida, in 18.5 meters of water. Most were identified as Pinus eliottii (slash pine), but oak and other species were also present. The trees were standing upright, firmly rooted in the bottom, but all were truncated at or below the sediment surface. The entire strand of timber covered an area of about 1 kilometer long and 19 to 30 meters wide, with an average of one tree for every 10 square meters of ocean floor.

The navy scientists concluded that this was probably part of an ancient shoreline whose trees were standing on dry land 30,000 to 40,000 years ago, when the sea level between ice ages was more than 18.5 meters lower than at present.

The prehistoric trees are not unique to the Panama City area. Similar trees have been sighted by divers off Pensacola Beach, Florida. But, midway down the Florida peninsula, south of Sarasota, there exists the most unique combination divers have ever found — the remains of a prehistoric forest, replete with the fossil remains of prehistoric animals.

In 1955, a retired air force Colonel, William Royal, started diving off Venice Beach, Florida, to see if he could find the source of the fossil shark teeth. As he was swimming out from shore, going deeper, but staying just above the bottom, he suddenly saw ahead of him a jumbled pile of rocks about 8 meters underwater. The rocks were really branches; and 6-inch-thick logs were everywhere, some pieces sticking up vertically out of the clay bottom. He was looking at the remains of a prehistoric forest.

Colonel Royal found fossilized bones in abundance among the trees. He had stumbled upon a prehistoric bone-yard. In the months that followed, the diver fanned up not only sections of prehistoric ivory, but fossil beaver teeth, whale vertebra, extinct land tortoises, teeth and bones of mammoths, mastodons, manetees and giant ground sloths, along with hundreds of fossil shark teeth, 7.5 centimeters to 15 centimeters (3 to 6 inches) long. Over the next few years, he recovered at least 2,000 of the giant carcharodon megalodon teeth completely intact, plus thousands of fragments of others. He asks himself the question: "Why were the fossil shark teeth in the same deposits as the mammoth remains?" Colonel Royal believed that the mammoths died before the sea level came up and deposited the clay beds over their bones. The presence of the shark teeth in those clay beds indicated to him that the 24 meter (80-foot) long megalodon was still living after mammoths 8,000 to 10,000 years ago. [1]

1. Robert F. Burgess, *Man 12,000 Years Under the Sea,* (New York: Dodd, Mead & Company, 1980), pp. 248-255.

This mystery can be unlocked only in light of biblical revelation. Those ancient forests in the Gulf of Mexico, about 2 kilometers off the Florida coast, belong to 2 categories. Those of Panama City, Florida, belong to the present creation, and others with fossil bones belong to the pre-Adamic era over 15,500,000,000 years ago. The ancient forest, about 2 kilometers (1.5 miles) off Panama City, is part of a submerged forest of the present creation. The sea water has risen so much during the past 4,336 years that large areas of land have been covered with water.

The sea water has been rising steadily, about 1.40 meters every 1,000 years. Mr. Burgess writes that, according to Mr. Dimitry Rebikoff, the sea water is rising about 12 to 20 centimeters (about 5 to 8 inches) a century, which is recorded by the tidal records of every harbor in the world. [2] If the sea water has been rising about 1.40 meters every 1,000 years, then there must be a cause. At this point, 3 factors must be taken into consideration.

1. A steady decrease of water by meteorologic cycle. The vast ice fields in the world, such as Antarctica, Greenland and the North Pole, are covered with ice up to 3 kilometers and deeper in some places. It is estimated that if all the ice in Antarctica melted, the sea water would rise by 70 meters (210 feet). This implies a continuous evaporation of sea water since the Flood (2348 B.C.) and precipitation. In the summer of 1988, I read in a newspaper that, towards the end of World War II, several American war planes were forced to make an emergency landing in Greenland because of fuel shortages. Now the plains, where they landed, are about 18.5 meters (60 feet) under ice.

2. A continuous increase of sediments in the seas. According to scientific study, each year the rivers bring about 4,850,000,000 metric tons of dissolved salts from the continents and deposit them in the seas, and about 32,500,000,000 metric tons of detrital material are stripped from the continents and deposited in the seas. This makes a total of about 37,350,000,000 tons a year, or 13.5 cubic kilometers (3.3 cubic miles) a year of seawater that is displaced by continental sediments. In 1,000 years, it would amount to about 13,500 cubic kilometers (330 cubic miles) of sea water that has been displaced by continental sediments.

The sea waters have decreased since the Flood (2348 B.C.) by

2. Ibid., p. 261.

)rming ice in the polar regions. It is estimated that the ice sheet verlaying the continent of Antarctica is approximately 30,000,000 ubic kilometers (over 7,000,000 cubic miles). Each year snow ccumulates at a rate equivalent to 17.2 centimeters (6.7 inches) of vater. It is estimated that the North Pole contains about 1,000,000 ubic kilometers of ice, and Greenland probably 2,000,000 cubic :ilometers, a total of 33,000,000 cubic kilometers of ice. This, lowever does not include the Canadian Arctic islands, covered with :e.

From the Noachian Flood to 1988 was about 4,336 years. On this)asis, I conclude that the forming of ice was about 7,610 cubic :ilometers a year. It is estimated that about 448,000 cubic kilometers)f ocean waters evaporate each year. Of this, about 7,610 cubic :ilometers remain in the Arctic regions in the form of ice, and 440,390 cubic kilometers return to the oceans by rain and by the rivers.

The study has already revealed that each year about 13.5 cubic kilometers of dissolved salts or sediments are deposited in the seas. In 100 years that would total about 1,350 cubic kilometers of sea water that has been displaced by continental sediments, while the ice in Arctic regions increased about 761,000 cubic kilometers. This should mean a great decrease of ocean waters, instead the water has increased by 1.40 meters in 1,000 years.

3. A slow and steady rising of the bottom of the seas. This is the only solution to this puzzle. In this century, there has been a great change in climate, increasing the melting of the ice in the Arctic regions. From 1890 to 1940, the mean thickness of sea ice in the polar regions decreased by about a third. In 20 years (1924-1944), the area covered by sea ice decreased by about 1,000,000 square kilometers. During this period, the westerly winds increased in speed in the North Atlantic by 20%, cyclones took a more northerly course, the Gulf Stream became stronger and penetrated farther north, and the surface temperature of the Norwegian Sea rose some 5 degrees Centigrade.

According to navy scientists, the ancient forest in the Gulf of Mexico, off Panama City, is 18.5 meters below the surface. This is evidence that, thousands of years ago, the shoreline was there and forests grew, but now the ancient shoreline is about 2 kilometers out in the sea.

During thousands of years, there has been an increase of water of about 6 meters or more. The waters in the seas rose about 1.4 meters each 1,000 years. From 2348 B.C. to 1988 is 4,336 years. Since then there has been an increase of water of about 6 meter (23.6 feet). Since there has been a continuous rising of the sea bottom, there must have also been some sinking of some areas in the Earth.

The ancient trees found by Colonel Royal, with the fossil bone among them, point back to the first perfect Earth, before the fall of Satan. It was then that forests and animals were swept together and perished. Some of the forests were buried deep under sand and rocks in some other areas they were buried only a few meters. In the State of Arizona, great petrified logs have been exposed by erosion, and are laying on the ground. Colonel Royal also found a fossil graveyard which has been exposed by the constant movements of water during thousands of years.

Navy scientists say that the ancient forest off Panama City is about 30,000 to 40,000 years old. This is only human conjecture and totally unacceptable, in light of the Word of God. Radio carbon-14 dating is highly unreliable and should never be accepted as an absolute fact.

The ancient forest off Panama City, in the Gulf of Mexico, cannot be pre-Adamic, because during the Ice Age all the waters were frozen to the bottom of the seas. The weight and movements of ice would have crushed them to pieces, but the trees are standing — which suggests an increase of water. This did not happen 30,000 years ago, but after the Flood, when water increase began.

Underwater Cities and Quays in the Seas

Mr. Burgess writes about Mr. Dimitri Rebikoff, who a few years ago made an extensive photographic aerial reconnaissance of drowned coastlines around the Mediterranean and Aegean seas. The photographs revealed old quays, harbors and sometimes the remains of cities beneath the sea, cultures that had simply been covered by gradually rising sea levels through the centuries. The deepest evidence of buildings Rebikoff has ever found was at Corinth, Greece, where he dived down to examine the bases of buildings 10 meters below the surface. [3]

This implies that the cities, at one time, were on the mainland, but during thousands of years the sea waters increased and submerged cities, harbors and quays.

3. Ibid., p. 261.

Another puzzle is a so-called Bimini Wall. This buried wall is off the island of Bimini in the Bahamas and was spotted by a commercial airline pilot, Robert Bush, who was flying a cargo plane from Miami to the Dominican Republic. He informed Dr. Valentine of the Miami Science Museum. Dr. Valentine and Mr. Rebikoff flew to study the wall of Bimini. Rebikoff noted that the material was typical masonry of the Middle-American type, possibly Mexican. Mr. Burgess writes that Mr. Rebikoff and Dr. Valentine returned in 1970 and were directed by a local fisherman to dive down about 1,000 meters off Paradise Point in North Bimini.

In 6 meters of water, they found huge blocks which were perfectly aligned and comparable to a giant causeway. Excavation trenches revealed a 600 meter wall, made up of pillow-shaped blocks up to 5 meters square. One end appears to form a right angle and three other walls nearby are over 65 meters long. At the base of the excavation, the underwater diggers found that blocks rested on pyramid- or cylindrical-shaped pillars that were 30 centimeters wide. The blocks were purposely set on supports some distance off the bottom to allow the passage of sea water, so that tidal fluctuations would not eventually push the blocks out of alignment.

Mr. Rebikoff and his group drilled core samples out of the rock, enabling others to make qualitative analysis of the material. The results revealed that the rock did not exist in its natural state in Bimini. The stone supports were assembled at the corners of the slabs, denoting a building technique akin to megalithic structures. Beneath the rocks, searchers found concrete made of ground-up shells. The radiocarbon date of the peat sample was more than 8,000 years.

The most obvious pavement-like stones or blocks form single or double lines roughly parallel to the present shoreline. The blocks are between 60 and 90 centimeters thick, somewhat pillow-shaped in cross section, their originally right-angled corners having been trimmed back, chiefly by boring mollucs and sea urchins. All of the blocks are of coarse-grained limestone, lying on a stratum of denser limestone of fine grain.

Most of the columns were found in deep grooves in the limestone that ran parallel to the shoreline, the same kind of grooves found just off the shoreline of other Bahamian Islands. Two of the columns proved to be marble and were fluted in the manner of Greek columns. Analysis showed the other columns to be made of cement coated

with a thin patina of marine lime deposits. Since marble is not nativ
to the Bahamas, it had to have been transported at least severa
hundred kilometers. Nor were the columns made of materia
indigenous to the Bahama islands.

The most striking aspect of the columns is the consistency in siz
and shape of the unbroken ones. They are all barrel shaped — thicke
in their middle than at their ends — about 70 centimeters (28 inches
long and 50 centimeters (20 inches) in diameter. These column
were formed by cement hardening in barrels or casks. The wooder
containers would have, by now, been broken up and lost. Scientist.
are unable to determine who built the stone walls. It is an enigma tc
all of them. [4]

Who built the Bimini causeway or harbor is almost impossible tc
determine. The work must have been done before the ocean watei
rose and covered the harbor, built by the people who lived at that time
in that area. No records can be found anywhere which would give
some hints about the approximate time of the building of the Bimini
harbor. It must be thousands of years old.

In this hemisphere, there are some strange, unexplainable and
unknown things to which no date can be fixed. One such thing is the
helmet which king Montezuma of Mexico inherited from his
ancestors. When the Spaniards invaded Mexico under Cortes in 1521
A.D. one of his soldiers had a unique helmet on his head. The Spanish
helmets were fashioned almost the same as the Imperial Roman
helmets. One of Montezuma's two ambassadors, Tendile, noticed it
and was excited because King Montezuma's god had one like that on
his head. He asked to take this helmet for King Montezuma to see.
When the King of Mexico saw the helmet, he was stunned to see one
just like his god, Huichilobos, had on his head.

No historical facts can be found as to how this European helmet
came to Mexico. The only answer is that, centuries earlier, some
European travellers or troops must have come to Central America,
but they were killed by the Mexicans, and all evidence of their visit to
Mexico was lost.

In 1976, I preached in southern Mexico, in the city of Chiapas.
There we visited the local museum. In that museum was a limestone
slab about 50 centimeters square. On that stone slab was carved a
Greek cross. This is evidence that sometime in the past Christian

4. Ibid., p. 262-266.

missionaries must have landed in Mexico, but were most likely killed by the savages and all evidence of Christianity disappeared. This must have happened centuries before the Spaniards arrived in this hemisphere.

The Bimini harbor builders must have been people of considerable ability and skill. They must have had ships to transport marble to the Bahama Islands and skill to build the harbor. They knew how to mix cement and how to make molds. They must have succumbed to disease or some other catastrophy which exterminated them totally, and no written records exist of them. However, the Bimini harbor cannot be more than 3,000 years old.

The Mystery of Underwater Caverns in the Bahamas

One of the great unresolved mysteries is the underwater caverns near the Bahama Islands. The evidence is quite convincing that, at one time, the caves were dry and above the water surface. Andros is the largest of the Bahama Islands, stretching about 160 kilometers long and about 65 kilometers wide. It lies close to the Tongue of the Ocean. At a depth of 3 meters, along the narrow shelf between the fragmented island and the abyss, dozens of strange blue holes can be found.

Mr. Burgess writes that in 1958, in Toronto, Canada, a chemist, Dr. George J. Benjamin, and team of divers began exploring them. 22 years later Dr. Benjamin was still exploring those remarkable cellars in the bottom of the sea. In 1970, he discovered evidence that at least some of these caverns had been formed in an air-filled environment. Dr. Benjamin's team dived down the 60 meter-deep (198 feet) hole and penetrated about 400 meters along a horizontal passageway leading to a large chamber festooned with stalagmites and stalactites. Since then, many other systems containing similar dry cave formations have been found. [5]

No one has ever been able to resolve the mystery of those underwater caverns. I do not intend to be dogmatic, but I would like to use the following hypothesis. Since stalactites (a deposit of calcium carbonate hanging from the roof or sides of a cavern) and stalagmites (a deposit of calcium carbonate formed on the floor of a cave by the drip of calcareous water) cannot form under water, these must have been, at one time, air-filled caverns, far above the water

5. Ibid., pp. 257-258.

surface. Now, this big chamber, with stalactites 9 meters long, is about 60 meters under water. This leads to the inevitable conclusion that some topographic changes took place thousands of years ago.

Since the Noachian Flood, the water, in general world-wide, has risen by about 6 meters to 6.5 meters (22 to 23 feet). But in some places the ocean's floor has also sunk considerably, and this is the solution to the caverns in the Bahaman sea. The caverns sank thousands of years ago. At that time the Bahama Islands must have been much larger than they are today.

A giant Ammonite (Museum of Natural History, Dallas, Texas, U.S.A.)

Plesiosaur front leg bone (Museum of Natural History, Dallas)

Vertebra of the Tenontosaurus (Museum of Natural History, Dallas)

Dinosaur footprint (Museum of Natural History, Dallas)

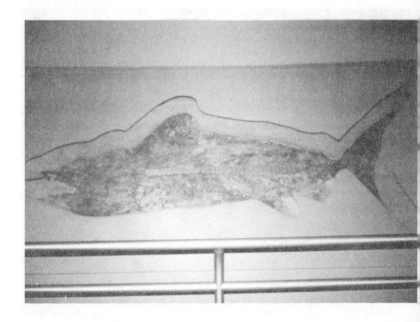

Glyptodont, a big fish (Museum of Natural History, Dallas)

**Section of mammoth tusk showing its layered growth
(Museum of Natural History, Dallas)**

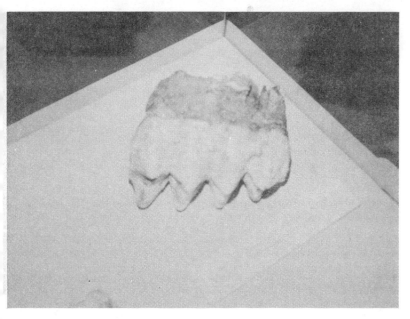

**Permanent mastodon molar tooth with sharp points for a diet of leaves and twigs
(Museum of Natural History, Dallas)**

Edophosaurus boanerges (The ship lizard of Texas)
(Museum of Natural History, Dallas)

A giant armadillo (Museum of Natural History, Dallas)

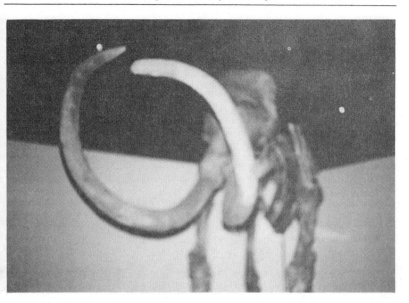

Mastodon (Museum of Natural History, Dallas)

A giant prehistoric bird (Museum of Natural History, Dallas)

CHAPTER X

THE RECREATION OF PLANET EARTH

The Difference Between "Create" and "Make"

The recreation of planet Earth itself is of paramount interest. The last clause of Genesis 1:2 states: *"...and the Spirit of God moved upon the face of the waters."*

This statement shows, in light of Genesis chapters 1 and 2, a gradual progress towards the completion of the recreation of planet Earth. In the study of this interesting subject, a distinction must be made between two important concepts.

1. Create: Bringing things into existence out of nothing.

2. Make: Making things out of existing matter. Both of these terms have been used in Genesis chapters 1 and 2, and must not be confused. "Created" and "made" are words which have been used in reference to living things, brought into existence. In Genesis 1:26-27, both of these words "made" and "create" have been used in reference to man, whom God created. Moses writes: *"And God said, Let Us make man in Our image, after Our likeness...."*

"And God created man in His image, in the image of God created He him; male and female created He them." A careful study reveals the twofold truth.

1. Man was made: His physical body was made out of dust — material that already existed.

2. Man was created: This has reference to the spirit and soul of man, the life principle which God had to create. So, man is both made and created.

Genesis chapters 1 and 2 mentions three distinct creations.

1. Plants
2. Fish and birds
3. Land animals and man

A third word used in Genesis 1:3-26 is "let." This word has been used 12 times by the Lord. "Let" means "to cause or effect a result." In Genesis 1:3-16, "let" has been used 6 times in connection with dead matter, to effect a result restoring things to their proper order. In Genesis 1:6-7, Moses wrote about God's command. "Let" simply implied a command and release of God's power to effect a result; the waters were divided from the waters. Again the Lord said: *"...let there be lights in the firmament of heaven to divide the day from the night....*

"And God made the two great lights, the greater light to rule the day, and the lesser light to rule the night...." [1] The lights spoken of are the sun and the moon, which derives its light from the sun.

The sun and the moon were created billions of years ago, but at the fall of Satan, God extinguished the sun. Now, the Lord through His might power restored the sun to its original usefulness. The sun again began to produce heat. However, the sun must have been reactivated sometime before the six day recreation began because the Spirit was moving upon the face of the waters. The word "let" is also used in connection with the living things created by God. Genesis 1:11 states: *"...let the earth put forth grass, herbs yielding seed, and fruit-trees bearing fruit after their kind wherein is the seed thereof, upon the earth: and it was so."* Fruit trees implies living things. There is a life principle in a tree. The Lord had to create new trees and plants, because all trees on the perfect Earth were of a tropical nature and perished in the ice.

Genesis 1:20 says: *"...let the waters swarm with swarms of living creatures, and let birds fly above the earth in the open firmament of heaven."* This passage of the holy Scripture reveals that, at the moment the word "let" proceeded out of God's mouth, His creative power was released; and all the fishes and living creatures were created. Genesis 1:21 states: *"And God created the great sea-monsters, and every living creature that moveth, wherewith the waters swarmed, after their kind, and every winged bird after its kind...."* In this one act, God filled the seas with fish and the firmament with birds.

There are about 30,000 different kinds of fish in the seas, and

---

1. *Genesis* 1:14,16.

15,000 species of birds in the world. Thus, the study has revealed that the word "let" was used by God in connection with dead matter to effect a result, as well as in connection to creating living things. Genesis 1:24-25 reveals that, on the sixth day, God created all the animals, creeping things, cattle and beasts of the Earth. Man was also created on the sixth day. So, in six days the Lord finished the recreation of planet Earth.

At this point, I want to take Genesis 1:2 once more into consideration. *"...and the Spirit of God moved upon the face of the waters."* This must mean that the sun was reactivated before the six day recreation process of the planet Earth began. However, no time is specified as to how long a time the Spirit was moving upon the face of the waters before God began to restore the Earth to its former usefulness.

Genesis 1:6-7 says: *"...Let there be a firmament in the midst of the waters, and let it divide the waters from the waters.*

"And God made the firmament, and divided the waters which were under the firmament from the waters which were above the firmament: and it was so." In this Scripture passage, two words should be taken into consideration.

1. The firmament — in Hebrew, "raqiya" — "an expanse"
2. The dividing of waters

The Lord made an expanse in the midst of the waters to divide the waters from the waters. Some waters were to be divided from some other waters. The waters which were under the firmament were divided from the waters which were above the firmament or expanse. This implies fog. Before the Lord began His restoration work, the sun had melted the ice in the Middle East area, but because there was no rotation of the planet Earth and no order as of yet, the fog, which is also water, had not separated itself from the water in the sea. At God's command the fog lifted and was separated from the waters in the sea, and became water vapor above.

Genesis 1:20 reveals that the birds were to *"...fly above the Earth in the open firmament of heaven."* This implies that air already existed on Earth, and the Lord did not create air at that particular time. The air remained on Earth from the perfect Earth, which perished at the fall of Lucifer. At the time of the fall of Lucifer, the Lord destroyed the first perfect Earth through a terrible judgment, and extinguished the sun. This resulted in the Ice Age. The entire globe was covered with ice. How thick the ice was on the entire Earth cannot be established. Scientists say that if the topography of the Earth were smoothed out, like a ball, the entire Earth would be covered with water up to 3 kilometers (2 miles). I have no way to prove whether the depth of the water was equal all over the Earth or not. For instance, during the Flood, the water reached only 15 cubits (22.5 feet) over the highest mountains, and at the same time the seas were several kilometers deep.

The ice in Europe was three kilometers thick, but in the Middle East it might have been only a few feet. In Europe, the evidence of an Ice Age is clearly seen. In my native country, Estonia, there is no native rock. Yet, there are huge boulders, some of which may weigh a hundred tons. They were all transported to Estonia by ice during the Ice Age. After the fall of Satan, the entire Earth was covered by ice for billions of years. There was no open water because the sun was extinguished. Yet Genesis 1:2 said: *"...and the Spirit of God moved upon the face of the waters."* This then reveals the fact that when the Lord began to recreate our planet Earth, a warmer climate existed. The ice had already melted, but to what extent cannot be established. How long a time was needed to melt the ice in the Middle East area is a very interesting question.

When the time came to recreate the Earth, the Lord reactivated the sun, which began to warm up the climate; and the ice began to melt. Since the Middle East was so much closer to the equator, the ice melted much faster there. During the melting process, the world was filled with vapor, and the sun was hidden behind a thick umbrella of fog. Genesis 1:3-5 states: *"And God said, Let there be light: and there was light.*

"And God saw the light, that it was good: and God divided the light from the darkness.

"And God called the light day, and the darkness He called night. And there was evening and there was morning, one day."

When the Lord said, "let there be light," He expelled the thick water vapor or fog, the sky was cleared, and the sun could shine in its strength. The statement, "there was evening and there was morning," shows clearly that the Earth began to rotate on its axis. The Earth's revolution around the sun establishes our year, its rotation on its axis establishes our day. The 23½ degree inclination on the Earth's axis and its journey around the sun cause the change of seasons and varying lengths of night and day.

According to scientists, the ice in Europe was three kilometers thick. I accept that as a fact; but how much time was needed to melt all that ice?

I want to use Antarctica as a comparative illustration. That continent has an area of about 13,109,000 square kilometers (5,100,000 sq. miles). The continent is almost wholly overlain by a continental ice sheet, containing approximately 30,00,000 cubic kilometers (7,000,000 cubic miles) of ice, representing about 90 per cent of the world's ice. The average thickness is about 2,440 meters (8,000 feet). The ice dome reaches a thickness of about 3,200 meters (10,500 feet) in the interior of the continent. This ice could cover the United States with a layer 3 kilometers (2 miles) thick.

How long would it take for nature to melt all this ice? If we take an average thickness of about 3,000 meters, it would give us an ice sheet of about 117,000 inches. If the ice melted about 1 inch per day, it would require nearly 321 years to melt all the ice on the continent of Antarctica, and the water in the sea would increase about 70 meters (210 feet). So in Europe, several hundred years were needed to melt the ice.

The Middle East, where the paradise of Eden was, the nursery of humanity, was so much closer to the equator, and had a warm climate, while up north the ice was just melting. It is the same today. Antarctica, North Pole, Greenland and many other islands have perpetual ice, while those islands to the south, near the equator, have perpetual summer.

That the ice in Europe took a long time to melt is confirmed by geological evidence. There are about 1,500 lakes in Estonia, about 12 in the area where I lived. You can see clearly how the running water has scooped out the sand, leaving a lake filled with water. Water, falling from a great height, has great power to carve out depressions. Some of the lakes I saw in Estonia were 30 to 35 feet deep.

The Purpose of Recreating the Planet Earth

The purpose of recreating our planet Earth reveals God's eternal purpose, stated in the decrees of God. In past eternity, God had a plan in His most holy counsel, to have a people for His name — the Church, through which He would receive glory and honor. Everything God does He does for His own eternal glory. That He created the universe, the planet Earth, all the angels, and the pre-Adamic race, was not for the happiness and the holiness of the creature. They were established with the view to His own glory. The same motive that caused God to establish His purposes also compelled Him to carry them out. The testimony of the Scripture shows clearly that He created all things for His own glory.

Psalms 8:1 says: *"O Jehovah, our Lord. How excellent is Thy name in all the earth. Who hast set Thy glory upon the heavens!"* Psalms 19:1 states: *"The heavens declare the glory of God, and the firmament showeth His handywork."* Isaiah 40:5 says: *"And the glory of Jehovah shall be revealed, and all flesh shall see it together...."* The Apostle Paul, writing to the church at Ephesus, reveals some of the mystery of God's most holy purpose and the reason for having the Church. Ephesians 1:11-12 states: *"In Whom also we were made a heritage, having been foreordained according to the purpose of Him who worketh all things after the counsel of His will.*

"To the end that we should be unto the praise of His glory, we who had before hoped in Christ."

Again the Apostle Paul writes in 2 Corinthians 4:6: *"Seeing it is God, that said, Light shall shine out of darkness, who shined in our hearts, to give the light of the knowledge of the glory of God in the face of Jesus Christ."*

Thus, the Scriptures reveal that all things the Lord does is for His own glory. To fulfill what He has decreed, in His most wise holy counsel, He needed the planet Earth to be the theater, the stage, on which He would manifest His marvelous plan to His creatures. Ecclesiastes 1:4 says: *"...that the earth abideth for ever,"* regardless of the fact that the original Earth was destroyed in a terrible judgment, but not annihilated.

On the planet Earth, Christ was to die for the Adamic race to redeem man. In God's holy purpose, the Earth will remain forever. It was on Earth that God would set up the kingdom of Christ, the Millennium, which will emerge with God's eternal kingdom. According to the Scripture, the Earth will be renovated with fire, recreated, and will become God's capital in His universe — from which He and His Church will rule throughout eternity. This is only the introduction to a marvelous study, which will explain a little of God's eternal plan.

The Symbolic Meaning of the Six Day Recreation

The Almighty God used six literal twenty-four hour days to set our planet Earth in order. The Lord, Who is Almighty, and for Whom all things are possible, could have restored the Earth to its original beauty in a second, but He did not do so. Instead He used six days for that purpose. Why did the Lord use six literal days, and not four days or five days? To understand the symbolic meaning of the six day history we must know biblical numerology, numbers in the Bible.

For instance, three is the number of manifestation. Genesis 1:11-12 reveals that, on the third day, life was manifested on Earth. The trees appeared, and they have a life principle in them. Three is the number of God: The Father, the Son, and the Holy Spirit. It is the number of the resurrection. Christ was resurrected on the third day —resurrection life manifested in its fullness.

Five is the number of favor and grace. The Brazen-altar was five cubits square. It was at the Brazen-altar that an animal was killed and an offender found mercy and grace, and returned home a forgiven man. Grace was manifested at the Altar. Ephesians 2:8 says: *"For by grace you are saved...."*

Six is the number of man. It symbolizes man's toil and labor in sin and in misery. The Lord used six literal days for the recreation of planet Earth. A day in the Bible symbolically can mean a thousand years. 2 Peter 3:8 says: *"But forget not this one thing, beloved, that one day is with the Lord as a thousand years, and a thousand years as one day."* The same thought occurs in Psalms 90:4. *"For a thousand years in Thy sight are but as yesterday when it is past, and as a watch in the night."*

So, by using six days, the Lord revealed the time period which He has designated for the history of mankind. Six days symbolizes six thousand years of human history. On the seventh day, the Lord rested. This is symbolic of the Millennium, when Christ will rule on Earth for one thousand years.

The six thousand years have been divided into seven dispensations. We are now in the dispensation of grace, which will end at the time of the first resurrection.

CHAPTER XI

THE CREATION AND FALL OF MAN

The Purpose of Creating Man

The Lord says in Genesis 1:26: *"...let Us make man in Our image, after Our likeness: and let them have dominion over the fish of the sea, and over the birds of the heavens, and over the cattle, and all over the earth, and over every creeping thing that creepeth upon the earth."*

The Bible teaches that God longed after fellowship with beings of His own order, and decided to create a pair of human beings. From this pair was to develop the Adamic race from which the Church would come. He made the body of man from dust and breathed into his nostrils, and man became a living soul. Thus, the Lord created man in His own image, referring to the soul — which is the immortal part of man. God is Spirit; the human soul is spirit. The essential attributes of a spirit are reason, sensibility, intellect and will. A spirit is rational and moral, and therefore a free agent. God endowed man with those attributes which belong to His own nature as a Spirit.

Thus, man belongs to the same order of beings as God Himself, and is, therefore, capable of communing with his Maker. Our first parents, Adam and Eve, had sweet communion with the Creator in the Garden of Eden. God had fellowship with His creatures of the same order as Himself. The first man and woman God created were placed in a beautiful garden called Eden.

The first couple were perfectly holy and in tune with God. This conformity of nature between man and God is also the necessary condition of our capacity to know God, and therefore, the foundation of our religious nature. If we were not like God, we could not know

Him. We would be as the beasts which perish. That man was created and endowed with great intellectual faculties is implied in the command to "dress the garden." Genesis 2:15 says: *"And Jehovah God took the man, and put him into the garden of Eden to dress it and to keep it."*

Adam also gave names to all the creatures which the Lord had created. Genesis 2:19-20 says: *"And out of the ground Jehovah God formed every beast of the field, and brought them unto the man to see what he would call them: and whatsoever the man called every living creature, that was the name thereof.*

"And the man gave names to all cattle, and to the birds of the heavens, and to every beast of the field...." Dr. Thiessen writes: "Here, then, in the earliest stage of Adam's life is speech; for he evidently calls out or pronounces these names. Here, too is the knowledge of language in its radical power; for these names are not empty, but significant. Here, also, is zoologic knowledge, the varying nature and qualities of the beasts and birds before Adam determine his action in naming them." [1]

Another purpose of creating man was the fact that Christ was to come from the Adamic race. The Apostle Paul wrote about it in 1 Corinthians 15:45: *"...The first man Adam became a living soul the last Adam became a life-giving spirit."* The Apostle writes further about it in 1 Corinthians 15:47: *"The first man is of the earth, earthly: the second Man is of heaven."*

The Significance of the Verb "Replenish"

The verb "replenish," significant in regard to filling the Earth, is translated from the Hebrew "mala" and means "to fill" or "to be full." But it is used in the sense "to fill again," especially after being emptied. This word is used by God in His address to Adam and Eve in Genesis 1:28. *"...Be fruitful and multiply, and replenish the earth...."* The Lord commanded them to multiply and fill again the Earth. In Genesis 9:1, the Lord said to Noah: *"...Be fruitful, and multiply, and replenish the earth."* The command to Noah and his sons was to refill the Earth that was emptied by the Flood.

The word "replenish" was used in prophecy in regard to Tyre. In Isaiah 23:1-2, the prophet writes: *"The burden of Tyre. Howl, ye ships of Tarshish: for it is laid waste, so that there is no house, no entering in from the land of Kittim it is revealed to them.*

1. Thiessen, op.cit., p. 220.

"Be still, ye inhabitants of the coast, thou whom the merchants of Sidon, that pass over the sea, have replenished."

This is a prophecy about the destruction of Tyre, destroyed by Nebuchadnezzar around 573 B.C. The merchants of Sidon had filled it with their merchandise, and again filled Tyre with their produce repeatedly.

In Ezekiel 27:25, the prophet Ezekiel wrote about the city of Tyre, which was built on an island about half a mile off shore. *"The ships of Tarshish were thy caravans for thy merchandise: and thou wast replenished, and made very glorious in the heart of the seas."*

The verb "replenish" is used here in the sense of filling the city of Tyre again with their merchandise. So, the conclusion is that "replenish" used by God in Genesis 1:28, *"...multiply, and replenish the earth...."* means to fill it again, to fill it once more. This is a strong indication that the Earth, before the fall of Satan, was inhabited by a pre-Adamic race.

The reader must not confuse this Tyre with the Tyre built on the mainland, and destroyed by King Nebuchadnezzar about 573 B.C. This Tyre was built on the island about half a mile off the shore and was destroyed by Alexander the Great around 322 B.C.

The Purpose of Tempting Man

How could a just God permit man to be tempted and allow him to fall into sin? This question is asked by many people. The answer to the question is that there was a need for probation. Man was a free moral agent. God placed a test before Adam and Eve, a test of their obedience to God. The Lord chose a tree to be the source of testing. Genesis 2:16-17 says: *"And Jehovah God commanded the man, saying, Of Every tree of the garden thou mayest freely eat.*

"but of the tree of the knowledge of good and evil thou shalt not eat of it: for in the day that thou eatest thereof thou shalt surely die." This tree was an ordinary tree like all the other fruit trees. There was no poison in it, no power of sin. The command was not to eat of that particular tree. The Lord endowed man with the power of choice, enabling him to choose contrary to the known will of God. The possession of this power was the necessary condition of probation. Probation was necessary, even though God foreknew it would result in the fall. Man had the opportunity to choose whether he would serve God or whether he would turn his back on the Lord. Genesis 3:1-7 is the story of Satan talking to Eve through a serpent. Satan

used only 46 words, but accomplished the greatest purpose of his cunning scheme.

The fall of the woman and the fall of the man were different. The fall of the woman was effected by the seductions of a serpent, whom Satan used for that purpose. Eve was deceived and enticed by the cunning words of Satan, and fell by deception. Adam, however, fell by affection. 1 Timothy 2:14 says: *"And Adam was not beguiled, but the woman being beguiled hath fallen into transgression."*

The conclusion is that, when Eve was deceived, Adam was not present. Adam, seeing that his darling had fallen, could not resist his affection, and deliberately and knowingly ate of the forbidden fruit. Nowhere is it stated in the Bible that it was Eve's sin that brought condemnation on mankind. Romans 5:12 says: *"Wherefore, as by one man sin entered into the world, and death by sin; and so death passed upon all men, for that all have sinned."*

The need of a tempter reveals God's benevolence in leaving a possibility for man's redemption. Satan sinned deliberately, spurred on by undue ambition, and thus originated his own sin, and became Satan — without hope of salvation, eternally lost or separated from God. Had man fallen without a tempter, he would have originated his own sin, and would have himself become a Satan. Then, there would have never been any possibility of man's redemption. He would have been hopelessly lost.

The Immediate Consequences of Adam's Sin

The consequences of the fall of man were far-reaching. The effects of sin upon Adam and Eve, and upon their environment will be treated only briefly in this section. On the day of transgression, man died spiritually, physically and eternally.

1. Spiritual death. Before the fall, God and Adam were in fellowship with each other. After the fall, their fellowship was broken. Instead of seeking fellowship with God, they now fled from the Lord. They knew they were guilty. Our first parents were separated from God — spiritually dead.

2. Physical death. When man came from the hands of God, he was innocent and holy. Now, Adam and Eve were sinners and had a sense of shame and pollution. They had something to hide. They were naked and could not appear before God in their fallen condition. Man now had a corrupt nature. Man now could live only a certain number of years. The Lord made man out of Earth, and man

was to return to it again. Because of sin, the death penalty of sin reaches every individual in the human family; none is exempt. The Apostle Paul writes in Romans 5:18: *"Through one trespass the judgment came unto all men to condemnation...."* Hebrews 9:27 says: *"And as it is appointed unto men once to die, but after this the judgment."* Every sin, of any nature, is an offense against God and subject to His wrath.

3. Eternal death. Man was separated from God forever. Without redemption there would have never been any chance for eternal life. On the day of transgression, the Lord promised the coming of a Savior.

4. The effect of man's sin on the environment. In Genesis 3:17, the Lord states: *"...cursed is the ground for thy sake; in toil shalt thou eat of it all the days of thy life."* The ground was cursed. Nature is groaning under the curse. Romans 8:21-22 shows that the curse will not be removed until Jesus returns to Earth in glory, to set up His kingdom, the Millennial reign. The Apostle writes: *"That the creation itself also shall be delivered from the bondage of corruption into the liberty of the glory of the children of God.*

"For we know that the whole creation groaneth and travaileth in pain together until now."

Man's Redemption Through Christ

God, in His unfathomable love, has prepared a way of escape through Christ, His Son. God's plan of redemption is magnanimous. In past eternity, the redemption plan was formulated by God, the Father; God, the Son, was to accomplish it at the cross; God, the Holy Spirit, was to apply redemption to the hearts of men, thus bringing about regeneration or the new birth.

You, being condemned to death, cannot pay the penalty for your sins yourself. Christ came to do that. God's eternal love, wherewith He has loved you, saw your poor, helpless condition. The Son of the living God died on the cross for you and paid the penalty for your sins. Now, by faith you can accept Christ as your personal Savior and Lord, and be forgiven of your sins. You can receive eternal life now instead of punishment.

Adam, who was placed in the Garden of Eden under the Adamic covenant with his wife Eve, was sinless and holy. Life was conditioned by perpetual obedience. They broke the covenant, forfeited life and became sinners. The sinner was to be eternally punished or satisfaction — an atonement — was to be made to God as a full legal equivalent for wrong done. The proper meaning of "the atonement" is "to make moral or legal restoration for fault or injury." God's holy nature and justice could not compromise with sin. Thus, an atonement was to be made which could completely satisfy a holy God. That atonement was Christ, the Son of God.

Since holiness is God's fundamental attribute, it is only reasonable that He should be given some satisfaction to remove the outrage of sin. The death of Christ at the cross supplied this satisfaction which satisfied the justice of God. God rightly exacts the penalty for a broken law. God cannot free the sinner until the demands of justice are satisfied. Christ's death fully satisfied these demands.

But why does God punish sin? Because of justice. The Great Creator, God, is an absolutely holy Justice. The moral perfection and absolute justice of God are interwoven in His nature. The moral perfection of God is essential and fundamental, and not a product of His self-determination. His essential perfection includes a principle of justice which makes the punishment of sin an end in itself. His justice cannot be resolved into disinterested benevolence. God's justice must be vindicated. The death of Christ did all this for us. Christ met the demands of God's law, and His justice was vindicated. Now, by faith in the risen Christ you can receive forgiveness of sins and eternal life.

The Almighty, loving Heavenly Father laid our guilt on the Lord Jesus Christ, His beloved Son. Philemon 10-18 affords a wonderful picture of Christ taking the guilt upon Himself. A slave of Philemon, Onesimus, wronged his master and fled to Rome, where he met the Apostle Paul. Through Paul's testimony Onesimus got saved. The Apostle sent him back to his master and wrote, asking Philemon to forgive him. He says in Philemon 18: *"If he hath wronged thee, or oweth thee ought, put that on my account."* Yes, thank God! Jesus said to the Father, "Put their sins on my account. I died for them on the cross." Now, God's promise of eternal life can be yours.

Titus 1:2 says: *"In hope of eternal life, which God, who cannot lie, promised before times eternal."* The Apostle Paul repeats God's promise in Titus 3:7. *"...being justified by His grace, we might be made heirs according to the hope of eternal life."*

As early as 609 B.C. the prophet wrote in Habakkuk 2:4: *"...the righteous shall live by his faith."* 650 years later the Apostle wrote in Romans 1:17: *"...the righteous shall live by faith."* So you, dear reader, if you have not yet accepted Christ as your personal Savior and Lord, you may do it by faith and receive forgiveness of sins and eternal life. God loves you with an everlasting love, and has made it possible for you to come to Him, through His Son Jesus Christ, Who died in your place on Calvary. He arose again, and today He is a living gracious, Savior.

CHAPTER XII

SATAN'S ATTEMPT TO STOP THE COMING OF CHRIST

The Human Blood Marred with Celestial Elements

Ever since his fall, Satan has been working against the purposes of God. He is very powerful, but not all-powerful. He cannot create, only the Lord can bring things into existence out of nothing. But the power of Satan is most real in the world and manifests itself through evil actions in the lives of evil men and women. Because of the sinful nature men have, the Devil has no difficulty in keeping them in his claws.

On the day that Adam and Eve fell into sin, the Lord made a promise of redemption. In Genesis 3:15 the Lord says: *"And I will put enmity between thee and the woman, and between thy seed and her seed: He shall bruise thy head, and thou shalt bruise his heel."* From that moment on Lucifer knew that a Savior would judge him and redeem man. The Devil has, ever since, tried to hinder the coming of the Son of God. Satan knew that the Redeemer would come of the seed of the woman. For this reason he has tried to mar the seed of the human race, to corrupt it and thus hinder the coming of the Lord Jesus.

The first attempt was made before the Flood, when he marred the human blood with celestial elements. Genesis 6:1-4 speaks of the sons of God: *"...the sons of God saw the daughters of men that they were fair; and they took them wives of all that they chose.*

"The Nephilim were in the earth in those days, and also after that, when the sons of God came in unto the daughters of men, and they bare children to them: the same were the mighty men that were of old, the men of renown."

This passage of the holy Scripture has been subject to great controversy. Some say that these were fallen angels, others that "the sons of God" were of the godly line of Seth. I have studied this passage very carefully to determine whether they were fallen angels, who assumed human nature to corrupt the human seed, and thus stop the coming of the Lord Jesus, or were godly men of the line of Seth. I have to conclude that the sons of God were fallen angels. In the Old Testament, men of the human race were never called "the sons of God." The angels of God were called "the sons of God." Job 1:6 says: *"Now it came to pass on the day when the sons of God came to present themselves before Jehovah, that Satan also came among them."* This same phrase is repeated in Job 2:1. *"...the sons of God came to present themselves before Jehovah...."* In Job 38:7 God said to Job, *"When the morning stars sang together, and all the sons of God shouted for joy."* This must have happened before the fall of Satan, probably at the time of the creation, when the beautiful universe came from the hands of God. The angels who were already created shouted for joy at the creation of the world.

So, this evidence points to the fact that the phrase, "sons of God," is a reference to angels, and not to men. The question now is, were the fallen angels able to take on human bodies with reproductive organs? Is Satan so powerful that he can make physical bodies? The answer to this question is 'yes.' Satan can turn dead objects into living things. This is demonstrated in the Old Testament. When God called Moses to go into Egypt to deliver His people from the bondage of slavery, the Hebrew man hesitated and objected. In Exodus 4:1-4 the Lord told Moses to cast his rod on the ground and it became a serpent. Exodus 7:10-12 shows that when Moses and Aaron stood before the king of Egypt, Aaron cast down his rod before the king and before his servants and it became a serpent. This happened in the power of the living God.

Then, Pharaoh called the sorcerers and they cast down their rods, and they became serpents. This happened in the power of Satan. All rods were changed into living creatures. There was no difference whatsoever. Aaron's rod became a living creature in the power of God, and the rods of the sorcerers became living creatures in the power of Satan. The only difference was that Aaron's rod or serpent swallowed up the other serpents. Exodus 8:6-7 again shows the power of Satan demonstrated. When Aaron stretched out his hand over the waters of Egypt, frogs came up in the power of God, so that all the waters were filled with frogs, and the land as well. The magicians did the same with their enchantments and brought up frogs. Again, living creatures were produced in the power of Satan. This has shown us that Satan is powerful enough to turn dead objects into living creatures.

Jude 5-6 confirms the fact that the fallen angels did have intercourse with women of the Adamic race. Jude writes: *"And angels that kept not their own principality, but left their proper habitation, he hath kept in everlasting bonds under darkness unto the judgment of the great day.*

"Even as Sodom and Gomorrah, and the cities about them, having in like manner with these given themselves over to fornication and gone after strange flesh, are set forth as an example, suffering the punishment of eternal fire."

The statement, "having in like manner with these given over to fornication," has great significance. It refers to the fallen angels, at least some of them, which did have sexual intercourse with the women of the Adamic race.

Many New Testament references speak of the evil work and miracles of demons. In 2 Thessalonians 2:9 the Apostle Paul writes about Antichrist, *"...whose coming is according to the working of Satan with all power and signs and lying wonders."* The Apostle John writes about the false prophet in Revelation 13:13-14 saying: *"And he doeth great signs, that he should even make fire to come down out of heaven upon the earth in the sight of men.*

"And he deceiveth them that dwell on the earth by reason of the signs which he was given him to do in the sight of the beast saying to them that dwell on the earth, that they should make an image to the beast who hath the stroke of the sword and lived." We can now see and understand the power of Satan, who will bring fire down from heaven to deceive the people of that day. So, he can do many miracles, the so-called "lying wonders," to deceive people everywhere.

Job 1:13-19 speaks about the disasters that struck him, and Job 1:16 says: *"...The fire of God is fallen from heaven, and hath burned up the sheep and the servants, and consumed them...."* "The fire from heaven" was the fire of Satan that burned up Job's sheep and his servants who were guarding the sheep.

Revelation 13:15 shows that Satan can give life to the image of the beast. The Apostle John writes: *"And it was given unto him to give breath to it, even to the image of the beast, that the image of the beast should both speak, and cause that as many as should not worship the image of the beast should be killed.''* This is the great power of Satan

Then, there is no doubt whatsoever that Satan could make physical bodies for his fallen angels. But what was the real purpose of his trying to mar the human race with unnatural seed? It was to destroy the purity of the seed of the woman, and stop the coming of Christ into this world. Satan knew that the coming of the Lord Jesus into this world as Savior would mean the end of his evil work, his confinement, that of his fallen angels in the lake of fire. Satan has tried four times to stop the Son of God from accomplishing redemption on the cross.

Satan's Attempt to Exterminate the Hebrew Race

The second scheme the Devil used was to try to exterminate the Hebrew race, since Christ was to come from that race. For this purpose, Satan used Pharaoh, the king of Egypt. It was a double scheme.

First, heavy slavery to prevent the multiplication of the Israelites. Exodus 1:8-10 says: *"Now there arose a new king over Egypt, who knew not Joseph.*

"And he said unto his people, Behold, the people of the children of Israel are more and mightier than we.

"Come, let us deal wisely with them, lest they multiply, and it come to pass, that, when there falleth out any war, they also join themselves unto our enemies, and fight against us, and get them up out of the land."

Satan used a political pretense. The king of the Hittites was preparing an invasion of Egypt, and the king of Egypt was concerned about the results of a possible war. Satan laid on the heart of Pharaoh, through whom he worked, to introduce heavy slavery to stop quick multiplication of the Hebrews. Exodus 1:11-12 says: *"Therefore they did set over them taskmasters to afflict them with their burdens. And they built for Pharaoh store-cities, Pithom and Raamses.*

"But the more they afflicted them, the more they multiplied and the more they spread abroad. And they were grieved because of the children of Israel."

This failure caused the Devil to introduce the killing of infants. The Hebrews were forced to commit infanticide. Exodus 1:16 reveals the king's mind in this matter. *"And he said. When ye do the office of a midwife to the Hebrew women, and see them upon the birth-stool; if it be a son, then ye shall kill him; but if it be a daughter, then she shall live."*

The scheme of Satan was most cunning — to kill the male children and thus exterminate the Hebrew race. Then, Christ, the Son of the Living God, could not come into the world. It must have been one of the most difficult times for the Hebrew people, especially the mothers, to have to take their own sons and throw them into the Nile and see them eaten by crocodiles. Satan thought that he would achieve his purpose, but he was not wise enough to know God's will. The Lord was ready to deliver His people from Egyptian bondage.

The third time Satan tried his luck was during the reign of Ahasuerus, who ascended the throne of Persia in 484 B.C. Esther 2:16 shows that Esther, a beautiful Jewess, was made Queen of Persia in the seventh year of his reign, or about 477 B.C. A year later the king exalted Haman to be the prime minister of Persia. This man hated the Jews because Mordecai, a godly Jew, did not bow down before him. He decided to exterminate the Hebrew race. Esther 3:8-10 reveals Haman's plot to destroy the Jews. He denounced the Jews to the king and asked permission to destroy them. Esther 3:9 shows Haman's request: *"If it please the king, let it be written that they be destroyed: and I will pay ten thousand talents of silver into the hands of those that have the charge of the king's business, to bring it into the king's treasuries."*

The Persian Empire consisted of 127 provinces, stretching from India to Greece. Satan's plot was to exterminate the Hebrews in all those regions and thus stop the coming of Christ into the world. The offer of ten thousand talents of silver was equivalent to ten million dollars. What was the reaction of the king? Esther 3:11 says: *"And the king said unto Haman, The silver is given to thee, the people also, to do with them as it seemeth good to thee."*

The Lord intervened again and frustrated the Devil's purpose in this matter, and the Jews were saved from total destruction. Esther 7:10 shows that Haman himself was hanged. Thus, God destroyed the enemy of the Jews and saved His people.

Satan's Attempt to Exterminate Christ

The fourth attempt was made by Satan through Herod, king of Judea. When the Lord Jesus was born, the wise-men from the East came to worship Him. Matthew 2:1-5 shows that, when the wise-men arrived in Jerusalem, they inquired about the location, where the King of the Jews was born. This reached the ear of Herod the Great, who sat on the Judean throne. Herod was one of the most wicked and jealous rulers in the history of Judea. When he heard about the wise-men and the purpose of their visit, he invited all the scribes and the chief priests to his royal palace, to inquire about the location of the birth of Christ, the King of the Jews.

The religious leaders referred to Micah 5:2, which foretold the location of the birth of the King of the Jews. *"But thou, Bethlehem Ephrathah, which art little to be among the thousands of Judah out of thee one shall come forth unto me that is to be ruler in Israel; whose goings forth are from of old, from everlasting."* Herod now knew the town where Christ was born. Next, he needed to find out in which house the child lived. With this purpose in mind, he invited the wise-men to his royal palace and asked them when the star had appeared. Matthew 2:7-8 shows that Herod cunningly encouraged the wise-men to go to Bethlehem and find the child, so that he could also go to worship Him. This was Satan's cunning trick. Herod had purposed in his heart to kill Jesus.

Matthew 2:12 reveals that the angel of God warned the wise-men not to go back to Jerusalem. They went home another way. When Herod saw that he was deceived by the Eastern visitors, he was very angry and ordered a general murder in Bethlehem and its vicinity. Matthew 2:16 says that Herod *"...sent forth, and slew all the male children that were in Bethlehem, and in all the borders thereof, from two years old and under...."* The Lord, however, had warned Joseph to flee with his family into Egypt. Thus, the Lord again frustrated Satan's schemes. In Matthew 2:17, the Apostle Matthew made reference to this experience as a fulfillment of Jeremiah 31:15. The prophet writes: *"Thus saith Jehovah. A voice is heard in Ramah, lamentation, and bitter weeping. Rachel weeping for her children; she refuseth to be comforted for her children, because they are not."*

CHAPTER XIII

THE NAMES
AND WORK OF SATAN

The Names and Work of Satan Revealed in the Scriptures

In the holy Scriptures, this archenemy of God is called by several names, which reveal qualities of character and methods of operation. In the Old Testament, he is mentioned in four books. He is spoken of in Genesis 3:1-17, when he tempted Eve to sin against God. In 1 Chronicles 21:1, he is seen opposing Israel. In Job 1:6-12 and Job 2:1-7, he is seen slandering Job before God. In Zechariah 3:1-2, he is revealed as an adversary of the high priest, Joshua. In the Old Testament, the noun "Satan" occurs only 19 times, 14 of them in the first two chapters of Job. In the New Testament, this noun occurs 37 times, 18 times in the gospels alone.

This superhuman being is a real being, a real person, to whom personal pronouns are applied in Job 1:8, Job 2:2 and Zechariah 3:2. In Matthew 4:10, the Apostle writes: *"Then saith Jesus unto him...."*

Personal attributes are ascribed to the Devil. In Isaiah 14:13-14, he says: *"I will."* Job 1:9-10 reveals that he has knowledge.

The Bible reveals that personal acts are performed by him. Job 2:7 says: *"So Satan went forth from the presence of Jehovah, and smote Job with sore boils from the sole of his foot unto his crown."* Matthew 4:1-11 reveals his personal acts in tempting Christ. 1 John 3:8 says: *"He that doeth sin is of the Devil for the Devil sins from the beginning. To this end was the Son of God manifested, that he might destroy the works of the Devil."*

There are at least 20 names for Satan in the Bible.

1. Satan. This is a transliteration from the Greek word "Satanas," and means "adversary," "the accuser." Zechariah 3:1 says: *"And he*

showed me Joshua the high priest standing before the angel of Jehovah, and Satan standing at his right hand to be his adversary." The Apostle writes in 1 Peter 5:8: *"Be sober, watchful, your adversary the Devil, as a roaring lion, walketh about, seeking whom he may devour."* Satan is the adversary of God and of man.

2. Devil. Devil is translated from the Greek word "Diabolos," which means "traducer." He is a slanderer who slanders God to man and man to God. This is not only New Testament terminology. In Genesis 3:1-7, he slandered God to Eve. In Job 1:9, he slandered Job to God. In Matthew 13:39, he is called *"the Devil."* In John 13:2, he is called *"the Devil."* In Matthew 4:1, Satan is called "the Devil who came to tempt Christ." In Revelation 12:10, he is called "the accuser." The Apostle John writes: *"...for the accuser of our brethern is cast down, who accuseth them before our God day and night."*

3. Serpent. In Genesis, he manifested himself in and through the serpent. In Revelation 12:9, he is called *"the old serpent."* The name "Serpent" denotes "a sly, cunning, and malicious person." In 2 Corinthians 11:3, the Apostle Paul shows that the serpent is a cunning deceiver. He wrote: *"...as the serpent beguiled Eve in his craftiness...."* "Serpent," then is a symbol of Satan as deceiver, it speaks of his crookedness.

4. Monster or dragon. In the King James Version of 1611, the name for Satan is translated "dragon." In the American Standard Version, the same word is translated "monster," which is more correct. "Monster" is translated from the Hebrew "tanniym," "a marine or land monster." "Tanniym" comes from "tan," an unused root and means "a monster preternaturally formed." The monster is spoken of in Isaiah 27:1. *"In that day Jehovah with his hard and great and strong sword will punish leviathan the swift-serpent, and leviathan the crooked serpent; and he will slay the monster that is in the sea."* "Leviathan" is translated from the Hebrew word "livyathan." This noun comes from the Hebrew word "levi," which means "joined," referring to its joined plate-armour-like scales. In Job 41:1, the Lord said to the old patriarch: *"Canst thou draw out leviathan with a fishhook... ?"* This means a sea animal or sea monster. "Leviathan" is mentioned 5 times in the Old Testament, and means "crocodile." In Ezekiel 29:3, the Lord says: *"...Behold, I am against thee, Pharaoh king of Egypt, the great monster that lieth in the midst of his rivers...."* Here, the king of Egypt is called the great monster, and Pharaoh himself was a type of Satan. So, the monster or dragon is a type of

Satan. This monster or dragon is in the sea, or in the waters. Water also typifies nations. This then refers to Satan and his activities in nations all over the world. "Dragon" is mentioned 13 times in the book of Revelation. Revelation 12:7-8 shows that he will fight against Michael and will be cast down to Earth. The Greek word "drakon" means "a fabulous kind of serpent."

"Dragon," then, symbolizes Satan's activities in the nations on Earth.

5. Tempter. In Matthew 4:3 he is called *"the tempter."* He came to tempt Jesus. As "the tempter" Satan endeavored to persuade the Lord to sin. It is Satan's business to induce people to commit sin against God. He leads God's people into sin. In 1 Thessalonians 3:5, the Apostle Paul expressed concern over the fact that the tempter might have tempted and ensnared the Christians in Thessalonica.

6. Lucifer. "Lucifer" means "light bringer" or "light bearer," the morning star. In Isaiah 14:12, Satan is called "Lucifer," or "Day-star." As light bearer, Satan is revealed as "an angel of light." The Apostle Paul writes in 2 Corinthians 11:14: *"And no marvel; for even Satan fashioneth himself into an angel of light."* This refers to certain moral and spiritual influences of a seductive nature, under some splendid semblance of truth and goodness. Satan can impose thoughts on God's people, which may sound like God speaking. In reality, this is Satan's cunning trick. Satan uses God's Word with wrong application and in this way also deceives people. Matthew 4:6 is a good example. *"...cast thyself down: for it is written, He shall give His angels charge concerning thee: and, on their hands they shall bear thee up. Lest haply thou dash thy foot against a stone."* This was a quotation from Psalms 91:11-12. Satan certainly knows the Scriptures well, but he misapplied them. The enemy uses God's Word, with wrong application, to deceive people in general, both saved and unsaved.

7. Beelzebub. Beelzebub was the Ekronite god of flies. The Jews, in ridicule changed "Beelzebub" into "beelzebul," god of dung. "Zebul" means "dwelling," thus, "lord of the lower world." In Matthew 12:26, Jesus identified "Beelzebub" with Satan. In Matthew 12:24, the Jews called Beelzebub *"...the prince of the demons."* The meaning seems to be that, since "zebul" means "dwelling," (lord of the house) that Satan wants to be master of human bodies, called in the Bible, tabernacle or house. In 2 Kings 1:2, Beelzebub is called "the god of Ekron."

8. Belial. "Belial" means "worthlessness," "recklessness," "lawlessness." It is not strictly a proper name, but is used so by personification. "Belial" is used in connection with worthless men. In Deuteronomy 13:13: *"Certain base fellows are gone out from the midst of thee, and have drawn away the inhabitants of their city, saying, let us go and serve other gods, which ye have not known."*

In 1 Samuel 25:25, Nabal is called a *"worthless fellow."* In 2 Corinthians 6:15, the Apostle Paul writes: *"And what concord hath Christ with Belial? or what portion hath a believer with an unbeliever."* "Belial" in the Greek is "Beliar." The ancients used "belial" as a name for Satan. As "Belial," Satan brings about all kinds of lawless practices in the midst of wicked people.

9. The Wicked One. In the American Standard Version, Matthew 13:19 is translated *"...then cometh the evil one, and snatcheth away that which hath been sown in his heart...."* The Greek "poneros," translated "wicked" and also "vicious," or "malicious," reveals Satan's character and work. He is cruel, wicked, malicious, and tyrannical over all that he can control. In Ephesians 6:16, the Apostle warns Christians against the *"...fiery darts of the evil one."*

10. The God of this World. In 2 Corinthians 4:4, the Apostle Paul writes: *"In whom the god of this world hath blinded the minds of the unbelieving, that the light of the gospel of the glory of Christ, Who is the image of God, should not dawn upon them."* The blinding of the minds implies that the mental perceptions of these people had been impaired and that they were deluded with sophistries until all original inclination to truth was gone. Their minds had no correct intellectual views.

The blinding is the work of "the god of this world," or Satan, who is the ruler of this world. Satan, as "god of this world," also has his own ministers. In 2 Corinthians 11:15, the Apostle writes: *"It is no great thing therefore if his ministers also fashion themselves as ministers of righteousness, whose end shall be according to their works."* In 2 Corinthians 11:14, the Apostle teaches that Satan fashions himself as "an angel of light," so also his servants or ministers fashion themselves as ministers of righteousness. Satan's ministers are those who prove to be his agents by their efforts to corrupt the work of God, and to disturb the churches. Satan has his doctrines. 1 Timothy 4:2-3 says: *"...giving heed to seducing spirits and doctrines of demons,*

"through the hypocrisy of men that speak lies...." In 1 Corinthians 10:20, the Apostle shows that Satan's ministers sacrifice to demons. Satan is behind all false religions and cults.

11. The Prince of the Powers of the Air. Here he is called a prince, 'the prince of the powers of the air." Satan is the head of an organized kingdom. He is the leader of evil spiritual forces that reside in the lower atmosphere. He directs the operations of the demons and the fallen angels. Satan has a vast number of emissaries that carry out his behests, and he rules with despotic power.

Matthew 25:41 shows that he is the leader of evil or fallen angels. *"...the eternal fire which is prepared for the Devil and his angels."* Matthew 12:24 and Revelation 16:13-14 reveal that he is the leader of demons. The Apostle wrote about spirits, like frogs that came out of the mouth of the dragon, and out of the mouth of the beast and out of the mouth of the false prophet; they were demon spirits.

According to Ephesians 6:12, our warfare is against evil spiritual forces, directed by Satan himself. He commands, as chief of the evil forces, to attack God's people anywhere at anytime there is opportunity.

12. The Prince of this World. In John 12:31 Jesus says: *"...now shall the prince of this world be cast out."* And in John 16:11, Jesus says: *"...the prince of this world hath been judged."* In 2 Corinthians 4:4, Satan was called *"the god of this world."* But the Lord called him 'the prince of the world."

The apostle John used the Greek word "archon" which means "a first," "chief," "ruler" or "prince." "World" is translated here from the Greek "kosmos," "orderly arrangement" including the inhabitants. Jesus, the Prince of peace, recognized Satan as the ruler of this world. When Jesus was tempted by Satan, the Lord did not dispute Satan's claim to this world. In Luke 4:6, the writer quotes Satan saying to Christ. *"...to Thee will I give all this authority, and the glory of them: for it hath been delivered unto me; and to whomsoever I will I give it."*

In Luke 4:5, Satan spoke about the kingdoms *"of the world."* This means the inhabited Earth. Satan does not own the planet, because the Bible says that the Earth is the Lord's.

As prince of this inhabited Earth, Satan has power to control the governments of this world. He is in the Kremlin to agitate the Russian leaders to attack God's people and persecute them.

13. Deceiver. Revelation 12:9 says: *"And the great dragon was cast down...the deceiver of the whole world."* Satan, as "deceiver," misleads and deludes the world. He tries to mislead God's own people too. The Apostle Paul made reference to Satan as a deceiver.

1 Timothy 2:14 says: *"And Adam was not beguiled but the woman being beguiled hath fallen into transgression."* In 2 Timothy 3:13, the Apostle speaks of the servants of Satan as deceivers. *"But evil men and imposters shall wax worse and worse, deceiving and being deceived."*

In 2 John 7, the Apostle says: *"For many deceivers are gone forth into the world, even they that confess not that Jesus Christ cometh in the flesh."* Satan has deceived multitudes of people, including the unsaved. He has deceived God's own people and some of them have fallen into sin as a result. Satan is always on guard to mislead some Christian who has become careless.

14. Accuser. Revelation 12:10 says: *"...for the accuser of our brethren is cast down, who accuseth them before our God day and night."* This is a very interesting passage of Scripture. Satan accuses the Christians before God. Whether this means that he can enter heaven and accuse the believers there, or if it means that Satan accuses God's people anywhere since God is omnipresent, is not clear. The Scriptures do reveal the amazing fact that Satan has, indeed, access to God's heaven.

Job 2:1 says: *"Again it came to pass on the day when the sons of God came to present themselves before Jehovah, that Satan came also among them to present himself before Jehovah."* Here it shows clearly that the Devil came before the Lord with the angels, but does not say whether it was on Earth, or in heaven. God is omnipresent. It may have happened on Earth. But I believe that it must have happened in heaven.

In 1 Kings 22:19, the prophet Micaiah says: *"...I saw Jehovah sitting on His throne, and all the host of heaven standing by Him on His right hand, and on His left."* The Scriptures reveal that God has His throne in heaven, and not on Earth or somewhere else. Isaiah 6:1 says: *"...I saw the Lord sitting upon a throne...."* The prophet Micaiah saw the Lord on His throne, which must have been in heaven. 1 Kings 22:20-23 reveals that it was like a council, because the Lord made reference to King Ahab of Israel with the intention of eliminating him. The reign of Ahab was so wicked that the king had to be judged. The Lord asked, *"...who shall entice Ahab, that he may go up and fall at Ramoth-gilead"* (1 Kings 22:20). Many answers and suggestions were given, but none was appropriate. 1 Kings 22:21 says: *"And there came forth a spirit, and stood before Jehovah, and said. I will entice him."* Notice, it does not say it was an angel. It says it was a spirit. This spirit said he was going to be a lying spirit in the mouth of all of Ahab's prophets. Good angels do not lie. It must have been a demon who could lie and deceive.

This, then, confirms the fact that the Devil does have access to heaven. Satan, as an accuser, charges God's people with faults and offences before the Lord, blaming the redeemed before the Great God of heaven. But he will be thrown down from the air, and will never again be able to bring his accusations into the courts of heaven.

Thank God that we have an Advocate at the right hand of the Father Who intercedes for us. 1 John 2:1 says: *"...And if any man sin, we have an Advocate with the Father, Jesus Christ the righteous."* His intercession is based upon His sacrifice, accomplished on the cross. The Father will hear Him and forgive the sinning child because of the holy, blessed blood of Jesus, the Lord.

15. Liar. Satan is also called a "liar," and he is the greatest liar in the universe. In John 8:44 the Lord Jesus says about the Devil. *"...for he is a liar, and the father thereof."* Satan, as a liar, utters lies with the intent of deceiving God's elect. He is called "the father of lies." This is appropriate because, before the fall of Satan, there were no lies. Satan uses any possible lie to deceive the Lord's people. His emissaries are also liars, deceiving the Christians.

1 John 2:22 says: *"Who is the liar but he that denieth that Jesus is the Christ? This is the antichrist, even he that denieth the Father and the Son."* People who deny that Jesus is the Christ are telling a lie, they are liars. 1 John 4:20 says: *"If a man say, I love God, and hateth his brother, he is a liar: for he that loveth not his brother whom he has seen, cannot love God Whom he hath not seen."*

Ephesians 4:25 states: *"Wherefore, putting away falsehood, speak ye truth each one with his neighbor...."* Colossians 3:9 also exhorts to practice honesty. *"Lie not one to another...."*

16. Murderer. In John 8:44 Jesus calls him "murderer." *"...he was a murderer from the beginning...."* The Lord here shows that the Devil was a "murderer" of men from the very beginning of human history. By the successful temptation of Eve and Adam, our first parents, he introduced first spiritual and then temporal murder and death into the world.

The fall is the beginning of human history, and of universal significance as the virtual fall of the whole race. Satan is the source of sin in general and murder in particular. There the Devil, in the shape of a serpent, proved himself both a murderer and a liar. 1 John 3:8

says: *"He that doeth sin is of the Devil; for the Devil sinneth from the beginning...."* This refers to the fall of Satan in past eternity, when he rebelled against God and sinned.

A murderer is one who unlawfully kills human beings with premeditated malice. Since Satan is a murderer, he is looking for any opportunity to kill God's people spiritually. Satan's purpose is to tempt men and lead them into sin and kill them spiritually. James 1:15 says: *"Then when lust hath conceived, it bringeth forth sin; and sin, when it is finished, bringeth forth death."* Death is separation from Christ, the source of life.

Sometimes Satan uses cold, indifferent relatives to keep lost souls hell-bound. Ruth 1:10-16 offers a good picture of this. *"And they said unto her, Nay, but we will return with thee unto thy people.*

"And Naomi said. Turn again, my daughters; why will ye go with me? Have I yet sons in my womb, that they may be your husbands.

"Turn again, my daughters, go your way; for I am too old to have a husband. If I should say, I have hope, if I should even have a husband tonight, and should also bear sons.

"Would ye therefore tarry till they were grown? Would ye therefore stay from having husbands? Nay, my daughters; for it grieveth me much for your sakes, for the hand of Jehovah is gone forth against me.

"And they lifted up their voices, and wept again; and Orpah kissed her mother-in-law; but Ruth clave unto her.

"And she said, Behold, thy sister-in-law is gone back unto her people, and unto her god: return thou after thy sister-in-law.

"And Ruth said: Entreat me not to leave thee, and to return from following after thee; for whither thou goest, I will go; and where thou lodgest, I will lodge; thy people shall be my people, and thy God my God."

The Eschatological Aspect of Satan's Work

1. A Star from Heaven. Revelation 9:1 says: *"...and I saw a star from heaven fallen unto the earth: and there was given to him the key of the pit of the abyss."*

There has been much controversy among Bible expositors regarding the meaning of "star" in this passage. Some say that "the star" is the Antichrist, others that it is Satan. I, myself, am forced to oppose the former view and accept the fact that "the star" symbolizes Satan. It cannot be the Antichrist for four reasons.

A. The star was fallen from heaven to the Earth, which means that the star had lost its former position.

B. Antichrist will not fall from his position until the end of the tribulation period — when Christ comes back, and casts him and his false prophet into the lake of fire.

C. The star symbolizes Satan, who will be dislodged from his headquarters in the middle of the tribulation period. His headquarters is now located in the atmospheric heaven. Revelation 12:9 says: *"And the great dragon was cast down...to the earth, and his angels were cast down with him."*

D. The star received a key to open the bottomless pit, or the abyss. The key symbolizes authority. Revelation 9:2-3 reveals that he opened the pit of the abyss and smoke came out. Out of the smoke came locusts.

No human being can have authority over demons, except in the power of Christ. The locusts symbolize demons, because Proverbs 30:27 says that the *"locusts have no king,"* while these symbolical locusts have a king over them. In Isaiah 14:12, Satan is called "the Day-star fallen from heaven."

So, the star in Revelation 9:1 is Satan. He is called "a fallen star" because, in past eternity, he lost his position as king and priest, and in the tribulation will lose his headquarters and be cast down as a helpless creature. But, he will receive authority from God to open the pit of the abyss, from which will come forth smoke, giving birth to those symbolical locusts. The smoke implies the darkening power of Satan, which darkens moral principles in the moral realm. The locusts are not literal, but symbolical.

2. The Angel of the Abyss. Those symbolic locusts will have a king over them is called "the angel of the abyss." This angel is Satan, and the locusts symbolize judgment which will be meted out on stubborn, unrepentant Israel. My purpose is not to write an exposition on Revelation 9:1-11, but to take into consideration only two words to prove that the locust plague is directed towards Israel.

A. "Furnace" is connected with judgment and destruction. Genesis 19:28 speaks about the destruction of Sodom and Gomorrah: *"And he looked toward Sodom and Gomorrah: and toward all the land of the plain, and behold, and, lo, the smoke of the land went up as the smoke of a furnace."*

"Furnace" also symbolizes affliction and suffering. In Deuteronomy 4:20, Moses said to Israel: *"But Jehovah hath taken you, and brought you forth out of the iron furnace, out of Egypt...."* Moses called Egypt an "iron furnace" because of the terrible suffering Israel endured in that country.

Daniel 3:19-26 is the story of three young Hebrew men who were cast into the burning fiery furnace, to be destroyed. God saved them by a mighty manifestation of His power. This is a picture of Israel in the tribulation, which will be like a burning, fiery furnace.

B. Locusts symbolize destruction in the form of judgment. In the Bible, locusts have been used by God as a rod of judgment to punish wicked nations, including Israel. Exodus 10:14-15 shows the tremendous devastation caused by locusts. Every green thing was eaten by them. In Nahum 3:17, the prophet uses locusts as a symbol of the sudden destruction of Nineveh, saying: *"Thy princes are as the locusts, and thy marshals as the swarms of the grasshoppers, which encamp in the hedges in the cold day, but when the sun ariseth they flee away, and their place is not known where they are."* Locusts lay their eggs under shelter of hedges; they are hatched by the sun's heat in spring; by June, the young are so matured as to be able to flee away. These rulers were wicked and destroyed human life for no reason. So, Nineveh was going to disappear, and its place would no longer be known.

In Revelation 9:1-3, the star, the furnace, the smoke and the locusts are all connected to the awful plague, meted out during the fifth trumpet judgment. It is to be noted that the locusts did not come from hell nor from the abyss, but from the smoke, "as the smoke of a great furnace." It was the smoke that gave birth to the symbolic locusts.

After Satan has been cast to the Earth, in the middle of the tribulation, he will receive authority from God to darken the moral life of Israel. Smoke symbolizes the great darkening power of Satan. Moral principles will be destroyed and total moral darkness will engulf Israel. In the midst of such total moral and spiritual darkness, extraordinary suffering will overtake Israel. The locusts symbolize demons who, under the command of their king, Satan, inflict indescribable pain and suffering on Israel. Satan, in his great hatred against Christ and the nation of Israel, uses his demons to cause unspeakable suffering to their conscience. All this terrible hate and wickedness comes from the abyss, which will be Satan's place of imprisonment for one thousand years.

3. Destruction — Abaddon. Revelation 9:11 says that *"...his name in the Hebrew is Abaddon,"* or "destruction." Satan is called "destruction" because he is the one who destroys all moral principles. He destroys the souls of men. Jesus referred to him as the destroyer of

soul and body in hell. [1] Walter Scott teaches that the reason the Hebrew word "Abaddon" precedes the Greek word "Apollyon" is because the Jew is more guilty than the Gentile. The Hebrew title "Abaddon," "destruction" emphatically asserts its certainty and finality of that judgment on apostate Israel. As the first woe has direct application to the mass of Israel, "Abaddon" is first named. [2] I agree with Mr. Scott, except that this judgment applies not to Judah only, but the entire nation of Israel.

4. Destroyer — Apollyon. Revelation 9:11 ascribes "Apollyon," "destroyer" to Satan. He destroys everything he possibly can. He destroys the souls and bodies of men in hell. During the tribulation, he will do much destruction. Mr. Scott thinks that the second judgment directly concerns the inhabitants of the Roman Empire, hence fittingly, the order of the name: first, Abaddon, second Apollyon. The order in grace, as in judgment, is the Jew first, then the Gentile. [3]

1. *Matthew* 10:28.
2. Scott, op.cit., p. 206.
3. Ibid., p. 206.

CHAPTER XIV

THE DEMONS IDENTIFIED

The Origin of Demons

What became of the pre-Adamic race? This question needs to be answered properly before one can understand the meaning of demons revealed to the reader of the New Testament. Many say that the demons, evil spirits, or unclean spirits are fallen angels. This however, is misleading. Demons and evil spirits are synonymous terms, but they are not fallen angels.

Demons are not spoken of as rulers of the kingdoms of this world, but are called evil spirits, or unclean spirits who seek embodiment. Nowhere is it stated in the Scriptures that fallen angels enter human bodies, but it is spoken so of the demons. In the King James Version of 1611, they are called "devils" which is wrong. There is only one Devil, the fallen Day-star of heaven, Satan. Matthew 8:16 says: *"And when even was come, they brought unto Him many possessed with demons: and He cast out the spirits with His word, and healed all that were sick."* Matthew 9:32 reads: *"...behold, there was brought unto him a dumb man possessed with a demon."*

"Demon" is translated from the Greek word "daimon" which means "a supernatural spirit." It is also called "evil spirit" or "unclean spirit." Luke 4:33 says: *"And in the synagogue there was a man, that had a spirit of an unclean demon; and he cried out with a loud voice."*

"Spirit" is translated from the Greek word "pneuma," which actually means "a current of air," "breath," or "a breeze." The "pneuma" is used in reference to the Spirit of God. Matthew 3:16 speaks about the Holy Spirit, Who descended on the Lord Jesus.

Here "the Spirit" is translated from the Greek "pneuma." The same Greek "pneuma" is also used in reference to "the unclean spirit."

"Angel" in the Greek is called "angelos," and means "a messenger," by implication "a pastor." An angel is simply a messenger who is sent by God with a message to some individual, or to some group of people. Angels are never identified with demons in the New Testament.

In Matthew 17:15-18, a father brought his epileptic son to the disciples of Christ to be healed. The Lord rebuked the spirit, and the demon went out of the boy. In Mark 9:25, the demon is called by Christ "dumb and deaf spirit." So, the evidence is absolutely clear that demons seek embodiment. In Matthew 12:43-45, Jesus makes it clear that demons are disembodied spirits, which at one time had bodies, but now do not. The Lord Jesus said: *"But the unclean spirit, when he is gone out of the man, passeth through waterless places, seeking rest, and findeth it not.*

"Then he saith, I will return into my house whence I came out; and when he is come, he findeth it empty, swept, and garnished.

"Then goeth he, and taketh with himself seven other spirits more evil than himself, and they enter in and dwell there: and the last state of that man becometh worse that the first...."

There is a significant statement in this Scripture passage — "I will return into my house whence I came out." Notice, the demon calls the human physical body, which he has entered, his house. This shows clearly, without any doubt whatsoever, that at one time they possessed physical bodies, but lost them. The human body, in the Scriptures, is called a "tabernacle" and a "house." Job 4:19 says: *"How much more them that dwell in the houses of clay, whose foundation is in the dust...."* Job was thinking of the human soul which dwells in a house of clay, or the physical body. In 2 Corinthians 5:1, the Apostle Paul says: *"For we know that if the earthly house of our tabernacle be dissolved, we have a building from God, a house not made with hands, eternal, in the heavens."* The Apostle was referring to the death of his present physical body, here figuratively called the destruction of his Earthly tabernacle. The body is thus described as the dwelling of the human soul.

In 2 Peter 1:13-14, the Apostle Peter writes the same about the physical body. *"And I think it right, as long as I am in this tabernacle to stir you up by putting you in remembrance;*

"knowing that the putting off of my tabernacle cometh swiftly, even

as our Lord Jesus Christ signified unto me." Here the Apostle Peter also calls the human body a tabernacle.

The statement by Christ, that a demon calls the physical human body his house which he had possessed, confirms the fact that, at one time, they possessed bodies, but were dispossessed of their bodies in past eternity.

Demons are the souls of people who lived on Earth before the fall of Satan.

Before the fall of Satan, there was no death on planet Earth. The pre-Adamic race must have lived for 15,000 years or more, multiplied, and the planet Earth was filled with many more people than we have now. Presently, we have 5,000,000,000 people and there is enough room on our planet to accommodate 5,000,000,000 more. Mark 5:1-9 speaks about a man in the country of the Gadarenes who was possessed by demons. Jesus asked the demon about his name and the evil spirit answered, "My name is Legion; for we are many." A Roman legion consisted of 6,000 men. One man alone had 6,000 demons. This shows the tremendous multitude of the demons loose in this evil world today.

We must not get confused about the souls of the wicked people, members of the present human race, who die. They are not loose in the atmosphere. At the moment of death their souls will be brought immediately to hell into the flames of the unseen world, to wait for the day of judgment.

Thus, the fact has been established that the demons are not fallen angels, but are the spirits of the pre-Adamic race which perished billions of years ago.

The Work of Demons

The work of these unclean spirits is diverse. I have been speaking about Satan and the origin of demons. All this refers to past eternity, to the time of Satan's fall, and the destruction of planet Earth. Now, in this section I want to study the different operations of these evil spirits with application to our present human race, during the past 6,000 years on the recreated Earth.

Satan is the commander in chief of all the evil forces, and he directs the operations of his forces in this evil world. Satan is not omnipresent like the Almighty God, Who is everywhere at the same time. Psalms 139:8-10 says: *"If I ascend up into heaven, Thou art there. If I make my bed in Sheol, behold Thou art there.*

"If I take the wings of the morning, and dwell in the uttermost parts of the sea;

"even there shall Thy hand lead me, and Thy right hand shall hold me." This passage of the holy Scripture confirms the fact that the Almighty God is everywhere at the same time.

Satan, however, is a created being and can never be omnipresent. He can only be in one place at a time. But he has an innumerable host of demons and fallen angels that do his bidding. The demons carry out the orders of their commander, Satan. I want to consider several types of work the demons do, in light of the Scriptures.

1. They bring disaster. In the dialogue between God and Satan, recorded in Job 1:6-12, attention is focused on the old Patriarch Job. It was not the Devil who slandered Job to God. The Lord Himself invited Satan's attention to this godly man, who served Him with all his heart. Satan complained that he could not touch Job because of God's protection around the old Patriarch. In Job 1:12, the Lord said to Satan: *"...Behold, all he hath is in thy power; only upon himself put not forth thy hand. So Satan went forth from the presence of Jehovah."*

Consider these two points:

A. God gave Satan permission to do what he wanted with the property of Job. "All that he has is in thy power."

B. Satan was not allowed to touch Job himself. "Only upon himself put not forth thy hand." Job 1:13-19 tells the reader what happened to Job's property.

A. The Sabeans attacked, took the oxen and asses, and killed all the workers.

B. Fire fell from heaven and burned up the sheep and the servants that attended the sheep.

C. The Chaldeans attacked, took all the camels and killed all the servants.

D. A great wind came from the wilderness and the house in which Job's daughters and sons were eating and drinking wine fell, killing them all.

2. Demons inflict disease. In the second dialogue which took place between God and Satan, the Lord again called Satan's attention to Job. The Devil complained because the Lord had not allowed him to touch the body of Job. The old Patriarch writes about this in Job 2:6-7. *"...Behold, he is in thy hand; only spare his life."*

"So Satan went forth from the presence of Jehovah, and smote Job

with sore boils from the sole of his foot unto his crown." In this passage, again, two points must be taken into consideration.

A. God's permission to Satan to inflict disease upon Job.

B. God definitely set the bounds as to how far Satan could go.

In the New Testament, the works of demons are clearly revealed. In Matthew 4:24, the Apostle wrote: *"And the report of Him went forth into all Syria: and they brought unto Him all that were sick, holden with divers diseases and torments, possessed with demons, and epileptic, and palsied; and He healed them."* Again the Apostle writes in Matthew 8:16: *"And when even was come, they brought unto Him many possessed with demons; and He cast out the spirits with a word, and healed all that were sick."*

There are demons who torment people and keep them bound with diseases. Jesus healed a woman who was bowed down and said: *"And ought not this woman, being a daughter of Abraham, whom Satan had bound, lo, these eighteen years, to have been loosed from this bond on the day of the sabbath?"* [1] Luke 13:11 says that *"this woman had a spirit of infirmity eighteen years."*

These few Scripture references suffice to prove the fact that demons inflict disease upon people. Every disease has a life, a germ which causes it to function. That evil life in the germ didn't come from God, because it kills and destroys human life. It is from Satan. It is that evil life, or spirit of infirmity that gives life to the disease, or growth, just as your spirit gives life to your body, and just as your body dies when your spirit leaves. So, the disease of a suffering person, when the spirit of infirmity is cast out, dies and disappears.

Luke 4:38-39 speaks of the healing of Peter's mother-in-law. *"And He rose up from the synagogue, and entered into the house of Simon. And Simon's wife's mother was holden with a great fever; and they besought Him for her.*

"And He stood over her, and rebuked the fever; and it left her: and immediately she rose up and ministered unto them." Here, the spirit of infirmity was cast out, the germ of the disease which caused the fever died, and the mother-in-law was delivered.

3. Demons cause mental disorders. Mark 5:4-5 speaks about a man that was crazy. *"Because that he had been often bound with fetters and chains, and the chains had been rent asunder by him, and the fetters broken in pieces: and no man had strength to tame him.*

---

1. *Luke* 13:16.

"And always, night and day, in the tombs and in the mountains, he was crying out, and cutting himself with stones." When Jesus cast the evil spirits out, the man was at once made whole. Luke 8:35 says: *"And they went out to see what had come to pass: and they came to Jesus, and found the man, from whom the demons were gone out, sitting, clothed and in his right mind...."* Many times doctors and psychologists wonder how a psychosomatic person can be cured? They try psychotherapy, to no avail. What they need is Dr. Jesus Christ to deliver those mentally ill people. They will be cured.

4. Demons lead many into moral impurity. Mark 3:11 says *"And the unclean spirits, whensoever they beheld him, fell down before him, and cried, saying, Thou art the Son of God."* Uncleaness is moral impurity. These are demons that stir up sinful people to practice sexual perversion.

Luke 4:33 speaks of another unclean demon: *"And in the synagogue there was a man, that had a spirit of an unclean demon and he cried out with a loud voice."* And Luke 6:18 reveals that Jesus healed them: *"And they that were troubled with unclean spirits were healed."* Acts 5:16 shows the deliverance of many people that were bound by the Devil. Luke writes: *"And there also came together the multitude from the cities round about Jerusalem, bringing sick folk, and them that were vexed with unclean spirits; and they were healed every one."*

It is amazing to see that there were so many demon possessed people among the Jews in the holy land. Luke 8:2 says that seven demons went out of Mary Magdalene. Christ delivered her from that terrible bondage. Praise the Lord! The demons are the authors of the filthy, unclean thinking, filthy speech and filthy conduct of men today.

Leviticus 18:6-30 presents a long list of sexual sins of which the Canaanites were guilty. Leviticus 18:24-25 says: *"Defile not ye yourselves in any of these things: for in all these the nations are defiled which I cast out from before you,*

"and the land is defiled: therefore I do visit the iniquity thereof upon it, and the land vomiteth out her inhabitants."

Deuteronomy 18:9-14 shows that it was because of spiritism that God would cast them out. Moses writes in Deuteronomy 18:10-12: *"There shall not be found with thee any one that maketh his son or his daughter to pass through the fire, one that useth divination, one that practiseth augury, or an enchanter, or a sorcerer, "or a charmer, or a consulter with a familiar spirit, or a wizard, or a necromancer.*

"For whosoever doeth these things is an abomination unto Jehovah: and because of these abominations Jehovah thy God doth drive them out from before thee."

5. Demons lie to people. There are so-called "lying demons" that lie and impose wrong thoughts upon people. 2 Chronicles 18:21 speaks of a lying demon: *"And he said, I will go forth, and will be a lying spirit in the mouth of all his prophets...."* In the counsels of God, King Ahab of Israel was to be removed from the human arena. The King was to be enticed to go fight against the Syrians at Ramoth-gilead and fall. A lying spirit offered himself to do the job. The lying demons were to say to the minds of Ahab's prophets that Ahab would win the war. This encouragement would send him to the battle field, where he would fall and die.

Lying demons deceive God's people by imposing wrong thoughts and feelings upon them. 1 Samuel 27:1 says: *"And David said in his heart, I shall now perish one day by the hand of Saul: there is nothing better for me that I should escape into the land of the Philistines; and Saul will despair me, to seek me any more in all the borders of Israel: so shall I escape out of his hand."* David was a very godly man and trusted in the Lord with all his heart, and the Lord preserved him. 1 Samuel 23:14 says: *"...And Saul sought him every day, but God delivered him not into his hand."*

Satan knew that the only way to get David was to fill his mind with wrong thoughts and feelings. What "David said in his heart" was not from himself, but from a lying demon. As soon as David yielded to this thought and decided to flee to Philistia, he stopped trusting in God. Through a lying spirit, Satan accomplished what he could not accomplish through King Saul. Friend, be careful as to the voices you hear. There are three voices that speak to us in our days on Earth.

A. The Holy Spirit speaks.

B. The human soul speaks. What you think in your heart, is your soul speaking. Many times simple minded Christians have mistaken the voice of their own soul for the voice of God, and have made frivolous mistakes, thinking that it was God speaking.

C. Lying demons speak. Therefore, it is important that you read the Bible and know it, so that lying demons cannot deceive you in your daily walk.

6. Demons cause people to gossip and criticize. The multitude of

words spoken in a malicious way by the ungodly is the work of demons. The people, however, do not realize it. Several years ago I read a testimony given by a businessman who had been converted. Before his conversion, he taught a Sunday School class in a denominational church. As soon as the class ended, he had to go out and speak to himself using very foul language. When he got saved, the Lord delivered him from the terrible power of a filthy tongue.

God's people are tempted to murmur and criticize others. Numbers 12:1-2 speaks of Aaron and Miriam, who criticized their brother Moses. The temptation to speak critically about a servant of God did not come from the Lord. This kind of criticism is generated by a demon. It was so bad in the sight of God in this case that the Lord punished Miriam. Numbers 12:10 says: *"...and, behold, Miriam was leprous, as white as snow...."*

James 3:6 calls the tongue "a fire." *"And the tongue is a fire the world of iniquity among our members is the tongue, which defiles the whole body, and setteth on fire the wheel of nature, and is set on fire by hell."*

We should dread an unruly tongue as one of the greatest and most pernicious of evils. There is such an abundance of sin in the tongue that it may be called a world of iniquity. The whole body is often drawn into sin and guilt by the tongue. Hell has more to do in promoting the fire of the tongue than men are generally aware of. When the tongue is set on fire by demons, there is mischief, producing rage and hatred, and all those things which serve the Devil's purpose.

Fire is a destructive force and so is the tongue, when controlled by evil spirits. It can cause much damage to the churches and to many people. Who is the master of your tongue?

King David of Israel once prayed: *"I said, I will take heed to my ways, that I sin not with my tongue. I will keep my mouth with a bridle"* (Psalms 39:1). In Psalms 141:3, David prays: *"Set a watch, O Jehovah, before my mouth; keep the door of my lips."* In 3 John 10, the Apostle mentions Diotrephes who spoke malicious words against the Apostle and the people of God. This is the sin of the tongue.

7. Demons disseminate false doctrine. 1 Timothy 4:1 says: *"But the Spirit saith expressly, that in latter times some shall fall away from the faith, giving heed to seducing spirits and doctrines of demons."*

Evil spirits bring wrong ideas into the minds of perverse people. False cults and their teachings are all a result of demon inspired doctrines. Nominal ministers preach a social gospel, omitting the true meaning of the resurrection of Christ and eternal life through faith in Him.

8. Demons impose fear on God's people. Exodus 14:10 says *"...And they were sore afraid: and the children of Israel cried out unto Jehovah."* At the Red Sea, demons of fear had their opportunity to attack God's people, through unprecedented circumstances. The people failed to resist fear by faith. The demons of fear attack God's people today at all times, but you too can resist them by faith. 2 Timothy 1:7 says: *"For God gave us not a spirit of fearfulness; but of power and love and discipline."* Friend, if you are tempted by this kind of demon, ask the Lord to set you free.

9. Demons oppose the spiritual growth of Christians. Evil spirits attack God's people in every possible way to mislead them. They use all types of temptations to lead a believer into sin, resulting in total defeat. The Apostle Paul writes in Ephesians 6:12: *"For our wrestling is not against flesh and blood but against the principalities, against the powers, against the world-rulers of this darkness, against the spiritual hosts of wickedness in the heavenly places."* That is why the Apostle encourages us to put on all the armor of God. Then, we shall be able to stand in this evil world. The Apostle writes in Ephesians 6:13-17: *"Wherefore take up the whole armor of God, that ye may be able to withstand in the evil day, and, having done all, to stand.*

"Stand therefore, having girded your loins with truth, and having put on the breastplate of righteousness,

"and having shod your feet with the preparation of the gospel of peace.

"Withal taking up the shield of faith, wherewith ye shall be able to quench all the fiery darts of the evil one.

"And take the helmet of salvation, and the sword of the Spirit which is the Word of God."

10. Demons are used sometimes by God in the carrying out of His purposes. Judges 9:23 shows that *"...God sent an evil spirit between Abimelech and the men of Shechem: and the men of Shechem dealt treacherously with Abimelech."* Abimelech was the son of Gideon by his Shechemite concubine. At Gideon's death, he murdered seventy of his brethren, all except the youngest. His mother's brethren influenced the Shechemites to make Abimelech king.

This murderer and imposter had to be punished. An evil spirit was permitted by the Lord to stir up enmity between him and the men of

Shechem, finally resulting in his death. 1 Samuel 16:14 speaks of an evil spirit which troubled King Saul of Israel.

The Three Types of Demon Manifestation

The first real manifestation of demonic power is in fortune-telling. Dr. Thiessen relates that the ancients believed in augury or foretelling the future by means of natural signs, such as the flight of birds, the disposition of the entrails; in hydromancy, or foretelling from the appearance of water poured into a vessel or of objects dropped in the water. The ancients also believed in astrology or the determination of the supposed influence of the stars on the destiny of a person. [2]

Ezekiel 21:21 says: *"For the king of Babylon stood at the parting of the way, at the head of the two ways, to use divination. He shook the arrows to and fro, he consulted the teraphim, he looked in the river."* The prophet Isaiah makes reference to Babylon saying: *"Thou art wearied in the multitude of thy counsels: let now the astrologers, the star-gazers, the monthly prognosticators, stand up, and save thee from the things that shall come upon thee."* [3]

These practices are a form of demon manifestation. Whenever a person attempts to read the future by a kind of divine inspiration, he is, in reality, doing so with the assistance of demons. Acts 16:16 reveals the power of demon manifestation in foretelling. *"And it came to pass, as we were going to the place of prayer, that a certain maid having a spirit of divination met us, who brought her masters much gain by soothsaying."* Future telling by demon power is real and cannot be denied.

2. The direct worship of demons and demon possession. Deuteronomy 32:17 shows that apostate Israel sacrificed to demons. *"They sacrificed unto demons, which were no God. To gods that they knew not...."* Several centuries later king David of Israel wrote in Psalms 106:37: *"Yea, they sacrificed their sons and their daughters unto demons."* The Apostle Paul, writing about the same thing in 1 Corinthians 10:20, says: *"...the things which the Gentiles sacrifice, they sacrifice to demons, and not to God: and I would not that ye should have communion with demons."*

The heathen did not intend to worship demons, and yet they did it. What would it avail, therefore, to the reckless Corinthians, who

2. Thiessen, op.cit., p. 209.
3. *Isaiah* 47:13

attended the sacrificial feasts of the heathen, to say that they did not intend to worship idols? Those in pagan countries who join in the religious rites of the heathen are just as guilty of idolatry and are just as certainly brought into fellowship with demons as the nominal Christians of Corinth, who, although they knew that an idol was nothing, and that there is but one God, frequented the heathen feasts. The Apostle warned the Corinthians not to frequent the heathen feasts, and said that, if they did, they would be in fellowship with demons. Dr. Henry Thiessen says that in some heathen countries in Africa people deliberately worship demons. During the tribulation period, there will be renewed demon activity and open worship of Satan. [4]

3. Demon manifestation in the form of spiritism. Dr. Thiessen teaches that spiritism is the belief that the living can communicate with the dead, and that the spirits of the dead can manifest their presence to men. It is also called necromancy. This is supposed to be done through the agency of a human being, known as a medium. The practice of necromancy is very old. A necromancer is often referred to as one who has "a familiar spirit." [5]

Moses writes about it in Leviticus 19:31: *"Turn ye not unto them that have familiar spirits, not unto the wizards; seek them not out, to be defiled by them...."*

1 Chronicles 10:13 shows that to consult a demon possessed person, called a familiar spirit, is a terrible sin. *"So Saul died for his trespass which he committed against Jehovah, because of the Word of Jehovah, which he kept not; and also for that he asked counsel of one that had a familiar spirit, to inquire thereby."* In these and many other Scriptures, Israel is warned against consulting those who profess to communicate with the dead.

I want to include a few Scriptural examples of media. 1 Samuel 28:3 says: *"...And Saul had put away those that had familiar spirits, and the wizards, out of the land."* Acts 8:9-24 speaks of Simon Magus. Luke writes in Acts 8:9: *"But there was a certain man, Simon by name, who before time in the city used sorcery, and amazed the people of Samaria, giving out that himself was some great one."* Acts 13:6-12 speaks of a sorcerer whom the Apostle Paul met in Cyprus. Acts 13:6 says: *"...they found a certain sorcerer, a false prophet, a Jew, whose name was Bar-Jesus."* These are biblical examples of media.

4. Thiessen, op.cit., p. 209.
5. Ibid., p. 210.

1 Samuel 15:23 speaks of this practice as witchcraft. Samuel writes: *"For rebellion is as the sin of witchcraft...."* In Nahum 3:4 Ninevah is called the *"...the mistress of witchcrafts, that selleth nations through her whoredoms, and families through her witchcrafts."* In Exodus 7:11, it is called sorcery. *"Then Pharaoh also called for wise men and the sorcerers: and they also, the magicians of Egypt, did in like manner with their enchantments."*

The Scriptures warn us to try the spirits to see whether or not they are of God. 1 John 4:1 says: *"Beloved, believe not every spirit, but prove the spirits, whether they are of God; because many false prophets are gone out into the world."* In 1 Corinthians 10:20, the Apostle Paul warns that we are not to have fellowship with people who commune with demons. The Apostle warns the Christians in 2 John 10-11: *"If any one cometh unto you, and bringeth not this teaching, receive him not into your house, and give him no greeting,*

"for he that giveth him greeting partaketh in his evil work."

The Eschatological Aspect of the Work of Demons

During the tribulation, there will be great demonic activity on planet Earth. Revelation 16:13-14 says: *"And I saw coming out of the mouth of the dragon, and out of the mouth of the beast, and out of the mouth of the false prophet, three unclean spirits, as it were frogs.*

"For they are spirits of demons, working signs; which go forth unto the kings of the whole world, to gather them together unto the war of the great day of God, the Almighty."

This passage of the Scripture reveals the unholy Satanic trinity in three persons.

1. Satan, the Dragon
2. Antichrist, the Beast
3. The False Prophet, a religious leader

To understand evil spirits working miracles you must understand the human agents through which the evil spirits work. These demons will be performing miracles in the power of Satan, to deceive the masses of humanity. They come out of the mouths of the Satanic trinity. The prophet writes about Christ in Isaiah 11:4: *"...and He shall smite the earth with the rod of His mouth, and with the breath of His lips shall He slay the wicked."* The same is said of Christ in Revelation 1:16: *"...and out of His mouth proceeded a sharp two-edged sword...."* In Revelation 2:16, Jesus says to the Pastor of Pergamum: *"Repent therefore: or else I come to thee quickly, and I will make war against them with the sword of My mouth."* These passages refer to judgment, which Christ will execute against those that do not repent and humble themselves before the Lord.

That these demons came out of the three persons — the Dragon, the Antichrist and the false prophet — indicates that the demons will deceive the people all over the world through lies and miracles, using human agents. The Apostle Paul wrote about it in 2 Thessalonians 2:9. *"Even he, whose coming is according to the working of Satan with all power and signs and lying wonders."* These demons will gather the kings of all the world to Palestine for the battle of Armageddon, the last battle of the world.

CHAPTER XV

IMMINENT FUTURE EVENTS

The First Resurrection — The Rapture

We are living at the very end of the dispensation of grace. God's clock is running much faster than most people realize. The Lord's six-day recreation symbolized six thousand years of human history in toil and labor. We are now living at the very end of the sixth day. The Church of Jesus Christ is almost complete, the rapture is at the door.

I have no intention of going into all the details of the doctrine of the resurrection, except to make a few brief statements. In light of this doctrine, two points must be taken into consideration.

1. The resurrection teaching revealed in the Old Testament; Psalms 16:10 says: *"For Thou wilt not leave My soul in Sheol. Neither wilt Thou suffer Thy holy One to see corruption."* This was a prophecy about the resurrection of Jesus Christ. In Daniel 12:2, the prophet spoke about the resurrection of the just and of the condemned.

2. The resurrection taught in the New Testament. Israel was conscious of the fact that a resurrection was to take place on the last day. In John 11:24, Martha says to Jesus: *"...I know that he shall rise again in the resurrection at the last day."* The Apostle Paul writes about the rapture in 1 Thessalonians 4:14-18, telling the Thessalonians that the dead in Christ shall be raised, and living saints translated. 1 Corinthians 15:52 says: *"In a moment, in the twinkling of an eye, at the last trump: for the trumpet shall sound, and the dead shall be raised incorruptible, and we shall be changed."*

The first future prophetic event that will take place is the resurrection of the New Testament saints and the translation of living believers in Christ. We are now at the close of this age. We have only a few years left, at the most nine or ten. Friend, are you ready to meet the Lord? When the trumpet sounds, it will be too late to get ready for His coming.

The Judgment of the Church

The next event after the rapture will be the judgment of the Church of Jesus Christ. This judgment will not be condemnation for sin, because Christ has delivered His people, the true believers, from everlasting condemnation. Romans 8:1 says: *"There is therefore now no condemnation to them that are in Christ Jesus."* But all believers will appear before the Judgment seat of Christ, to be judged or rewarded — according to their works done on Earth during their lifetime. This idea is revealed in 1 Corinthians 3:13-15. *"Each man's work shall be made manifest: for the day shall declare it, because it is revealed in fire; and the fire itself shall prove man's work of what sort it is.*

"If any man's work shall abide which he built thereon, he shall receive a reward.

"If any man's work shall be burned, he shall suffer loss: but he himself shall be saved; yet so as through fire."

2 Corinthians 5:10 reads: *"For we must all be made manifest before the judgment seat of Christ; that each one may receive the things done in the body, according to what he hath done, whether it be good or bad."*

There are many other Scripture passages that speak of the same matter, but these Scripture references will suffice to show that the believers will appear before the judgment seat of Christ to receive their rewards for the work done during their life time on Earth.

Three writers of the New Testament speak of a crown which Christians will receive at the day of judgment. In Philippians 4:1 the Apostle Paul calls the Philippian converts his *"...joy and crown...."* Again in 1 Thessalonians 2:19, the Apostle calls his Thessalonian converts his *"...joy, or crown of glorying...."* James 1:12 calls it *"...the crown of life, which the Lord promised to them that love Him."* There are seven references in the New Testament to the crown that believers will receive at the day of judgment. These crowns simply mean the various areas, work or ministry for which a Christian will be rewarded. In Revelation 2:10, Jesus encourages His followers to be faithful and promises that He will give them a crown of life. In Song of Solomon 3:11, it is spoken of as a festal ornament.

The Reviving of the Roman Empire in Prophecy

The prophet Daniel saw the rise and fall of the Roman Empire, and the reviving of the same. Nebuchadnezzar's dream of a great image in Daniel 2:31-35 reveals the four successive world empires. Daniel 2:37-45 is the interpretation of the dream. The image represented four world empires that would rule on Earth, and a fifth one, the kingdom of Christ, the Millennium. I want to mention these empires chronologically.

1. The new Babylonian Empire was founded by King Nabopolassar, father of Nebuchadnezzar, in 625 B.C. This first world empire was represented in Nebuchadnezzar's dream as the head of gold. This empire lasted for 89 years and fell in 536 B.C.

2. The Medo-Persian Empire was represented by silver in the image. Persia conquered Babylon in 536 B.C. The Persian Empire lasted for 203 years and was destroyed by Alexander the Great of Macedonia in 333 B.C.

3. The Grecian Empire, represented by brass, lasted for only a few years. Alexander defeated Persia in 333 B.C. He himself died in 323 B.C. and his empire was divided among his generals.

4. The Roman Empire was represented by iron and clay in the image. Rome became a world empire under General Octavian, who became ruler of Rome in 29 B.C. under the name of Ceasar Augustus. The Roman Empire lasted for more than 500 years. Rome fell in 476 to the barbarians, and the Western half of the Roman Empire ceased to exist. The Eastern half of the Roman Empire lasted 977 years longer, until Constantinopole fell to the Turks in 1453.

The remarkable prophecy about the rise and fall of Rome is in Daniel 2:40-44. *"And the fourth kingdom shall be strong as iron, forasmuch as iron breaketh in pieces and subdueth all things; and as iron that crusheth all these, shall it break in pieces and crush.*

"And whereas thou sawest the feet and toes, part of potters' clay, and part of iron, it shall be a divided kingdom; but there shall be in it of the strength of the iron, foreasmuch as thou sawest the iron mixed with miry clay.

"And as the toes of the feet were part of iron, and part of clay, so the kingdom shall be partly strong, and partly broken.

"And whereas thou sawest the iron mixed with miry clay, they shall mingle themselves with the seed of men; but they shall not cleave one to another, even as iron doth not mingle with clay.

"And in the days of those kings shall the God of heaven set up a kingdom which shall never be destroyed, nor shall the sovereignty thereof be left to another people; but it shall break in pieces and consume all these kingdoms and it shall stand for ever."

In Daniel 7:2, the prophet speaks about a vision saying: *"...I saw in my vision by night, and behold, the four winds of heaven brake forth upon the great sea."* The four winds mean the political movements and the sea the Gentile nations. The prophet saw the rise of four Gentile world-dominions about which he writes in Daniel 7:4-8, but at this time he saw the four world empires in the form of four ferocious beasts which reveal the character of each world empire.

1. The lion with eagle's wings, and the head of gold in the image typified the Babylonian Empire.

2. The bear, and the silver in the image typified the Medo-Persian Empire. The bear was raised up on one side which meant that the Persian element in the Empire was stronger than the Median. The bear had three ribs in its mouth, signifying the three conquests of Persia.

    A. Susiana

    B. Lydia

    C. Asia Minor

3. The leopard with four wings and four heads, was a type of the Grecian Empire under Alexander the Great, corresponding to the thighs of brass in the image.

4. A terrible beast with ten horns, corresponds to the feet and toes part of potters clay, and part of iron in the image. This beast typified the Roman Empire.

Thus, the prophet Daniel, through the interpretation of the image of Nebchadnezzar's dream and the beast vision, has given a line of prophecy, a span of 2,600 years, extending from the reign of Nebuchadnezzar to the full and complete establishment of the kingdom of Jesus Christ, the Millennium.

In the vision of the beast in Daniel 7:7, the rise of the Roman Empire is revealed and in Daniel 7:8, the Roman Empire revived and *"...a little horn...,"* the Antichrist, the Emperor of the restored empire. Thus, Daniel 7:7-8 reveals five factors about the Roman Empire in world affairs.

1. The rise of Rome to a great Gentile world power

2. The disappearance of the Roman Empire, though not so stated

3. The restoration of the former great Gentile world power, the Roman Empire

4. The last Emperor of Rome, the Antichrist

5. Antichrist in his rise to power will overthrow three governments in Europe. Daniel 7:8 says: *"I considered the horns and, behold, there came up among them another horn, a little one, before which three of*

the first horns were plucked up by the roots...." Revelation 13:1-3 is a prophetic utterance about the revived Roman Empire in a ten kingdom form. *"...And I saw a beast coming up out of the sea, having ten horns and seven heads, and on his horns ten diadems, and upon his heads names of blasphemy.*

"And the beast which I saw was like unto a leopard, and his feet were as the feet of a bear, and his mouth as the mouth of a lion: and the dragon gave him his power, and his throne, and great authority.

"And I saw one of his heads as though it had been smitten unto death; and his death-stroke was healed and the whole earth wondered after the beast...."

In this passage of Scripture, the Apostle calls the empire a beast which came up from the sea. The sea refers to its future historical rise. The beast's historical appearance will be in a ten-kingdom form. One of the heads of the beast had a deadly wound, or death-stroke, which healed. This miracle causes the world, the European nations and the Middle East nations, including the nation of Israel, to surrender their power to the Antichrist.

"Head" or "heads" in the Bible sometimes symbolize a government. This is seen in Daniel 7:6. *"...and, lo, another, like a leopard, which had upon its back four wings of a bird; the beast had also four heads; and dominion was given to it."* The leopard typified the Grecian Empire under Alexander the Great. The wings denoted the swiftness with which Alexander conquered the Persian Empire. It took him only six years to destroy Persia. The four heads symbolized four different governments or kings which would emerge from Alexander's Empire. This is confirmed by Daniel 8:8. *"And the he-goat magnified himself exceedingly: and when he was strong, the great horn was broken; and instead of it there came up four notable horns toward the four winds of heaven."* After the death of Alexander the Great in 323 B.C. his Empire was divided among his four generals. In this way, there came into existence four different governments or kingdoms. The four kingdoms which emerged from Alexander's Empire were represented by the four heads.

Daniel 8:3-8 is a distinct prophecy about the Persian and Grecian Empires. Daniel 8:3 says: *"...there stood before the river a ram which had two horns: and the two horns were high; but one was higher than the other, and the higher came up last."* The two-horned ram represents the Medo-Persian Empire. The higher horn represented the Persian element, which was more powerful in the Empire than the Median element. The Median kingdom existed before Persia became a kingdom. In 558 B.C. Cyrus became king of Persia and united Media with Persia, founding the Medo-Persian Empire. Thus, the prophecy about the two-horned ram was fulfilled.

The statement in Revelation 13:1 is of interest: "...And I saw a beast coming up out of the sea, having ten horns, and seven heads, and on his horns ten diadems, and upon his heads names of blasphemy." This Scripture reveals four important factors.

1. A beast
2. The sea
3. Ten horns which had diadems on them
4. Seven heads, having the names of blasphemy

In Revelation 12:3, the Apostle writes about the same matter in a different way saying: "...And behold, a great red dragon, having seven heads and ten horns, and upon his heads seven diadems." Here the dragon has the heads and horns. This prophecy also reveals three factors.

1. A great red dragon
2. Seven heads, each head having a diadem
3. Ten horns with no diadems

But, in this Scripture passage, the order is different. The heads are mentioned first instead of the horns as in Revelation 13:1. And in Revelation 12:3 the heads have diadems, while in the former Scripture passage the heads had no diadems. In Revelation 17:3, the horns and heads are again spoken of. "And he carried me away in the Spirit into the wilderness and I saw a woman sitting upon a scarlet-colored beast, full of names of blasphemy, having seven heads and ten horns." Here the heads and horns are associated with the woman. The heads are mentioned first and then the horns. The woman typifies the world religious system, or church, headed by the papacy in Rome.

The dragon had seven heads with diadems and ten horns. The beast had seven heads and ten horns with diadems. "Diadem" is translated from the Greek "diadema," as "bound about the head," "a fillet." The heads of the dragon are encircled with a golden fillet, or diadem, the emblem in the East of arbitrary, despotic power. The dragon and the beast are distinct, however, closely related. Both the dragon, or Satan, and the beast are connected with the heads and horns. All three actors on the political arena of the last Gentile world power are connected with the heads and the horns — the dragon, the beast, and the woman.

Revelation 17:9-10 teaches that the heads typify governments. *"Here is the mind that hath wisdom. The seven heads are seven mountains, on which the woman sitteth:*

"and they are seven kings; the five are fallen, the one is, the other is not yet come; and when he commeth, he must continue a little while."

The Apostle shows here that the seven heads are seven mountains, and they in turn are seven kings, which, in other words, means governments. Many Bible scholars say that the seven mountains here mean the seven-hilled city of Rome, because Rome is built on seven hills. Revelation 17:18 seems to strengthen this position. *"And the woman who thou sawest is the great city, which reigneth over the kings of the earth."* The woman typifies the world church headed by the pope during the tribulation.

The papacy has its headquarters, the center of operations, in Rome. Therefore, the city of Rome is also called the woman.

However, the Apostle calls the seven heads seven kings, or seven governments. "The seven heads are seven mountains." "Mountain" in the Bible typifies a government, as has been already explained. The dragon had seven heads and they were crowned.

Mr. Scott teaches that the seven crowned heads of the dragon refer to the concentration of Earthly power and wisdom in cruel and despotic exercise. His ten uncrowned horns point to the future limits of the Empire as distributed into ten kingdoms, the government of which he administers. If his heads are crowned, there is no need for the horns. When we come to actual history, the ten horns or kings are crowned. The simple thought is that the heads of the dragon are crowned, while his ten horns signify that his power is exercised administratively through the Empire in its ten-kingdom form. The dragon represents the unseen force behind the Empire; hence the diadems are on his heads, not on his horns. His heads are encircled with the golden fillet, or badge of royalty, as expressing his complete power and wisdom on Earth —centered in the beast, the royal power then dominant on earth. [1]

I do agree with Mr. Scott, but he does not seem to explain the real significance of the heads of the dragon. The seven heads of the dragon are crowned, but the seven heads of the beast are not

---

1. Scott, op.cit., p. 250.

crowned. The ten horns of the dragon are not crowned, but the ten horns of the beast are crowned. Upon the seven heads of the beast are the names of blasphemy.

In light of the historical context, the seven heads and ten horns do not exist now, but will appear in the political sphere after the rapture. Six of the seven heads have already existed, the seventh will be manifested after the rapture, in the beginning of the tribulation. The dragon possessed the seven heads, which denote seven governments in the history of Rome.

Each form of government exercised full power over its subjects. All the governments have been in operation historically and therefore are crowned. However, all the characteristics of the former governments will be included in the form of the last government of the revived Roman Empire. Because Satan is the energizing, unseen power behind the government of Antichrist, the heads of the dragon were crowned. The ten horns of the dragon were not crowned, because they symbolize kings that will rule at the end of the last Gentile world power under the Antichrist — after the rapture. That is why the horns on the dragon were not crowned.

The beast possesses the heads also. The biblical revelation teaches that Satan and the Antichrist will be working in unison. What belongs to Satan belongs to Antichrist also. Satan is the unseen power behind the revived Roman Imperial government. The dragon is in control of all the political movements in the revived last Gentile world power, working through his representative, the Antichrist, who is in total submission to the dragon. The seven heads typify the government of Antichrist in Rome. Six of the seven heads typify the government of Antichrist in Rome. Six of the seven heads also denote the former governments of Rome in its historical context. The city was founded in 753 B.C. and had several different governments in succession. The Apostle John writes about these heads or governments in Revelation 17:9-10. At the time Revelation was written, in 96 A.D. five of the governments of Rome had already fallen and one was in existence. And the seventh had not yet come.

The seven heads of the beast, therefore, represent seven successive forms of government from the rise of Rome on through its history. The Apostle wrote: "Five have fallen." These five forms of government have ceased to exist.

1. Kings
2. Consuls

3. Dictators
4. Decemvirs
5. Military Tribunes

"One is." That was the sixth, the one that existed at the time of the writing this revelation by the Apostle John, in 96 A.D. It was the Imperial form of government set up by Julius Caesar before his assassination in 44 B.C.

"The other hath not yet come." This is the seventh head. It is the rise of the fallen Roman State under new conditions, and will be formed of ten kingdoms. Each state will have its own king, but will be in total subordination to the great Gentile chief, the Antichrist, who will control the empire and hold all with a firm grasp.

The Purpose of Reviving the Roman Empire

I want to include three reasons for reviving the Roman State at the end of this age.

1. To fulfill prophecy. Whatever God has foretold in the Scriptures must be fulfilled. Daniel 2:40-44 spoke about Rome's rise and its latter restoration. In Daniel 7:7-8 again the prophet wrote about its rise, and the end time Empire under the rule of Antichrist. The Apostle John writes in Revelation 13:1-3 about the revived Roman State in the last form at the end of this age. In 2 Thessalonians 2:4, the Apostle Paul writes about the Gentile chief, the leader of the revived empire.

Revelation 11:15 contains the great prophecy about the second coming of Christ in glory, to set up His kingdom, the Millennium. *"The kingdom of the world is become the kingdom of our Lord, and of His Christ."* These are a few Scripture passages that show the reader the first reason why the Roman Empire will be restored in its ten kingdom form after the first resurrection.

2. To prepare the nation of Israel for the coming of Christ. In the beginning of the tribulation, the Jews will accept the Antichrist as their messiah. Jesus said: *"I am come in My Father's name, and ye receive Me not: if another shall come in his own name, him ye will receive."* This is Christ's prophecy about the rule of the revived Roman Empire under the Antichrist, whom the Jews will accept as the expected messiah.

According to Daniel 9:27, the Antichrist will make a covenant with the Jews for seven years. This covenant is called, in Isaiah 28:18, *"covenant of death."* The prophet writes: *"And your covenant with death shall be annulled, and your agreement with Sheol shall not stand when the overflowing scourge shall pass through, then ye shall be trodden down by it."* Daniel 9:27 reveals that, after three and a half years, Antichrist will break the covenant, and then begins the great tribulation, which is called by Jeremiah 30:7 *"...Jacob's trouble...."*

The tribulation period will be used by God to punish the ungodly world, and the ungodly Israelites. Terrible persecution will be used by the Lord to prepare the stubborn nation of Israel for acceptance of Christ as their Messiah. In Moses' time, God used Egypt to make the life of the Israelites so sour that they were ready to leave Egypt in a hurry.

So also, the tribulation under Antichrist will be so terrible that the Jews, in despair, will have no other way to escape except to call on the name of the Lord to save them from total annihilation. In Matthew 23:39, Jesus says: *"For I say unto you. Ye shall not see Me henceforth till ye shall say. Blessed is He that commeth in the name of the Lord."* When the Lord ascended into heaven, two angels stood by the disciples and prophesied about the coming of the Lord: Acts 1:11 says: *"Who also said, Ye men of Galilee, why stand ye looking into heaven? This Jesus, Who was received up from you into heaven, shall so come in like manner as ye beheld Him going into heaven."* This, His second coming, will fulfill the prophecy of Zechariah 12:10: *"And I will pour upon the house of David, and upon the inhabitants of Jerusalem, the spirit of grace and of supplication; and they shall look unto Me Whom they have pierced; and they shall mourn for Him, as one mourneth for his only son...."*

3. The Gentiles in the tribulation. The time period, called by the Lord in Luke 21:24, "the times of the Gentiles" — *"...and Jerusalem shall be trodden down of the Gentiles, until the times of the Gentiles be fulfilled."* — is one of the important time periods in prophetic Scripture. The "times of the Gentiles" began with the Babylonian captivity, when Jerusalem fell into the hands of the Gentiles in 606 B.C. continues to the present time, and will continue through the tribulation period — at which time the Gentile power will be judged — a period of about 2,600 years.

The last seven years of this age, called by Christ in Acts 1:7, *"the times and the seasons"* appointed for Israel, will also be the last seven years of the times of Gentiles — the tribulation period. The beast spoken of in Revelation 13:1-3 is a composite beast, partaking of the

eatures of the leopard, the bear, and the lion; and this form of world
ower is marked by ten horns.

The tribulation is a period of time when God pours His judgment
pon the ungodly world. In the middle of the tribulation, the Soviet
Union will invade Israel. Ezekiel 39:1-6 is a prophecy about the
destruction of the Russian hords in the Republic of Israel. God
Himself will destroy the armies that come with Russia to Israel.

The book of Revelation speaks of many judgments the Lord will
use to punish the ungodly world. The tribulation will end with the
destruction of all the armies that come against Jerusalem to destroy
it.

CHAPTER XVI

ANTICHRIST, EMPEROR OF THE REVIVED ROMAN EMPIRE

Identification of Antichrist

One of the greatest objects of interest for many has been the identity of Antichrist. All kinds of explanations have been given about the numbers in Revelation 13:18. *"Here is wisdom. He that hath understanding, let him count the number of the beast; for it is the number of a man; and his number is six hundred and sixty and six"*(666). Some of the interpretations of this Scripture have been very fancy and ridiculous. Later, I will give the interpretation.

It is not difficult to identify Antichrist in light of the Scripture. The Antichrist will be an Italian politician. In Daniel 9:26-27, Antichrist is revealed as an Italian. Let us read it carefully: *"...And the people of the prince that shall come shall destroy the city and the sanctuary....*

"And he shall make a firm covenant with many for one week: and in the midst of the week he shall cause the sacrifice and the oblation to cease; and upon the wing of abominations shall come one that maketh desolate; and even unto the full end, and that determined, shall wrath be poured out upon the desolate."

The identification of Antichrist is not difficult here. Notice: "the prince that shall come." The prince the prophet wrote about is the Antichrist. But the statement, "the people of the prince that shall come shall destroy the city and the sanctuary," is important. The people of the prince, the Antichrist, that destroyed the city of Jerusalem and the Temple in 70 A.D. were the Romans, or Italians; and the prince here is identified with the Italians.

On this basis, the future ruler of the Revived Roman Empire will be an Italian politician. He is not Judas Iscariot, the one who betrayed

Jesus, because Satan does not have the power of resurrection. Only Christ has the power to resurrect the dead. He is not a Jew, as some believe and teach. Daniel 7:3 says: *"And four great beasts came up from the sea...."* The beasts here are the four world empires, including the Roman Empire. All the rulers were Gentiles, not Jews. And Revelation 13:2 says: *"...And I saw a beast coming up out of the sea, having ten horns and seven heads...."* In Revelation 13:4-5, Antichrist is also spoken of as the beast, and unto him was given "a mouth speaking great things." The noun "beast" is used interchangeably. The Roman Empire is called "the beast" and the Antichrist is called "the beast."

Water typifies the Gentile nations. And because the beast came up from the sea, he is a Gentile and not a Jew. However, the false prophet will be a Jew because Revelation 13:11 says: *"And I saw another beast coming up out of the earth...."* Earth sometimes symbolizes the nation of Israel.

Thus, in light of these Scripture passages, the conclusion is that the future Emperor of the Roman Empire, in the form of ten kingdoms, is an Italian politician. He must be in his 30s. He is now a statesman, a politician in Rome today. He is not of any particular fame or prominence at the present time. He is an ordinary politician like the rest of the Italian statesmen, until the rapture takes place. After the Church is translated, then Satan will fill him with demons, and he will become the Antichrist, the ruler of the last form of the Gentile world power. He will be Satan's great masterpiece in the imitation of the program of God during the tribulation.

The Rise of Antichrist to Power

The future ruler of the last Gentile world power is spoken of in eleven books of the Bible. He has about thirty names in the holy Scriptures. We now see how extensive the revelation of this person is. I do not intend to go into every detail, but a few things should be included. I want to include four factors that will make his rise to power possible.

1. The Antichrist is marked by his intelligence and persuasiveness. In Daniel 7:8, the Gentile chief is spoken of as the little horn in which were eyes like the eyes of a man, and a mouth speaking great things. The "eyes" symbolize intelligence, wisdom. The same is repeated in Daniel 7:20. *"...Even that horn that had eyes, and a mouth that spake great things, whose look was more stout than its fellows."*

In Daniel 8:23, the prophet again writes about the wisdom of Antichrist calling him *"...king of fierce countenance, and understanding dark sentences...."* This shows the intelligence he has when he appears on the political arena after the rapture.

2. In Ezekiel 28:4-5, the prophet writes about his subtlety and graft. *"By thy wisdom and by thine understanding thou hast gotten thee riches, and hast gotten gold and silver into thy treasures,*

"by thy great wisdom and by thy traffic hast thou increased thy riches, and thy heart is lifted up because of thy riches."

When this person appears in the political arena, he will have satanically-inspired wisdom, which brings him riches and glory. He will be great and mighty in riches and in politics.

Through his policies of graft, business will prosper. The nations in Europe will readily submit themselves to Antichrist, and the ten kingdom federation will be established.

3. Revelation 17:12-13 says: *"And the ten horns that thou sawest are ten kings, who have received no kingdom as yet; but they receive authority as kings with the beast for one hour.*

"These have one mind, and they give their power and authority unto the beast."

Thus, the Scripture reveals that his rise to power in Rome, and his position over the nations in Europe is by their own consent.

4. At the time of his rise to power, Antichrist is elevated through the instrumentality of the harlot, the corrupt religious system, the world church — headed by the papacy in Rome, which consequently seeks to dominate the beast. Revelation 17:3 shows it clearly: *"And he carried me away in the Spirit into a wilderness and I saw a woman sitting upon a scarlet-colored beast, full of names of blasphemy, having seven heads and ten horns."* The woman here typifies a false religious system, the world church having its headquarters in Rome. The pope controls the government in the beginning and helps the last world dictator rise to power. Later, the papacy will be destroyed. Revelation 17:16 says: *"And the ten horns which thou sawest, and the beast, these shall hate the harlot, and shall make her desolate, and naked, and shall eat her flesh, and shall burn her utterly with fire."* Here is the prophecy about the destruction of the papacy in Rome.

The number of the Antichrist, "666," is of paramount interest. Bible scholars in the past have interpreted it in many different ways. There is only one correct interpretation for every passage of

Scriptures. No Bible scholar can interpret the Scriptures properly without understanding biblical numerology.

Number six in the Bible symbolically means man's toil or labor in sin and struggle. Number six is the number of man and is applied to Antichrist in Revelation 13:18: *"...and his number is six hundred and sixty and six"*(666). Mr. Walter Scott explains it well.

Man was created on the sixth day. His appointed days of labor and toil are six days. The Hebrew slave was to serve six years. For six years the land was to be sown. Under the sixth seal an appalling and universal catastrophe upon mankind ensues. Six being short of that signifies human imperfection and toil. But in the growing development of man's history he goes from bad to worse, hence six combined with six increases in moral significance till man is witnessed in open and direct opposition to God. In the yet future development of man in his progressive evil history the culmination is reached in the ominous signification of 666, the number of Antichrist. The image of gold set up by Nebuchadnezzar for his own glorification was sixty cubits high and six cubits broad. Under threats of an awful death the image of gold must be worshiped.

The golden image spoken of in Daniel 3:1-7 points forward to the yet even deeper and truly Satanic evil of Revelation 13:18. In both Scriptures the pride, self-will, and haughty independence of God by men placed above human law is the sad picture. The significance of the trinity of six is this. The 666 means the fullest and highest development of man under direct Satanic control. It is the combination of civil, religious, and political power Satanically inspired. It is as far as man can go, the complete setting aside of God as the Supreme Ruler and a man taking His place. [1]

The Character of Antichrist

The last ruler of this great Gentile world power, the Antichrist bears the characterization of a blasphemer because of the assumption of deity. His blasphemous character is revealed in Ezekiel 28:2. *"...Thus sayth the Lord Jehovah: because thy heart is lifted up, and thou hast said. I am a god, I sit in the seat of God, in the midst of the seas; yet thou art man, and not God, though thou didst set thy heart as the heart of God."* This Scripture reveals Satan's purpose and desire to be worshipped as God. This was his plan and desire when he rebelled against God in past eternity. In the person of Antichrist

1. Scott, op.cit., pp. 286-287.

during the tribulation, the Devil will be worshipped as God — when Antichrist sits in the Temple in Jerusalem, and declares that he is God.

The character of the Antichrist is also revealed in Daniel 7:25. *"And he shall speak words against the Most High, and shall wear out the saints of the Most High; and he shall think to change the times and the law...."* His blasphemous character is also spoken of in Revelation 13:5-6. *"And there was given to him a mouth speaking great things and blasphemies, and there was given to him authority to continue forty and two months.*

"And he opened his mouth for blasphemies against God, to blaspheme His name, and His tabernacle, even them that dwell in the heaven."

Mr. Scott says that God, and all His in Earth and heaven, are openly railed upon, and spoken against in words not recorded, but bitter enough surely, as the expression of an apostate heart inspired by the Devil. Words bold and bad are uttered. What is said is not revealed, but it is sure that the utmost of undying hatred to God which the malice of the Devil can suggest is publicly and loudly expressed.

In the pride of his heart the Antichrist boasts and blasphemes. Who he is and what he has done constitute the sum of the great things spoken, and added to this are the significant words and blasphemies.

The Doom of Antichrist

The Scripture reveals the end of several wicked evil persons. When the children of Israel came out of Egypt, they were persued by Pharaoh and his armies. The wicked, proud king of Egypt in his blindness followed the Israelites into the Red Sea and perished. Exodus 14:28 says: *"And the waters returned, and covered the chariots, and the horsemen, even all the host of Pharaoh, that went in after them into the sea; there remained not so much as one of them."* That was the end of one wicked leader of evil.

2 Kings 1:9-12 speaks of the fifty men whom the king of Samaria sent to Elijah to bring him to king Ahaziah. Two groups were burned up by fire from heaven. The king himself died also. Again, in the Old Testament, another wicked, evil person who was destroyed suddenly was Queen Jezebel of Samaria. She was the one who introduced Baal worship into the northern kingdom of Israel. 2 Kings 9:30-35 shows that the Queen was thrown out of a window, and her blood sprinkled

on the wall, and on the horses. That was the end of an evil woman who dared to fight against the Almighty God, the Lord of heaven and of Earth.

Ezekiel 21:25-27 shows the doom of Antichrist, who is called the wicked prince of Israel. Daniel 7:11 is another prophecy of the doom of Antichrist. *"I beheld at that time because of the voice of the great words which the horn spake. I beheld even till the beast was slain, and its body destroyed, and it was given to be burned with fire."*

In 2 Thessalonians 2:8, the Apostle also speaks of the doom of the Antichrist. *"And then shall be revealed the lawless one, whom the Lord Jesus shall slay with the breath of His mouth, and bring to nought by the manifestation of His coming."* The most terrific prophecy of the doom of Antichrist is in Revelation 19:20. *"And the beast was taken and with him the false prophet that wrought the signs in his sight, wherewith he deceived them that had the mark of the beast and them that worshipped his image: they two were cast alive into the lake of fire that burneth with brimstone."* These two men are not killed as their deluded followers are, but grasped by the hand of Omnipotence, and cast into the lake of fire. That is the end of the last world ruler, the Antichrist, Satan's masterpiece to deceive and lead people to worship Satan. One thousand years later Satan also will be cast into the lake of fire.

CHAPTER XVII

THE CAMPAIGN OF ARMAGEDDON

The Purpose of the Campaign of Armageddon

The great battle of Armageddon will not be one single battle fought in Palestine. It will be a series of battles fought between nations culminating at the end of the tribulation, and ending at the second coming of Christ to Earth in great glory and power. It begins with the Russian invasion of Israel in the middle of the tribulation and will continue until the coming of the Lord.

According to Ezekiel chapters 38 and 39, the northern confederacy, headed by the leader of the Soviet Union, will be destroyed by God Himself.

The Emperor of the revived Roman Empire is an ally of Israel. An attack against one is an attack against the other. The Antichrist will rush to Palestine, but before he reaches the holy land, God already will have destroyed the northern confederacy. At the same time Egypt will attack Israel, and the Antichrist will invade Egypt and defeat it. These battles will continue until they result in the final battle called the battle of Armageddon. There, God deals in judgment with the nations. The purpose is two-fold:

1. Because of their persecution of Israel. Joel 3:2 says: *"I will gather all nations, and will bring them down into the valley of Jehosaphat; and I will execute judgment upon them there for My people and for My heritage Israel, whom they have scattered among the nations: and they have parted My land."*

2. Because of the sinfulness of the nations, and because of their godlessness. Revelation 16:9 says: *"And men were scorched with great*

heat: and they blasphemed the name of God Who hath the power over these plagues; and they repented not to give Him glory." In Revelation 19:15, the Apostle writes about the judgment upon the ungodly nations. *"And out of His mouth proceedeth a sharp sword, that with it He should smite the nations: and He shall rule them with a rod of iron: and He treadeth the winepress of the fierceness of the wrath of God, the Almighty."*

The Battle of Armageddon

The battle of Armageddon will be the last and most terrific battle ever fought on planet Earth. Many great, decisive battles have been fought in the history of the world. The first great battle recorded in world history was fought about 956 B.C. between king Jeroboam of the northern kingdom of Israel and Abijah the king of Judah. King Jeroboam had 800,000 men under his command, and Abijah of Judah had 500,000 men under his command. In the ensuing battle, which lasted only a few hours, Jeroboam was totally defeated, losing about 500,000 men. The king of Judah was victorious because he trusted in the Lord Who protected him, and he had no casualties. The divine institutions were saved.

I would like to include two or three more great battles that changed the history of the world. One of the great, decisive battles was fought in June, 451 A.D. at Chalons, 153 kilometers (95 miles) northeast of Paris, France. The attack was led by the king of Huns. The Mongol tribes recruited about 500,000 men. They were fierce fighters who hated Rome. Attila, the king of the Huns, decided to destroy the Roman Empire, so that he could rule the whole world. The Huns camped in Hungary, close to the present day city of Budapest, their residence for many years. On their way to attack the Roman Empire, they ravaged the country, burning and killing everything in their way.

The Huns were met by the Romans and their allies at Chalons, France, by General Aetius, under whose command were about 500,000 men. The battle lasted for about six hours. In this terrific campaign, over 1,000,000 men fought for their lives and for their kings. In this battle, about 300,000 men fell, but Attila and his Huns were defeated, and Christianity was saved from total destruction.

Another decisive battle was fought on the 18th of June, 1815, at Waterloo, about 19 kilometers (12 miles) south of Brussels. The French Army of 125,000, led by Napoleon I, was encountered by the

Allies. The Prussians, commanded by General Blucher, numbered about 120,000 men, and the English, Belgian and Dutch, and various German contingents, commanded by the 1st Duke of Wellington of England, numbered about 70,000 men. In this great campaign, Napoleon was defeated, and his dream to build a mighty French Empire in Europe was terminated in a one-day battle. This changed the course of European history.

One of the most important battles fought in the Second World War was that at Stalingrad, close to the Caspean Sea. In this decisive battle, which began on August 24, 1942, and ended on February 2, 1943, the Germans lost an entire army. The Germans suffered 300,000 casualties, and 93,000 surrendered. Each of the opposing armies at Stalingrad was comprised of over 1,000,000 men. The outcome of this battle gave the Germans a mortal blow. From this time on, the Germans never again mounted a large-scale advance.

More than 68,000,000 men fought in the Second World War. The Allies mobilized 46,271,000 and the Axis powers 21,775,000 men.

All these important battles in world history are nothing in comparison to the battle of Armageddon. This battle will be fought in Palestine at the close of this present age.

The Russian confederacy will be destroyed by the Lord Himself on the mountains of Israel. The armies of Egypt will be destroyed by the army of Antichrist. The Roman army will be victorious under the leadership of Antichrist. Then, the armies of the East come to test the strength of the revived Roman Empire. All other armies have already been destroyed, and now the armies of Antichrist and the armies of the East are drawn up in battle array. Before the battle can be joined, there appears a sign in the heavens, the sign of the Son of man, the Lord Jesus Christ. This unexpected sign causes the armies to turn from their hostility toward each other, to unite to fight against the Lord Himself.

Therefore, the battle of Armageddon will not be fought between opposing military forces, but between the Lord Jesus Christ and the Gentile armies in Israel. Revelation 19:19 says: *"And I saw the beast, and the kings of the earth, and their armies, gathered together to make war against Him that sat upon the horse, and against His army."* This universal assemblage of powers is not effected by human authority. Satan himself is behind this universal gathering.

How incredible to see human beings fighting against the Almighty God and His Army! But sin and pride have blinded the minds of those men so much that they cannot see the futility of such an effort. They make war against Christ and His Army but are destroyed.

I want to include Revelation 14:20 and show its connection with the battle of Armageddon. *"And the winepress was trodden without the city and there came out blood from the winepress even unto the bridles of the horses, as far as a thousand and six hundred furlongs."* Thus, the reader will get a little idea of the battle of Armageddon which will be fought at the conclusion of this age. Joel 3:2 is a prophecy about the gathering of the nations in the valley of Jehoshaphat. *"I will gather all nations, and will bring them down into the valley of Jehoshaphat; and I will execute judgment upon them there for My people and for My heritage Israel whom they have scattered among the nations: and they have cast lots for My people, and have given a boy for an harlot, and sold a girl for wine, that they may drink."*

The Valley of Jehosahphat is an extended area east of Jerusalem. The battle will not be fought at Megiddo alone. The entire land of Palestine will be a battlefield. The Apostle John writes in Revelation 16:14 about the combatants involved. *"...to gather them together unto the war of the great day of God...."* War is translated from the Greek word "polemos" which means "war" in the sense of a campaign. It is not a single day battle, but a long campaign starting with the invasion of Israel by Russia in the middle of the tribulation and followed by the armies of the East, or Asiatic peoples.

The statement in Revelation 14:20 that blood will reach horse bridles has been a confusion and misinterpretation for a long time. The area referred to as the Valley of Jehosahphat is about 1,600 furlongs long. 1 furlong is about 203 meters (660 feet). This makes a distance of about 268 kilometers or 166 miles.

The Asiatic armies number about 200,000,000 and the Antichrist may have about 50,000,000 — making a total of 250,000,000 combatants. It is estimated that a human being has about 5 to 6 liters of blood. If one allows 6 liters of blood per man, this would make about 1,500,000,000 liters of human blood. If a bullet goes through a person it is unlikely that half of his blood would run out. If we say 3 liters per man, that would make about 750,000,000 liters of blood. This would create a lake of 1 square kilometer about 75 centimeters (2.5 feet) deep.

There will be great rain which will wash all the blood into a valley, and the water mixed with blood will seem like blood.

An experience of similar nature occurred in the history of Israel in the ninth century B.C. Water appeared to the people as blood. When crown prince Jehoram ascended the throne of Israel in 849 B.C. the King of Moab rebelled against Israel. This forced King Jehoram to declare war on Moab. Jehoram also invited Jehoshaphat, King of Juda, and the King of Edom to be his allies in the ensuing battle.

In the desert the allies faced a shortage of water. On the request of King Jehoshaphat, Elisha prophesied that the Lord would supply the water. 2 Kings 3:20-23 says: *"And it came to pass in the morning, about the time of offering the oblation, that, behold, there came water by the way of Edom, and the country was filled with water.*

"Now when all the Moabites heard that the kings were come up to fight against them, they gathered themselves together, all that were able to put on armor, and upward, and stood on the border.

"And they rose up early in the morning, and the sun shone upon the water, and the Moabites saw the water over against them as red as blood;

"and they said. This is blood; the kings are surely destroyed, and they have smitten each man his fellow: now therefore, Moab, to the spoil."

The Moabites saw the water in the valley, where the army of Israel and her allies were encamped, and supposed it was blood. They knew the valley to be dry, and could not imagine it should be water. The sun shone upon it, probably the sky was red and lowering, making the water look red. This made them willing to believe it was blood.

The same thing will occur at the conclusion of the battle of Armageddon. There will be such a great rain that the valley of Jehoshaphat will be filled with water. The rain water will wash all the blood of the dead into the valley and the water will appear as blood. There will be bright sunshine which will reflect or strengthen the red color.

CHAPTER XVIII

THE SECOND COMING
OF CHRIST

The Lord's Promise of His Return to Earth

Before His death on the cross, Jesus made a promise to His followers, that He was going to prepare a place for His people and that He would come again. There are two aspects to the second coming of Christ at the end of this age.

1. His promise to come and take them to Himself — the rapture. In John 14:3, the Lord says: *"And if I go and prepare a place for you, I come again, and will receive you unto Myself; that where I am, there ye may be also."* This is in reference to the first resurrection, when the dead in Christ shall be raised and the living saints translated.

2. His return to Earth in great glory and power. Jesus said: *"And then shall appear the sign of the Son of man in heaven: and then shall all the tribes of the earth mourn, and they shall see the Son of man coming on the clouds of heaven with power and great glory."* [1] When Jesus ascended into heaven, two angels appeared to the disciples and delivered a prophecy to them, stated in Acts 1:11. *"...ye men of Galilee, why stand ye looking into heaven? This Jesus, Who was received up from you into heaven, shall so come in like manner as ye beheld Him going into heaven."*

At the end of the tribulation, when Christ appears on the clouds and destroys the Gentile armies in Palestine, He will descend to the Mount of Olives. Revelation 19:11-18 is the prophecy of His second coming in glory as a Victor on a white horse. Revelation 19:11 says: *"And I saw the heaven opened and behold, a white horse, and He that*

1. *Matthew* 24:30.

sat thereon called Faithful and True; and in righteousness He doth judg *and make war."* The horse is not literal, but symbolic. The whit horse symbolizes the victorious end of a battle. When Jesus ascende into heaven from the Mount of Olives, He did not go on horsebac He just ascended slowly, until He disappeared in the clouds. Th angels said that the Lord would return in the same manner. He wi descend to the Mount of Olives slowly until His feet touch th mountain.

This is the second coming of Christ, spoken of in so man Scripture passages. When He comes down to Earth in glory, then H shall judge the nations. Matthew 25:31 says: *"But when the Son o man shall come in His glory, and all the angels with Him then shall H sit on the throne of His glory."*

The Judgment of Israel

The Old Testament prophets depicted the judgment of Israel at th return of the Lord in glory when He will regather His people; bu before they can enter the promised land and the Millennial blessing this judgment must take place. To them was promised, through th covenants, a kingdom over which the Messiah, David's son, shoul reign. Before this kingdom can be instituted, there must be judgment on Israel to determine who will enter the promise kingdom. The unsaved will be excluded from the believing remnan Only the saved can enter the Millennium. Jesus says in John 3:3 *"...Verily, verily, I say unto thee, Except one be born anew, he cannot se the kingdom of God."* The regathering and judgment of Israel i depicted in Ezekiel 20:34-38. *"And I will bring you out from th peoples, and will gather you out of the countries wherein ye ar scattered, with a mighty hand, and with an outstretched arm, and wit wrath poured out.*

"And I will bring you into the wilderness of the peoples, and ther will I enter into judgment with you face to face.

"Like as I entered into judgment with your fathers in the wildernes of the land of Egypt, so will I enter into judgment with you, saith th Lord Jehovah.

"And I will cause you to pass under the rod, and I will bring you int the bond of the covenant.

"And I will purge out from among you the rebels, and them tha transgress against Me; I will bring them forth out of the land where they sojourn, but they shall not enter into the land of Israel: and ye shal know that I am Jehovah."

The same judgment is also spoken of in Malachi 3:2-3. The prophet writes: *"But who can abide the day of His coming? and who shall stand when He appears? For He is like a refiner's fire and like fuller's soap.*

"And He will sit as a refiner and purifier of silver, and He will purify the sons of Levi, and refine them as gold and silver; and they shall offer unto Jehovah offerings in righteousness."

The Apostle Paul writes about this judgment in Romans 11:26-27. *"And so all Israel shall be saved: even as it is written. There shall come out of Zion the Deliverer; He shall turn away ungodliness from Jacob.*

"And this is My covenant unto them, when I shall take away their sins."

This judgment will take place at the second coming of Christ to the Earth in glory. According to Matthew 24:31, the Lord will gather His ancient people together to Palestine, where they will be judged before they can enter the Millennial reign. Matthew 24:31 says: *"And He shall send forth His angels with a great sound of a trumpet, and they shall gather together His elect from the four winds, from one end of heaven to the other."* It is through the angelic ministry that the remnant of His elect will be led back to the land of their forefathers — fulfilling many of the Old Testament prophecies. [2]

The Judgment of the Gentile Nations at the Second Coming of Christ

Jesus, in His parabolic discourse in Matthew 13:47-50, spoke about the net, the good fish and the bad fish. The net was cast into the sea, which typifies the Gentile nations, and the net was drawn to shore. The good fish were gathered into vessels, but the bad cast away. This implies a separation which will take place at His second coming to Earth. Matthew 25:32 says: *"And before Him shall be gathered all the nations: and He shall separate them one from another, as the shepherd separateth the sheep from the goats."*

Christ will judge the nations and then put the sheep, the righteous nations, on His right hand, to enter His eternal kingdom; while the wicked nations, typified by the goats, will go to eternal condemnation. That this happens at the end of this age is attested by Matthew 13:49. *"So shall it be in the end of the world (age): the angels shall come forth, and sever the wicked from among the righteous."*

2. *Deuteronomy* 30:1-9; *Jeremiah* 32:37-38; *Ezekiel* 11:16-21.

The judgment of the Gentile nations at that time is to determine who will enter the Millennium. This judgment will be on an individual basis. Christ will not judge a nation with one pronouncement, because a nation cannot believe. Only individuals can believe. All those who believed and accepted the message preached by the 144,000 during the tribulation will enter the Millennium, while those that rejected the message and the messenger will perish.

The nations will be judged on the basis of a reception or rejection of the message of the gospel of the kingdom. Since this message requires faith and a resultant new birth, those being judged will be judged on a personal basis — according to their individual response.

Jude 14-15 also speaks of a separation. He writes: *"...Behold, the Lord came with ten thousands of His holy ones,*

"to execute judgment upon all, and to convict all the ungodly of all their works of ungodliness which they have ungodly wrought and of all the hard things which ungodly sinners have spoken against Him."

In each of these Scriptures, which depict this same process of judgment in separating the unsaved from the saved prior to the Millennium, it is always an individual judgment.

CHAPTER XIX

THE MILLENNIAL REIGN
OF CHRIST

The Millennium in Prophecy

The rapture will be followed by the rule of Antichrist for seven years. At the time of the battle of Armageddon, Christ will return and set up His own kingdom. Christ will rule from David's throne in Jerusalem for one thousand years in perfect peace and great prosperity. The reign of the Lord Jesus on Earth is foretold in the Bible by many prophets, both in the Old Testament and the New Testament.

God's kingdom occupies a large portion of Scripture. The eternal kingdom must be studied from two viewpoints.

1. The kingdom of God as eternal
2. The kingdom of God as temporal, with a definite historical beginning, progress, and termination

The timeless aspect of God's kingdom is seen in the Scriptures. Psalms 10:16 says: *"Jehovah is king for ever and ever...."*

Jeremiah 10:10 states: *"But Jehovah is the true God; He is the living God, and an everlasting king...."* And Lamentations 5:19 says the same.

So, God Almighty has always been king Who rules over the universe. The primary meaning of the New Testament word for kingdom, "basileis," is "reign" rather than "realm" or "people." In the New Testament, the Millennial reign of Christ is spoken of in two ways.

1. It is called "the kingdom of God"
2. It is called "the kingdom of heaven"

Both terms are used in reference to the future Millennial kingdom. Matthew 3:2 says: *"Repent ye; for the kingdom of heaven is at hand."* John the Baptist calls the Millennial reign of Christ "the kingdom of heaven." Matthew 5:3 says: *"blessed are the poor in spirit: for theirs is the kingdom of God."* In Luke 19:11, it is called "the kingdom of God." *"...because they supposed that the kingdom of God was immediately to appear."* Both terms are used in respect to the Millennial kingdom. Matthew 6:33 says: *"But seek ye first the kingdom and His righteousness...."* Again in Matthew 18:3-6, Jesus speaks of "the kingdom of heaven." And in Mark 10:14 the Lord mentioned "the kingdom of God." Both terms are used in reference to the eternal kingdom.

Isaiah 2:4 speaks about the Millennium. *"And He will judge between the nations, and will decide concerning many peoples; and they shall beat their swords into plowshares, and their spears into pruning hooks; nation shall not lift up sword against nation, neither shall they learn war any more."* All together about 14 of the Old Testament writers depicted the reign of Christ — the Millennium.

The reign of Christ on Earth for 1,000 years will be a glorious rule characterized by many glorious aspects.

1. The Millennial reign will be characterized by righteousness
2. It will be characterized by obedience
3. It will be characterized by holiness
4. It will be characterized by truth
5. It will be characterized by the fullness of the Holy Spirit

The prophecy about the outpouring of the Holy Spirit will then be fulfilled. Joel 2:28 says: *"And it shall come to pass afterward, that I will pour out My Spirit upon all flesh...."* On the Day of Pentecost, there was only a partial outpouring of the Holy Spirit. Acts 2:17 says: *"...I will pour forth of My Spirit upon all flesh...."* And in Acts 2:18, the Apostle Peter says: *"...in those days I will pour forth of My Spirit...."* In these two statements the Apostle Peter quoted from Joel 2:28, but notice the wording: "of My spirit." In other words, he meant a partial outpouring of the Spirit of God. There are tribes and nations in the world today where there is no evangelical work whatsoever. Many of the tribes in the world have not yet heard the name of Christ. But in the Millennium, the Lord will pour out His Holy Spirit in its fullness on all nations. The outpouring of the Holy Spirit in the Millennium will be powerful in its transforming ability. The Holy Spirit will impart miraculous gifts to the saints and will so pervade in and over he Jewish nation that all shall be righteous, from the least to the greatest. It will be so wide-reaching over the Gentiles that they shall rejoice in the light bestowed and so extended in its operation that the whole Earth shall ultimately be covered with glory. In the Millennium, oel 2:28 will be fulfilled.

Habakkuk 2:14 says: *"For the earth shall be filled with the knowledge of the glory of Jehovah, as the waters cover the sea."* Haggai 2:19 speaks also of the Millennial glory during the reign of Christ on Earth.

Conditions Existing Within the Millennium

Many Bible prophecies are devoted to describing the blessings and glory poured out upon Earth through the beneficence of the Lord Jesus Christ in the Millennium. I want to list just a few of them.

1. The removal of the curse. The original curse, placed upon creation, will be removed, so that there will be abundant productivity in the Earth. The animal kingdom will be changed, so as to lose its venom and ferocity. Isaiah 11:6-9 says: *"And the wolf shall dwell with the lamb, and the leopard shall lie down with the kid; and the calf and the young lion and the fatling together; and a little child shall lead them.*

"And the cow and the bear shall feed; their young ones shall lie down together; and the lion shall eat straw like the ox.

"And the suckling child shall play on the hole of the asp, and the weaned child shall put his hand on the adder's den.

"They shall not hurt nor destroy in all My holy mountain: for the earth shall be full of the knowledge of Jehovah, as the waters cover the sea."

2. Sickness will be removed. There will be no more sick people on Earth. The deformed will be healed. Accompanying this ministry will be the healing of all deformity at the inception of the Millennial reign of Christ. Jeremiah 31:8 says: *"Behold, I will bring them from the north country, and gather them from the uttermost parts of the earth, and with them the blind and the lame, the woman with child and her that travaileth with child together: a great company shall they return hither."*

3. Unified language. God confounded the language at Babel, but according to Zephaniah 3:9, this curse will also be removed. The prophet writes: *"For then will I turn to the peoples a pure language, that they may all call upon the name of Jehovah, to serve Him with one consent."*

4. World-wide peace. The cessation of war through the unification

of the kingdoms of the world, under the reign of Christ, will result in world-wide peace. War will be known no more. Isaiah 2:4 says: *"An He will judge between the nations, and will decide concerning man peoples; and they shall beat their swords into plowshares, and the spears into pruning-hooks; nation shall not lift up sword against natior neither shall they learn war any more."* The prophet Hosea write about the same matter in his book. Hosea 2:18 says: *"And in that da will I make a covenant for them with the beasts of the field, and with th birds of the heavens, and with the creeping things of the ground: and will break the bow and the sword and the battle out of the land, and wi make them to lie down safely."*

After the advent of Christ to Earth, Satan and his demons will b bound for 1,000 years. There will be no outside force to agitate th nations one against the other. Perfect peace will reign under the iro rule of Christ. All the Gentiles and the Jews that enter the Millenniun will live in peace together and enjoy great happiness. They will fee comfortable and satisfied. Isaiah 40:1-2 states: *"Comfort ye, comfor ye My people, saith your God.*

"Speak ye comfortably to Jerusalem; and cry unto her, that he warfare is accomplished, that the iniquity is pardoned, that she hat. received of Jehovah's hand double for all her sins."

5. Reproduction by the living people. Those who go into th Millennium will beget children throughout the age. The Earth' population will soar. Those born during the Millennium will be bor with a sinful nature, so salvation will be required for them. Zecharial 10:8 says: *"...for I have redeemed them, and they shall increase as the have increased."*

6. Increase of light. Isaiah 30:26 states: *"Moreover the light of th moon shall be as the light of the sun, and the light of the sun shall b sevenfold...."*

7. The perpetuity of the Millennial state. That which characterize the Millennial age is not viewed as temporary, but eternal. Joel 3:2(says: *"But Judah shall abide for ever, and Jerusalem from generation t generation."* Isaiah 60:19-20 says: *"The sun shall be no more light b day; neither for brightness shall the moon give light unto thee: bu Jehovah will be unto thee an everlasting light, and thy God thy glory.*

"The sun shall no more go down, neither shall thy moon withdraw itself; for Jehovah will be thine everlasting light...."

Satan's Last Rebellion

The last rebellion of Satan, at the conclusion of the Millennia reign of Christ, will also be the last drama of hatred to be enacted on his Earth. According to Revelation 20:7-8, the Devil will be loosed from his prison. *"And when the thousand years are finished, Satan shall be loosed out of his prison,*

"and shall come forth to deceive the nations which are in the four corners of the earth, Gog and Magog, to gather them together to war: the number of whom is as the sand of the sea."

Four corners of the Earth means a universal gathering of the Gentile nations against God's people, and the holy city, Jerusalem. The number of the wicked under Satan is so great, so numerous that the only comparison is to the sand of the sea. This vast assemblage is metaphorically spoken of as Gog and Magog. The northern confederacy under Gog invaded Israel with the purpose to destroy Israel completely, but God intervened and saved the nation from a total destruction.

The last attack under Satan again is against Israel in Palestine. During the Millennium all Israel is saved. Isaiah 59:20-21 says: *"And a Redeemer will come to Zion, and unto them that turn from transgression in Jacob, saith Jehovah.*

"And as for Me, this is My covenant with them, saith Jehovah: My Spirit that is upon thee, and My words which I have put in thy mouth, shall not depart out of thy mouth, nor out of the mouth of thy seed, nor out of the mouth of thy seed's seed, saith Jehovah, from henceforth and forever." The Apostle Paul says in Romans 11:26: *"And so all Israel shall be saved...."* But not so with the Gentiles. Large numbers will be saved, but vast multitudes also will be unsaved. They have obeyed Christ the King during the Millennial reign because of fear, but not in obedience of faith.

After Satan is loosed, he will deceive vast multitudes to go and attack Israel and the city of Jerusalem. Such is man's depraved nature. The Gentiles live in peace and great prosperity during the reign of Christ, but Satan stirs them up. So readily they follow the deceiver of humanity. This attack ends in judgment. Fire falls from heaven and devours them all. Satan is cast into the lake of fire, followed by the Great White Throne judgment, and the renovation of the Earth by fire.

CHAPTER XX

THE DESTINY
OF PLANET EARTH

The Renovation of the Universe by Fire

After the Great White Throne judgment, the greatest conflagration will take place. The entire universe will be set on fire. This is God's way of purging the universe and the Earth. Even the universe is not clean in His sight. Job 25:5 says: *"...the stars are not pure in His sight."* Satan's wicked, filthy presence has stained the universe, and it needs to be purged of all filth before the eternal state can be ushered in.

2 Peter 3:10-13 says: *"But the day of the Lord will come as a thief; in the which the heavens shall pass away with a great noise, and the elements shall be dissolved with fervent heat, and the earth and the works that are therein shall be burned up.*

"Seeing that these things are thus all to be dissolved, what manner of persons ought ye to be in all holy living and godliness.

"Looking for and earnestly desiring the coming of the day of God, by reason of which the heavens being on fire shall be dissolved, and the elements shall melt with fervent heat.

"But, according to His promise, we look for new heavens and a new earth, wherein dwells righteousness."

Scientists say that there are about 10,000,000,000 galaxies in the universe, a guess, of course, because the end of the universe cannot be seen. The most distant galaxy detected lies at a distance of about 15,000,000,000 light years. It is said that the Earth is in the center of the universe. So, there will be another 15,000,000,000 light years in the opposite direction, making a total of 30,000,000,000 light years. But the universe is much longer than 30,000,000,000 light years.

And the Apostle Peter stated that the heavens will be on fire and shall be dissolved. What a tremendous sea of fire that will be! This is indeed incomprehensible. What a tremendous heat that fire will produce!

Scientists tell us that the temperature in the Earth's center is about 5000 degrees Centigrade. In such heat all rock melts. The lava which spews out of volcanos is molten rock. The central temperature of the sun is about 15,000,000°C. This gives the reader a little idea of what terrific temperatures exist in the heavenly bodies. The fire, with which the Lord will renovate the universe, must be millions of degrees. It will dissolve everything in the universe.

2 Peter 3:10 says: *"...the heavens shall pass away with a great noise, and the elements shall be dissolved with fervent heat, and the earth and the works that are therein shall be burned up."* According to this statement, the present, existing galaxies and the Earth will simply melt, and everything flammable on the planet Earth will burn up. The rock will not burn up or cease to exist. Only things that burn will be burned up. Only molten rock will be left. In this way, the Almighty God will purge His entire universe of all that is unclean in His sight.

The Recreation of the Universe

The Lord has promised in His Word to create a new universe. Isaiah 65:17 says: *"For, behold, I create new heavens and a new earth; and the former things shall not be remembered, nor come into mind."* The heavens are plural just as in the New Testament, but the Earth is singular. God again will bring into existence the billions of galaxies, and the planet Earth will be recreated. King David wrote in Psalms 104:5: *"Who laid the foundations of the earth, that it should not be moved for ever."* And Solomon wrote in Ecclesiastes 1:4 that *"...the earth abideth for ever."*

Thus, the Bible establishes the fact that the Earth will never be annihilated. It will only be renovated by fire. Then, the Lord will create a new Earth out of the molten rock, and this new Earth will remain forever. The Heaven of heavens itself will not undergo any changes. The very heaven itself is the dwelling place of the Mighty Creator God. It subsists in moral and physical perfection.

On the new Earth, the conditions will be vastly different. There will be no more sea or water. Water is the source of life on our Earth. Where there is no water, there is no life; there is desert and death. About 50% of the oxygen is produced by the phytoplankton of the ea, and the rest of the oxygen is produced by plant foliage. If there is no water, there will be no oxygen, and without oxygen no life can exist on Earth.

Because there will be no water on the new Earth, there will be no oxygen. Breathing or respiration will be absent. A totally new system will be inaugurated by God. The Bible does not reveal much about life on the new Earth, but the absence of water implies a different condition on the renovated planet. On the new Earth, no nation will exist as they do today. It will be God and men on an Earth without sea. The conditions of life will be so different in the everlasting state that time conditions of life and happiness are no longer needed.

The total surface area of planet Earth is about 510,100,000 square kilometers (197,000,000 miles), of which 148,300,000 square kilometers is land area, and the water area is about 361,800,000 square kilometers. The land area of the total surface is only about 30% and the water area about 70%. On the new Earth, all the total surface area of 510,100,000 square kilometers will be habitable. So, the people on the new Earth will have 70% more living space than we now have.

The New Jerusalem — God's Capital

The New Jerusalem occupies a great part of prophecy in the New Testament. On the new Earth will be the New Jerusalem — God's capital, from which He rules His universe. Everything in the universe will be new. Revelation 21:5 says: *"...Behold, I make all things new...."* In this sentence is fixed the character of the eternal state. This is the Father's house Jesus spoke about in John 14:2-3. *"In My Father's house are many mansions; if it were not so, I would have told you; for I go to prepare a place for you.*

"And if I go and prepare a place for you, I come again, and will receive you unto Myself; that where I am, there ye may be also." This is Christ's promise to His Church of being united with Him again. This promise can be realized only through the resurrection. In Galatians 4:26, the Apostle Paul makes reference to the New Jerusalem, saying: *"But the Jerusalem that is above is free, which is our mother."* Father Abraham knew that such a city existed. Hebrews 11:10 says: *"For he looked for the city which hath the foundations, whose builder and maker is God."* In Hebrews 13:14, the writer says: *"For we have not here an abiding city, but we seek after the city which is to come."* Thus, the Word of God reveals very clearly that the New Jerusalem does exist, and that the city is to descend onto the new Earth.

The New Jerusalem is a literal city, not a mystical city as many believe. Revelation 21:10-27 gives a precise description of the golden city. It is made of pure gold, which symbolizes God's city. This marvelous city is built by God Himself and is very large. There are 24 points that should be taken into consideration which confirm that the New Jerusalem is a literal city and not figurative.

1. The holy city, Jerusalem
2. The New Jerusalem has the glory of God
3. The new city's light is as it were a jasper stone
4. A great high wall built of jasper
5. The city has twelve gates
6. At the gates, twelve angels — one angel at each gate
7. On the gates are written the names of the twelve tribes of Israel
8. The city is foursquare, and on each side are three gates
9. The wall of the city has twelve foundations
10. On the foundations are written the names of the twelve Apostles of the Lamb
11. The city is twelve thousand furlongs long, and the breadth and height is the same. It is a huge city, about 2,415 kilometers (1,500 miles) high, long and broad
12. The wall of the city is 144 cubits high or 66.5 meters (216 feet), made of jasper, typifying the divine glory
13. The twelve foundations are adorned with all manner of precious stones
14. Each gate of the city is made of a single pearl
15. The street of the city is of pure gold
16. God and the Lord Jesus are the temple thereof. The Temple in Israel was the place where the nation worshipped God. The Father God and the Lamb will be worshipped
17. The glory of God lightens the city, and the lamp thereof is the Lamb
18. The nations shall walk amidst the light thereof
19. The kings of the Earth bring their glory into it
20. The gates of the city shall always be open
21. In the New Jerusalem there will be no night
22. All the glory and honor of the nations shall be brought into it
23. No unclean thing shall enter into it
24. Only those written in the book of life will enter the city

In regard to the New Jerusalem, I want to bring four more important points to the readers attention.

1. The inhabitants of the New Jerusalem. In light of the Word of God, the inhabitants of the New Jerusalem consist of several different groups and the Almighty God.

A. The triune God will dwell in the holy golden city — God the Father, God the Son, and God the Holy Spirit. Revelation 22:3 says that *"...the throne of God and of the Lamb shall be therein, and His servants shall serve Him."*

B. The glorified Church, the Bride of Christ, will dwell in the eternal city with Christ, her Redeemer.

C. The redeemed of Israel.

D. The redeemed of all ages. The Old Testament saints from Abel to Pentecost, apart of the nation of Israel.

E. The tribulation saints also will be resurrected, and will live in the New Jerusalem. Those tribulation martyrs are not a part of the Church of Jesus Christ. All saints of all ages, and the Church will enter the New Jerusalem by resurrection. At the rapture, when the Church will be married to Christ, the Church enters her eternal abode. Only rapture and resurrection make entrance possible. When the Church is raptured and rewarded, she enters her eternal state, which will never be changed.

F. The holy angels. Hebrews 12:22 shows that the angels of God also will dwell in the New Jerusalem.

2. The relation of New Jerusalem to the Millennium. During the reign of Christ in the Millennium, the golden city will be suspended over the Earth. Revelation 21:10 shows that the New Jerusalem descends from heaven, *"...coming down out of heaven from God."* And Revelation 21:4 reveals that the city will stay above the Earth. *"And the nations shall walk amidst the light thereof: and the kings of the earth bring their glory into it."* The nations spoken of are the Millennial scene. They will bring honor and glory unto the Lord. The nations will pay court to the heavenly city.

3. The relation of New Jerusalem to eternity. In Revelation 21:2 is seen the descent of the city at the commencement of the eternal state. This descent takes place after the renovation of the Earth by fire. It is then that the New Jerusalem will descend to Earth, and this marvelous, huge, golden city will be God's capital, from which He will rule the universe throughout all eternity. Christ's promise to His

Church was that she should be with Him. Revelation 22:5 says: *"...and they shall reign for ever and ever."* The saints in the New Jerusalem shall never cease to reign. As long as Christ is on the throne, so long also will the saints reign with Him eternally.

4. Life in the New Jerusalem. The New Jerusalem will be the residence of the triune God and of all the redeemed of all ages. However, the saints will not stay in the golden city all the time, but will be moving around at will in the service of the Almighty God, the Great Creator of the universe and of all intelligences.

Life in the eternal city will be a life of fellowship with the blessed Lord. The Apostle Paul writes in 1 Corinthians 13:12: *"...now I know in part; but then shall I know fully even as also I was fully known."* 1 John 3:2 says: *"...We know that, if He shall be manifested, we shall be like Him; for we shall see Him even as He is."* In the golden city, there shall be a life full of knowledge, a life of eternal happiness and joy, without end. The glorified saints shall serve Him Who has bought them with His holy blood. It will be a life full of glory. 2 Corinthians 4:17 says: *"For our light affliction, which is for the moment, worketh for us more and more exceedingly an eternal weight of glory."*

Life on the New Earth

On the new Earth people will live forever. I am not referring to the Church, the Bride of Christ, nor to the Old Testament saints glorified, but to people that will live as immortals on the new Earth forever. There are two different nations that will live on in eternity.

1. The nation of Israel. Israel, as God's chosen nation, will be transferred to the new Earth. The Lord made four covenants with Israel which are eternal in character. The first one is found in the Abrahamic Covenant and reveals three everlasting aspects, guaranteeing three important things to the nation. It is stated in Genesis 17:7: *"And I will establish My covenant between Me and thee, and thy seed after thee throughout their generations for an everlasting covenant, to be a God unto thee, and to thy seed after thee."* In Genesis 17:19, the Lord reconfirmed His Covenant making a reference to Isaac: *"... and I will establish My covenant with him for an everlasting covenant for his seed after him."* Several hundred years later king David of Israel made reference to the Abrahamic Covenant stated in 1 Chronicles 16:16-17. *"The covenant which He made with Abraham, and His oath unto Isaac.*

"And confirmed the same unto Jacob for a statute. To Israel for an

everlasting covenant." I shall briefly name the three everlasting aspects which this Covenant guarantees to Israel.

A. A permanent national existence. This nation is not to exist on planet Earth only in this age and the Millennium, but also in eternity as a distinct nation. Isaiah 66:22 says: *"For as the new heavens and the new earth, which I will make shall remain before Me, saith Jehovah, so shall your seed and your name remain."* Notice that the Lord ascribes the same permanent character to the national existence of Israel as He ascribes to the new heavens and the new Earth. The angel, Gabriel, said to Mary *"And He shall reign over the house of Jacob forever, and of His kingdom there shall be no end."* [1]

B. An everlasting title to the land of promise. In Genesis 17:8, God said to Abraham. *"And I will give unto thee, and to thy seed after thee, the land of thy sojournings, all the land of Canaan, for an everlasting possession, and I will be their God."* After the last judgment, at the conclusion of the Millennial reign, God will renovate the planet Earth by fire and recreate it. Then Israel, which will be removed from the Earth during the renovation, will be settled on the new Earth to live on forever as the nation of Israel.

C. The Abrahamic Covenant guarantees material and spiritual blessing through Christ, the Messiah, to Israel and guarantees the Gentiles a share in the blessings of redemption and of material abundance.

The Palestinic Covenant: Dueteronomy 30:3-5 reveals that God guarantees to the nation of Israel a permanent restoration to the land, which is known in the Bible as "the promised land."

The Davidic Covenant guarantees a permanent dynasty, a dynasty in perpetuity in Christ. The promises in the Davidic Covenant are stated in 2 Samuel 7:11-16. It promises Israel a house, a throne, a king, and a kingdom. In this covenant the Lord made a promise to David that his throne would be established forever. This then connotes that Christ must reign on David's throne over David's people forever on the new Earth.

The New Covenant is stated in Jeremiah 31:31-40. The New Covenant guarantees Israel redemption and spiritual blessing. Now the reader begins to understand the possibility of life on the new Earth, and if there will be people on the new Earth, then there is a need of governing authority, as well.

1. *Luke* 1:33.

During the Millennium, man's nature will be changed considerably, enabling people to live a thousand years. But man will still be mortal, a sinner by nature, and he must be born again in order to become a member of the family of God. In eternity, the human body will be changed totally, and people will never die nor get any older.

2. The nation of the Gentiles. The saved Gentiles, at the conclusion of the Millennial reign, will be transferred to the new Earth, and they will live on eternally.

There has been a great controversy among different schools of interpretation. Some say that there will be nations in eternity as in the Millennium, others that there will be no nations but men in relationship with Christ. I decided to study to find the answer to this problem. I think that there is a misinterpretation on the part of the translators, and also a mistranslation in the Authorized Version of 1611. It is in the statement of Revelation 21:24, *"And the nations shall walk amidst the light thereof, and the kings of the earth bring their glory into it."* Here "nations" is translated in the plural as well as "kings," but this is during the Millennial reign under Christ on the present Earth, not in eternity. That we have different nations and languages is the result of the curse. Before the Flood, there was only one people or one nation, having the same language, throughout the world. It was at Babel that God confounded their language. Genesis 11:6-7 says: *"And Jehovah said, Behold, they are one people, and they have all one language....*

"Come, let us go down, and there confound their language, that they may not understand one another's speech." The statement, "they are one people," is "am" in the Hebrew and is singular. God said to Rebekah, in answering her request, *"...Two nations are in thy womb, and two peoples shall be separated from thy bowels."* [2] "Peoples" is translated from the Hebrew "goy" which is singular and means "nation" or "people."

In Zephaniah 3:9, the Lord says: *"For then will I turn to the peoples a pure language...."* This is a quotation from the American Standard Version. "Nations" here is translated from the Hebrew "am," which is singular. The translators, of course, were thinking in terms of the many nations and languages that exist on Earth today. In the King James Version, "am" is translated "people," which is correct.

In the sight of God there are only two nations, the Hebrew nation

2. *Genesis* 25:23.

and the Gentiles, but geographically they are called "nations." Jesus, in His statement, confirms the fact that there are only two nations on Earth. Addressing the Jews, the Lord said: *"...The kingdom of God shall be taken away from you, and shall be given to a nation bringing forth the fruits thereof."* [3] The Apostle Matthew, used the Greek "ethnos" which is singular, and means only one "nation." Christ was referring to the Gentiles as one nation on Earth, although divided into different groups geographically. Thus, it shows that the Gentile nations should be translated always as singular, "nation," and not in the plural, "nations." The Apostle writes in Matthew 25:32: *"And before Him shall be gathered all the nations, and He shall separate them one from another...."* In this passage, the Apostle again uses the Greek "ethnos," which means Gentile, and is in the singular. The real meaning would be "the nation of the Gentiles." In Revelation 13:7, the Apostle John writes: *"...And there was given to Him authority over every tribe and people and tongue and nation."* Again the Apostle used the Greek "ethnos," and in Revelation 21:24 "nations" is translated from Greek "ethnos," singular and not plural. Thus, the conclusion is that "the nations" spoken of in Revelation 21:24 is in reference to the Gentiles in general, and refers to the Millennial reign of Christ, and not to the eternal state. In eternity there will be only two classes of people on Earth, the Jewish nation, Israel, and the Gentiles that were saved during the Millennium. The Gentiles that were saved and transferred to the new Earth will not be looked upon as different, distinct nations, but as men in relationship with Christ, the eternal King — the King of kings and Lord of lords.

God's eternal plan reveals that the Lord will inhabit the universe with people. On the new Earth there will be procreation, and planets and galaxies will be populated by human beings. God's plan is magnanimous and the eternal age will reveal His wisdom to His people. God will reveal His plan step by step in eternity. Praise the Lord for His great plan, and thank God that He included me and you. Praise the Lord!

This can be confirmed by God's promise in Deuteronomy 7:9. *"Know therefore that the Lord thy God, He is God, the faithful God, which keepeth covenant and mercy with them that love Him and keep His commandments to a thousand generations."*

God's promise to His people that keep His commandments and

---

3. *Matthew* 21:43.

love Him was to a thousand generations. Many Bible scholars say that a generation is about forty years — which the author disagrees with. If we accept the forty year theory, then a thousand generations would be forty thousand years. From Adam to the present generation would be about one hundred and fifty generations. If God is going to bless the descendents of those who love Him and keep His commandments to a thousand generations, then this can be fulfilled only on the new Earth. On this basis there must be procreation in eternity as well as now. We have now seen God's marvelous plan. Because God will inhabit the universe in eternity, there will be a God-worshipping universe, and we shall reign with Christ unto the ages of the ages.

There will be new manifestations, a new unfolding of God's purpose and glory: His plan from eternity to eternity.

SCRIPTURE INDEX

BIBLIOGRAPHY

Copyright Acknowledgments

The following have been consulted or quoted in the preparation of this publication. Every effort has been made to locate the owners of copyright material used. Upon notification, the Publisher will make proper correction in subsequent printings.

Burgess, Robert F. *Man 12,000 Years Under the Sea,* New York: Dodd, Mead & Company, 1980.

Castillo, Bernal Diaz del. *The Discovery and Conquest of Mexico,* Mexico City: 1956.

Colliers Encyclopedia, 1987.

Encyclopedia Americana, 1986.

Fenton, Carrol L. & Mildred A., *The Fossil Book,* Garden City: Doubleday & Company, Inc., 1958.

Howorth, Henry H. *The Mammoth and the Flood,* London: Sampson Low, Marston, Searle & Rivington, 1987.

Hugg, James. *Science and the Bible,* McKinney: Lamb and Lion Ministries, 1988, tape.

Lucas, Frederic A. *Animals of the Past,* New York: American Museum of Natural History, 1929.

Merit Student Encyclopedia, 1982.

Morris, Henry M. *The Bible and Modern Science,* Chicago: Moody Press, 1951.

Silverberg, Robert. *The Morning of Mankind, Prehistoric Man in Europe,* New York: Graphic Society Publishers LTD. 1967.

Scott, Walter. *Exposition of the Revelation of Jesus Christ,* London: Pickering & Inglish LTD., 1914.

The New Encyclopedia Britannica, 1987.

Thiessen, Henry C. *Introductory Lectures in Systematic Theology*,
    Grand Rapids: W.B. Eerdmans Publishing Co., 1949.
World Book Encyclopedia, 1982.